12
Best Foods
Cookbook

12 Best Foods Cookbook

Over 200 Delicious Recipes
Featuring the 12 Healthiest Foods

Dana Jacobi

RODALE

© 2005 by Dana Jacobi

Printed in the United States of America
Rodale Inc. makes every effort to use acid-free ♾, recycled paper ♻.

Photographs by Maren Caruso
Food styling by Kim Konecny and Erin Quon
Photo assistance by Faiza Ali
Book design by Joanna Williams

Library of Congress Cataloging-in-Publication Data
Jacobi, Dana.
    12 best foods cookbook : over 200 delicious recipes featuring the 12 healthiest foods / Dana Jacobi.
        p.   cm.
    Includes bibliographical references and index.
    ISBN-13 978–1–57954–965–7 paperback
    ISBN-10 1–57954–965–9 paperback
    1. Cookery.   I. Title: Twelve best foods cookbook.   II. Title.
TX714.J325 2005
641.5'63—dc22   2004028428

Distributed to the trade by Holtzbrinck Publishers

4   6   8   10   9   7   5   paperback

LIVE YOUR WHOLE LIFE™

We inspire and enable people to improve their lives and the world around them

For more of our products visit **rodalestore.com** or call 800-848-4735

To Joan, Kevin, and Peggy

CONTENTS

ACKNOWLEDGMENTS

If you enjoy reading cookbooks, imagine the pleasures of creating one. For the *12 Best Foods Cookbook*, I have enjoyed getting to know dozens of generous people. They have shared their knowledge—and some, their energy—assisting me with the research, cooking, and physical production of this guide to eating well in every sense of the word.

Particular thanks to the culinary, agricultural, and nutritional experts and the creative scientists whose work keeps revealing new ways in which good food supports our health; also, to the organizations that support their work and make it accessible. For culinary information: Elizabeth Andoh, Corrado Assenza, Rick Bayless, Cara DeSilva, David Karp, Molly Katzen, Mani Niall, Michel Nischan, Julie Sahni, Suvir Saran, Elizabeth Schneider, Arthur Schwartz, and William Shurtleff.

For agricultural and commercial information: the Alaska Seafood Commission, Tim Bennett at Muir Glen, Blue Diamond Growers, Geri Burdak at Solae, California Walnuts, Mike Caron and Chris Clarke at Louisiana State University, Nancy Chapman at Soyfoods Association of North America, the Environmental Working Group, Mark Federman at Russ & Daughters, Tanya Fell of the National Onion Association, Linda Funk at the Soyfoods Council, Wayne Garber of Garber Farms, Bertille Glass at M&M/Mars, Peter Goldbitz at SoyaTech, Myra Goodman at Earthbound Farms, Gary Hamaguchi, Ken Hamaguchi, Jasch and Kathleen Hamilton at Diamond Organics, Stanley Karp at University of Georgia, Pat Kearny at the Tree Nut Council, Phil Kimball at the Michigan Bean Commission, Michael Langeborg at Spectrum Organics, Henry Lovejoy of EcoFish, Bryce Malone, Lindsay Martinez of Boscovitch Farms, Kathy Means at the Produce Marketing Association, Joe Miucci at Mann Packing, the Organic Trade Association, J. M. Procacci, Chris Cunane and Rita Neczypour of Procacci Bros., Eric Samstadt at Cornell University's Agricultural Extension Station, John Sarve of the U.S. Highbush Blueberry Council, John Scharffenberger of Scharffen Berger Chocolate, Greg Toku of Happy Boy Farm, and the United Soybean Board.

For nutritional information and guidance: Richard Delaney, M.D.; John W. Erdman, University of Illinois, Urbana-Champaign; Elizabeth Fassberg, R.D.; Irvin Goldman, University of Wisconsin; Carl L. Keen, University of California, Davis; Cyril Kendall, University of Toronto; John LaPuma, M.D.; Bernard Levin, University of Texas; Mark Messina, Loma Linda

University; Jackie Newgent, R.D.; the Oldways Preservation and Exchange Trust; Jeff Prince and Melanie Polk, R.D., at American Institute for Cancer Research; Carol Sloan, R.D.; Walter C. Willett and the Harvard School of Public Health.

For testing and tasting, culinary assistants Ellen Fried, Rachael Macchiese-Cheung, Judy Marshall, Renee Marton and Karen Praslick, and the Chocolate Crew—Nancy Armstrong, Freya Clibansky, Elizabeth Fassberg, Nancy Jessup, Hilary Maler, Carol Prager, Regina Ragone, Akasha Richmond, and Diana Sturgis.

Thanks also to Ellen Fried for research expertise; Hilary Maler for turning drafts into error-free recipes; and to Sheila Darnborough, Beth Shepherd, and Joan Emery for vetting the manuscript and other invaluable support.

Thanks to the staff at 460 East 79th Street for your health-conscious appetite and sweet tooth, and to AppleCare. Eternal gratitude to Barney Stein, Akasha Richmond, Joan Emery, and Muriel Miller for listening when the process seemed endless, and to Alice Fixx for long walks and talks.

Deepest thanks to Mehmet Oz, M.D., for your gracious introduction.

Finally, to everyone at Rodale who helped make this an enticing volume: Margot Schupf, whose passion brought me to Rodale; Miriam Backes and Shea Zukowski, the smartest, most supportive editors ever; Kathy Dvorsky for her relentless attention to the copyediting details; and Carol Angstadt and Joanna Williams for the perfect cover and brilliant interior design. Huge hugs to Maren Caruso and Faiza for the luscious photos and fabulous music; to Kim Konecny and Erin Quon for styling the food to perfection and creating the best lunches in San Francisco; and deepest appreciation to Meghan Phillips for orchestrating wonders.

Last, but never least, to Angela Miller for your vision, enthusiasm, and down-to-earth guidance. You are the best.

FOREWORD

As a surgeon, I am as dedicated to helping people stay healthy as I am to treating my heart patients. This is why in my television programs for the Discovery Health Channel, I not only show how disease affects our bodies but also explain what you can do to significantly reduce your risk of heart disease, cancer, and other chronic diseases.

Diet is one of the most powerful tools we have to help in avoiding epidemic diseases, including diabetes, heart disease, and cancer. Using this connection between food and health is hardly new, dating back to the ancient practice of Ayurvedic and Chinese medicine, but modern science has taken our understanding of what foods can do to new heights. Clinical research has demonstrated that the omega-3 fatty acids abundant in salmon and flax help reduce dangerous LDL blood cholesterol levels and elevate beneficial HDL levels. It has proven that the antioxidant activity in thousands of carotenoids found in fruits and vegetables combats free-radical damage that is implicated in aging, heart attacks, strokes, cancer, the blindness caused by age-related macular degeneration, and more. Today we are even looking at their ability to possibly act as a natural sunblock to aid in preventing skin cancer.

Working with patients, I also see how the word *diet* produces resistance. It implies restriction and deprivation, imposing discipline, and worst of all, lack of pleasure. But I know this doesn't have to be. My Turkish heritage includes a cuisine rich with the Mediterranean diet, which loaded our table with vegetables, bulgur and other whole grains, fresh and dried fruits and nuts, yogurt and cheeses, plus some fish, poultry, and occasionally lamb, combined with olive oil, paprika, and other spices and herbs. Today my erratic and demanding schedule means I rely on my wife, Lisa, to keep me and our four active children well fed. (Actually, the oldest, who is in college, has written her own diet book to get fellow dorm residents on the right track.) Lisa is a strict vegetarian, but since I am not, we have fish, usually salmon, twice a week. I urge patients to eat a diet based primarily on fresh fruits and vegetables, whole grains, legumes, and soy, with moderate fat. At home, Lisa prefers organic and sustainable choices, but I realize that simply shifting to fewer processed and refined foods requires as much discipline as most people can handle.

I met Dana Jacobi at The Ross Institute in East Hampton, New York, during a program on holistic health. Watching her soy demonstration, I was impressed by her culinary talent, her simple techniques, and her passion for delicious food. Her double-chocolate bread pudding made with soymilk and succotash made with edamame proved that her dishes can satisfy the most sophisticated taste and delight everyone. Talking with her, I was struck equally by her grasp of science and her understanding of what makes individual foods healthy.

In *12 Best Foods Cookbook*, Dana provides over 200 recipes combining her creativity and nutritional savvy in dishes loaded with flavor and life-changing power. Her focus on these 12 foods is empowering. She shows how to take advantage of the health benefits of phytochemicals and vital nutrients as a lifestyle, no matter how busy you are, without rules and restrictions. You get delicious variety in recipes with modest amounts of the right fats, whole grains, and all the information you need to keep going on your own. Lisa and I use this cookbook and guide to better incorporate these powerhouse foods as regularly as we know we should, with more enjoyment than ever.

—Mehmet Oz, M.D.

Vice chairman and professor of surgery at Columbia University, director of the Cardiovascular Institute, and founder of the Complementary Medicine Program at New York Presbyterian Medical Center

INTRODUCTION

I am passionate about food—so passionate that I left a successful marketing career with Chanel to go to France to apprentice with three top chefs. When I returned to New York, I started a catering service, where I found that my clients were often conflicted. They wanted to eat lavishly, but also were concerned about health and had special requests. I eventually developed a reputation for providing extravagant food using healthy cooking techniques. Clients loved my lean smoked salmon dip and a meatless version of my signature dish, chicken in pungent mustard and coriander sauce. Among my desserts, I was known for a stunning chocolate mousse that was actually cholesterol-free.

I was uniquely able to fuse haute cuisine with healthy cooking because I inherited from my family both a love of delicious food and a deep appreciation for the connection between food and health. In the 1930s, my grandmother followed Gaylord Hauser, one of the earliest holistic gurus. My mother, continuing Gran's interest in health food, was an Adelle Davis fan. Davis's books *Let's Cook It Right* and *Let's Eat Right to Keep Fit* were family bibles. I even had a cousin, Ethel, who in the 1950s ran a health food store in New York City. I was mad for her baked farmer cheese with strawberry sauce. At the same time, mom was also an adventurous gourmet cook, so we enjoyed an eclectic combination of health food and wonderful food of all kinds.

Other kids ate peanut butter and jelly on white bread; my mother made whole wheat sandwiches with almond butter and sliced banana. For special occasions, though, she made an ethereal three-layer Lady Baltimore cake full of butter, eggs, and sugar. Sometimes dinner consisted of buttery kale, a baked sweet potato, and lentils stewed with garlic and carrots. Other nights we had succulent, onion-smothered pot roast. From her, I learned to cook grains and greens decades before they became fashionable, and I learned to make them taste so good even my meat-and-potatoes boyfriends liked them. Along with fond memories of enjoying food, my family gave me an understanding of the link between food and health long before we had today's detailed scientific proof of that connection.

I think that's why I started writing cookbooks—to show others how healthy food and delicious eating truly can go together. This particular book began taking shape in my mind as I talked with students in cooking classes, people at the supermarket, neighbors in my apartment building, and the man sitting next to me on a flight to Chicago. Seeing "10 Best" lists of superfoods in magazines, hearing information on TV and radio about how diet can reduce the risk of cancer and chronic diseases like type 2 diabetes, osteoporosis, and heart disease, they were eager to eat the healthiest foods they could find. They also had endless questions.

They asked me, "Are strawberries as good for you as blueberries?"

"Does frozen spinach provide the same benefits as fresh?"

"Should I eat broccoli raw?"

"How do you make soy taste good?"

"Aren't nuts full of fat?"

Most of all they asked, "How can I possibly eat all these foods, so many times a week, for the rest of my life?" Clearly they wanted a lot more flavorful, varied, and exciting recipes than they were finding.

Here are the answers to all those questions and more in a cookbook with over 200 recipes that prove the best foods are easy, enjoyable, and always enticing. And because I wanted to make sure you could use these recipes even on the most hectic day when you are eating on the run, I selected 12 foods that offer the best combination of nutrients *and* versatility in the kitchen. I gave myself three basic guidelines to work with:

Seek Foods with Maximum Vitality

Of course most foods give vitality—life and energy. But a wide body of research proves that some food groups—including cruciferous vegetables, whole grains, legumes, soy, and nuts—provide more nutritional bang for their caloric buck. These food groups naturally became a springboard for deciding which foods should make my list.

I leaned toward broccoli when I found that it was the most potent cruciferous vegetable. A dark leafy green would also be essential to the list, as well as other fruits and vegetables, to provide as many antioxidants and as much fiber as possible. The list would certainly require a whole grain. And among protein sources, I knew fish rich in omega-3 fatty acids as well as nuts and soy would be important. After much research, it was a pleasure to see chocolate make the cut because of its proven antioxidant powers.

Because variety matters, too, I decided early on that the recipes in *12 Best Foods Cookbook* would incorporate scores of other nutrient-dense foods—from red bell peppers, strawberries, and citrus fruits to shrimp and dairy foods—but that each recipe would include at least one of the 12 Best.

Consider Versatility and Convenience

On a trip, wearing one suit with different blouses or shirts and ties is easier than packing several outfits. Borrowing the same logic, I've found that when it comes to food, becoming expert in ways to prepare one choice, such as spinach, is much easier than keeping a list of all the other dark leafy greens and learning the best ways to cook each of them. Also, some foods are easier to make delicious than others. Trust me, you can do much more (and you can do it more easily, especially on a busy weeknight) than you can with Brussels sprouts and collard greens, though I love them, too. Look at the recipes and see for yourself how to eat broccoli more than a dozen ways without getting bored.

A visit to Scotland taught me that oats are not just for breakfast—they're good in savory and main dishes too. This makes them the most versatile whole grain. I chose black beans because they can be seasoned in more ways than other beans (nutritionally, they also rank at the top). For their many health benefits, alliums are essential—I picked onions because they can be used in greater quantity, more often, and in more ways, both raw (which is the best way to reap their nutritional benefits) and cooked.

For every food, I also considered if it comes in several forms. Blueberries, for example, are good fresh or frozen and in jam, juice, and sorbet. And there are so many sensational ways to enjoy soy—from tofu to tempeh—that this chameleon ingredient appears throughout most of the book. See chapter 1 (page 1) for more about each of the foods that eventually made my list of the 12 Best Foods.

Enjoy Voluptuousness, Always

It sounds sexy, but *voluptuous* means "delighting the senses." And for most of us, myself included, the food we eat must ignite our senses or we're unlikely to eat it (no matter how healthy it is). Though I have saved this indispensable requirement for last, in these recipes, pleasure always comes first.

That's why you'll find a half dozen velvet-smooth dips and butters, including one made from sweet potatoes that is as perfect served with crudités as it is spread on a warm muffin.

Breakfasts you want to wake up to include a Best Everyday Oatmeal (page 286) that is transformed with a topping of Maple-Walnut Crunch (page 287) and a French Toast with Hidden Blueberries (page 298) that is as much fun to make as it is to eat. The vivid colors in Nine-A-Day Salad (page 100) are guaranteed to dazzle—and tasting it, your family might even overlook the fact that it's a nutritional powerhouse.

Because I believe that, even when you're short on time, every meal can be voluptuous and healthy, I've included plenty of simple dishes—those ready in less than 30 minutes are marked with a ◯ near the recipe title. Here and there I offer more lavish creations, great for entertaining, such as Salmon Paillard with Napa Cabbage and Spinach Slaw and Soy and Honey Drizzle (page 150). Other dishes are simple, but equally delectable: picture-perfect Garlic-Roasted Tomatoes (page 222) are divine paired with golden braised tofu, or beef, if you like. With these recipes, it's easy to go in any direction—especially since all roads lead to great-tasting, good-for-you food.

Chapter 1 offers plenty of reasons why you should include the 12 Best Foods in your life, as well as a wealth of information to make it easier to do so. But the *12 Best Foods Cookbook* is, first and foremost, a cookbook—one that I hope you will love and use often. It is full of bold and wonderful flavors—and terrific surprises. Enjoy!

THE 12 BEST FOODS

Here are the 12 Best Foods, in alphabetical order. Every entry features a brief explanation of why the food is so important for your well-being; practical culinary advice on buying, storing, and preparing it; and plenty of suggestions for great ways to eat each food, including ways to enjoy it without any cooking.

The "Benefits at a Glance" boxes highlight only the key nutrients each food offers, as well as suggest other foods that provide similar benefits.

Black Beans

High in folate and ranking at the top among legumes for antioxidants and (along with kidney beans) for fiber, black beans are clearly the Best legume because eating them helps to lower cholesterol and LDL levels, scavenge free radicals, moderate insulin resistance, and reduce cancer risk. Many people also find them easier to digest than other beans, and they are such a versatile ingredient that eating them will never leave you bored.

BENEFITS AT A GLANCE

Serving size: ½ cup cooked or canned

Vitamins: Folate, thiamine

Minerals: Magnesium, iron, potassium

Phytonutrients: Lignans, phytic acid, protease inhibitors, flavonoids

Also provides: Fiber, protein

- Folate helps reduce blood levels of homocysteine, an amino acid that, when elevated, is associated with the risk of heart disease. Folate is vital to women who are or might become pregnant because it reduces the risk of birth defects.

- Fiber helps reduce blood cholesterol and stabilize blood sugar levels.

- Flavonoids include those that may reduce the risk of breast, prostate, and colon cancers.

- Recommended servings: Try to eat two servings a day, including black beans and other legumes.

- Also eat: kidney, pinto, great Northern and navy beans, chickpeas, and lentils.

Everyday Ways

Black beans harmonize with Hispanic, Asian, Caribbean, and Mediterranean flavors.

Use them in salads and soups, stews and chili, salsas, burritos, and huevos rancheros. Creamy mashed black beans make perfect refried beans and velvety hummus.

Buying and Storing

Canned black beans work as well as, or better than, dried.

If you prefer to use dried beans, buy them at a store with high turnover and store them in a sealed container in a cool, dry place. After 1 year, cook whatever is on hand or throw them out.

Cooking Dried Beans

Cold-soaking is best because it draws off less folate and other water-soluble nutrients than the quick-soak method (which involves boiling beans for 1 to 3 minutes, leaving them in the hot water for an hour, then draining them).

To preserve even more nutrients, skip soaking altogether. Cook the beans at a gentle simmer; even though they cook for a longer time, the beans will retain more nutrients.

To make the most of those nutrients, don't discard the water. Instead, for chili, stews, and soups, add the other ingredients in stages to the dried beans as they cook.

Using Canned Black Beans

Draining but not rinsing canned beans preserves the most flavor. Adding some of the drained liquid enhances flavor and nutrition in soups, stews, and other dishes. If sodium is a concern, buy organic brands, which have 15 to 140 milligrams of sodium per serving versus the 400 to 480 milligrams of conventional brands. Some brands of black beans are quite firm, while others are softer. For salads, soups, and most other dishes, use firmer beans, such as Bush's, Goya, S&W, Westbrae, and Eden. For refried beans and pureed dishes, use the softer ones from Green Giant or Progresso, or Whole Foods Market's 365 brand.

Blueberries

Blueberries contain the most health-protecting antioxidants of all fresh fruits and vegetables. They are cultivated using significantly less pesticide than other berries. They are also the least perishable and most versatile of all the berries.

Everyday Ways

Consuming blueberries *au naturel* is a good idea, since heat diminishes the benefits of the phytonutrients they contain. (Health experts agree that eating cooked berries, fresh or frozen, still provides significant benefits.)

While fresh berries are available nearly year-round these days, keeping frozen blueberries in the freezer and dried ones in the pantry guarantees this native fruit is always on hand.

Add fresh or frozen blueberries to breakfast cereal, blend them into smoothies, toss them into fruit salad, or mix them into muffin and pancake batters (and top with blueberry syrup!). Make blueberry jam your spread of choice. For dessert, old-fashioned pies, cobblers, crisps, grunts, and slumps are sweet ways to enjoy blueberries. So is sorbet. For an easy iced treat, whirl frozen blueberries with some blueberry fruit spread in a food processor or blender to make luscious blueberry ice. (Freeze this in molds for portable, child-friendly ice pops.)

Properly done, dehydration concentrates antioxidant content, making dried berries an even richer source than fresh or frozen fruit. So make liberal use of them—in granola, trail mix, and cookies, for example. And if you haven't already, try blueberry juice.

BENEFITS AT A GLANCE

Serving size: ½ cup fresh or frozen, ¼ cup dried

Vitamins: A, C, E, beta-carotene

Minerals: Potassium, manganese, magnesium

Phytonutrients: Anthocyanins, chlorogenic acid, ellagic acid, catechins, resveratrol

Also provides: Fiber

- Ounce for ounce, blueberries provide more antioxidants than any other fresh fruit or vegetable, including ellagic acid, plus cancer-fighting chlorogenic acid.

- Recent studies indicate that eating blueberries may improve memory, intelligence, and coordination.

- Recommended servings: Every day is ideal, but try to eat berries at least three times a week.

- Also eat: blackberries, cherries, cranberries, raspberries, strawberries, and purple grapes.

Visiting Maine and parts of
eastern Canada in late
summer, you can taste the
best blueberries in the
world. Tiny and firm, these
tart-sweet berries pack ex-
quisitely intense flavor and
are even more loaded with
phytonutrients than other
blueberries. Increasingly,
wild blueberries are available frozen, dried, and in
juice. Food manufacturers
are using them in breakfast
cereals, baked goods, and
snack foods.

Buying and Storing

Fresh blueberries should be firm and have a silvery coating, or bloom. Size is no indication of maturity, ripeness, or sweetness.

Because the nutrients and phytonutrients in blueberries are heat sensitive, buy them from a refrigerated case. At outdoor markets, shop early, when the day is still cool, or ask for baskets of berries stored in a cool area and get them home promptly. Naturally, avoid containers with juice stains or moldy berries.

If using them within 24 hours, refrigerate fresh blueberries in their container, picking them over and rinsing them just before using. (Unlike other berries, a bad blueberry ruins only its immediate neighbors in the container.)

Freeze fresh unwashed blueberries in one layer on a baking sheet, then transfer the frozen berries to a resealable plastic bag. They will keep for up to 3 months.

Commercial frozen blueberries are usually sold unsweetened. They are as rich in phytonutrients as fresh, and they are often an excellent value.

Most dried blueberries are sweetened. They may also be coated with a touch of oil to keep them moist.

When buying blueberry juice, read the label. Some are straight blueberry juice, like R.W. Knudsen's Just Blueberry. Others are naturally sweetened with other fruit juices, including Wyman's Wild Blueberry, which tastes like summer in Maine.

Cooking with Blueberries

The less you cook blueberries, the more nutrients they retain. As noted, there are many delightful ways to enjoy them raw—even in a pie (just fill a prebaked pie crust with fresh blueberries mixed with melted blueberry jam). Pancakes, waffles, and muffins cook so quickly that the fruit in them is just briefly heated.

Frozen blueberries work as well as fresh in baked goods and most desserts. Do not defrost frozen berries before using them, except when making pancakes, which cook so quickly that the berries may not have time to thaw out.

Toss blueberries with a bit of flour before adding them to a batter or dough, both to keep them from sinking to the bottom and to help keep the area around them from turning blue.

Broccoli

Broccoli is a crucifer (like cauliflower and Brussels sprouts) whose abundance of antioxidants (see Benefits at a Glance, below) makes it one of the healthiest vegetables you can eat.

Preparing broccoli various ways not only keeps it interesting but also ensures that you make the most of the nutrients it has to offer: Raw broccoli contains the most vitamin C and folate, while cooking actually makes some of its other nutrients more available. In cooking, heat softens this sturdy vegetable's cell walls so your body can more readily use its beta-carotene and other phytonutrients.

Everyday Ways

To eat broccoli without boredom, have it raw, lightly blanched, or cooked.

Use it in dips, casseroles, soups, lasagna, stir-frys, and salads, on a crudité platter, on pizza, tossed with pasta, pureed as a side dish, blended into vegetable pâté, and added to frittatas and quiche.

Chop up leftover cooked broccoli and add it to chili, Sloppy Joes, soups, and other dishes when you reheat them, or whirl it with cream and nutmeg for a yummy puree.

BENEFITS AT A GLANCE

Serving size: ½ cup raw, 1 cup cooked

Vitamins: A, C, K, beta-carotene, folate

Minerals: Potassium, phosphorus

Phytonutrients: Sulforaphane, indoles, quercetin, lutein, zeaxanthin

Also provides: Fiber

- Broccoli contains cancer-fighting sulforaphane, indoles, and carotenoids (all of which help to detoxify carcinogens and pollutants and flush them out of the body), plus eye-healthy beta-carotene (which may help protect against cataracts) and lutein and zeaxanthin (which may protect against age-related macular degeneration).

- Broccoli has antibacterial properties that kill *Helicobacter pylori*, bacteria that cause ulcers and play a role in stomach cancer.

- Recommended servings: Try to eat ½ to 1 cup of cruciferous vegetables every day.

- Also eat: bok choy, Brussels sprouts, cabbage, cauliflower, collard greens, kale, and mustard greens.

Buying and Storing

Fresh broccoli is available year-round, although prices may be lower from January to March.

Good broccoli is dark green, with a firm, compact head of small, tightly closed buds. The more color, the more nutrients it contains, so pick the darkest bunches, particularly those with a blue cast or a purple blush. Leaves should be perky and bluish green. Stems should not have brown spots. Avoid broccoli with yellowed florets or flowers or a strong odor that smells like cabbage.

To preserve its nutrient content, broccoli must be kept very cold from the moment it's picked until the moment you cook it. Store broccoli up to 3 days in the refrigerator in a loose plastic bag in the vegetable drawer.

Frozen broccoli, which is mostly florets, may actually have more nutrients than fresh, including up to 35 percent more beta-carotene, because most of its supernutrients are in the florets and because frozen broccoli is processed rapidly.

Cooking Broccoli

Drier, briefer cooking methods retain more of broccoli's water-soluble vitamin C and folate. Sautéing, stir-frying, and steaming are best. Steam 1-inch florets and sliced stems for 3 minutes, either in a steamer basket over a saucepan of boiling water or in a deep, narrow saucepan with less than an inch of boiling water in the bottom. Drain immediately and plunge into a waiting bowl of ice water to stop the cooking process and preserve the vegetable's bright color.

For crudités, blanching florets in boiling water for 2 minutes takes away the raw, cabbagelike taste many people dislike. Blanched broccoli will keep for several days in the refrigerator. Blanch a bunch at a time and keep it on hand, ready to pack for lunches and snacks.

Chocolate

This may be the best nutritional news ever: Dark chocolate has the highest antioxidant content of any food. A number of studies in which people ate dark chocolate or drank cocoa have demonstrated heart-protecting benefits, including increased HDL (good cholesterol) levels and reduced LDL (bad cholesterol) levels, as well as slower LDL oxidation.

The darker the chocolate, the higher its antioxidant content is likely to be, although the antioxidant content in all chocolate depends on how it is processed.

Chocolate also contains mood-altering substances, though a link between eating chocolate and feeling good has yet to be proven scientifically.

Everyday Ways

Since chocolate contains sugar and fat, it is fortunate that just a little can be good for us. Plan a daily chocolate treat, setting aside 1 ounce for a snack. Put away the rest of the bar.

Eat the darkest chocolate you can. The darker the chocolate, the less sugar—and possibly the more antioxidants—it contains. How cocoa beans are processed determines how much of their antioxidants remain in the finished product. Dove is currently the only readily available chocolate bar with optimal antioxidants.

Much of the fat in chocolate is "neutral," with no apparent effect on cholesterol, and some is monounsaturated, like olive oil. Cocoa is much lower in fat, containing 10 to 24 percent versus up to 50 percent in unsweetened chocolate. This makes hot chocolate made with

BENEFITS AT A GLANCE

Serving size: 1 ounce

Minerals: Iron, magnesium, phosphorus, potassium, calcium (especially in milk chocolate)

Phytonutrients: Catechins, theaflavins

Also provides: Fiber

- Dark chocolate can be higher in antioxidants than any other food. It is rich in flavonols and proanthocyanins, flavonoids that boost good HDL cholesterol levels.

- Dark chocolate (70% and higher) can provide 3 grams of fiber per 1-ounce serving.

- Recommended servings: Enjoy a 1-ounce serving of flavonol-rich dark chocolate daily.

- Also eat: grapes, red wine, green tea.

Nibs: Shattered, hulled, roasted cocoa beans. Used to make chocolate liquor.

Chocolate liquor: Cocoa nibs ground to a paste. Contains cocoa solids and cocoa butter.

Cocoa butter: The fat component in cocoa and chocolate.

Cocoa powder: Ground cocoa solids with 75 to 85 percent of the cocoa butter removed. Also available fat-free.

Dutch process: Alkali treatment that reduces the acidity in cocoa powder. Makes the cocoa milder tasting and darker in color than natural cocoa powder.

low-fat milk or soymilk a leaner choice. Since some studies indicate that milk somehow reduces absorption of chocolate's antioxidants, many of the chocolate recipes here use soymilk in place of dairy milk. Cocoa and egg whites make lovely, low-fat meringue cookies. A simple smoothie of banana, soymilk or fruit juice, and cocoa powder is another possibility. I also recommend adding a tablespoon or two of unsweetened cocoa to chili, black bean stews, Mexican mole, tomato-based sauces, and sautés including tomatoes, as I do in a few recipes here. Cocoa nibs are another intense form of chocolate to enjoy.

Buying and Storing

Every brand of chocolate tastes different. Taste several, then buy the one you like best.

Store chocolate tightly wrapped in plastic wrap, then foil, and keep it in a cool, dry place away from foods with a strong odor.

Temperatures above 70°F can cause chocolate to "bloom." This white, powdery effect simply means that some of the cocoa butter has migrated to the surface. You can still use it. Refrigerating chocolate can make it sweat when it returns to room temperature but does not affect its taste. However, never freeze chocolate. Properly stored, dark chocolate keeps for a year or more; milk chocolate, for several months.

Cooking with Chocolate

The amount of cocoa butter and sugar in chocolate affects how it will perform. (For more information about this fascinating aspect of chocolate, read *Bittersweet* by Alice Medrich, the doyenne of chocolatiers.) Before shopping, check your recipe to see if it specifies a particular level of cocoa solids, e.g., bittersweet (70%).

When melting chocolate, if even a drop of water gets into it, the chocolate turns rock hard. Melting it with a bit of butter, oil, or Silk soy coffee creamer helps prevent this seizing up.

To melt chocolate in the microwave, zap chopped chocolate in 5- to 15-second bursts, stirring after each one to see when it is soft—it will not lose its shape when it melts. To melt it on top of the stove, place the chocolate in a heatproof bowl set in the middle of a deep skillet filled with a couple inches

Crunchy cocoa nibs are the raw material of chocolate, with a complex flavor that is rich, somewhat bitter (tannic), and intriguing. Use them for garnishing soups, salads, and chocolate desserts.

of gently simmering water. (This method produces less steam than a double boiler so there's less risk of the chocolate seizing up, and less risk of burning the chocolate too.) Also make sure to cool melted chocolate almost to room temperature before adding it to other ingredients.

Let baked chocolate desserts rest 8 hours to overnight before serving so the volatile flavor compounds in the chocolate can settle down and meld after being heated.

To lend a professional look to desserts, shave chocolate with a swivel-blade vegetable peeler to make long curls or use a microplane grater for grated chocolate.

Oats

No matter how old you are, you need to eat your oatmeal—or some form of oats, because they provide fiber that lowers blood cholesterol levels and thus reduces the risk of heart disease. With the appealing recipes that follow—including Muesli in a Glass (page 297), Oat Muffins with Pear and Pecans (page 215), Sesame-Oat Chicken Fingers (page 123), and Oat Cranachan with Raspberries (page 256)—you'll find it easy to reap the health benefits of oats.

Everyday Ways

To make eating oats every day a pleasure, start by learning to make great oatmeal. I'll be giving you five possibilities to choose from, and by eating a big bowlful you'll bank a good portion of

BENEFITS AT A GLANCE

Serving size: 1 cup cooked, ½ cup uncooked rolled oats, ¼ cup steel-cut

Vitamins: Thiamine

Minerals: Selenium, magnesium, potassium, zinc

Phytonutrients: Lignans, caffeic and ferulic acids

Also provides: Fiber, protein

- One cup of oatmeal made from old-fashioned rolled oats contains 4 grams of fiber, half of it soluble, half insoluble, all of it beneficial (see "Fiber Fundamentals," page 10).

- Eating oats regularly may reduce insulin resistance and help stabilize blood sugar.

- Researchers are currently investigating whether eating oats helps stabilize mood.

- Recommended servings: Eat at least three servings a day of whole grains, including oats.

- Also eat: barley, beans and lentils, and apples.

Fiber (or dietary fiber, as nutritionists call it) is the part of fruits and vegetables that we cannot digest.

Fiber may be soluble or insoluble. Soluble fiber absorbs cholesterol from the blood and carries it away. It also helps you feel full. Oats, barley, legumes, and apples are good sources. To help reduce blood cholesterol, you must consume at least 3 grams a day of soluble fiber. Rolled oats provide 4 grams of total fiber in a 1-cup serving; steel-cut up to 8 grams, half of it soluble. Oat bran also provides up to 8 grams a serving.

Insoluble fiber speeds digestion and may reduce the risk of colon cancer. Wheat bran, bulgur, dried fruits, whole grain bread, and whole wheat pasta are good sources.

Adults 50 or younger should consume a daily total of 25 grams of fiber for women, 38 for men. Over age 50, women require 21 grams daily, men 30 grams.

your day's fiber first thing in the morning. Spark them with a repertoire of toppings. Brown sugar and maple syrup are popular, but fresh and dried fruits are better. A couple tablespoons of raisins or dried blueberries add healthful antioxidants and boost the fiber by 2 grams or more. Other toppings include Walnut Honey (page 291) and Maple-Walnut Crunch (page 287), a crunchy combination that adds flax, with its omega-3s, and more fiber. Cooking oatmeal with fruit juice makes Wild Blueberry Oatmeal (page 292) a glorious wake-up call.

Forget about precooked, pasty instant oatmeal. Instead, try oat bran, which cooks almost as fast. (If you must eat instant oatmeal, buy a good brand like McCann's and add healthful toppings.)

Quick-cooking oats are more tender than other types and therefore often best in baking and other cooking. Use them in pancakes, muffins, quick breads, scones, cookies, and yeast breads, and in place of breadcrumbs as a coating for poultry.

Buying and Storing

Premium American brands and imported Irish and Scotch oats, sometimes called porridge oats, have fuller flavor and are chewier than less expensive choices. Ones I like include The Silver Palate Thick & Rough Oatmeal, all forms of McCann's Irish Oatmeal, Bob's Red Mill, Hamlyn's pinhead oats, organic Country Choice oats, and Scott's Porridge Oats, which are sold at Myers of Keswick in New York City, and online (see Resources, page 321).

Oats contain oil that goes rancid if not stored properly. Stored in a dry, dark, cool place or in the refrigerator, they will keep for 3 months or longer. Groats keep in the freezer for up to 6 months.

Cooking Oats

For best results, always start with good-quality oats.

To enhance the flavor, toast oats in a dry, heavy skillet over medium heat before you cook them. To toast rolled and quick-cooking oats, stir occasionally for the first minute, then constantly for 2 minutes more, until the oats are fragrant and just slightly colored. For steel-cut oats, begin stirring after the first minute. They take 4 minutes to toast.

When cooking oatmeal, water produces the densest, chewiest, nuttiest porridge; milk or soymilk, the most tender and creamy. The fat content of the milk affects the texture, as does combining water and milk in varying proportions. Using fruit juice, such as blueberry or apple cider, makes chewy, sweet oatmeal.

For chewy and dense old-fashioned oatmeal, skip the package directions. Instead, cook ½ cup rolled oats in 1¼ cups boiling water for 15 minutes. For thick-cut oats, start with ¼ cup more liquid than called for in the package directions and simmer for 15 to 20 minutes.

Always add a pinch of salt to your oats to bring out their sweetness.

Onions

Onions are a Best choice because, in addition to the sulfur compounds that give all alliums their bite and are good for the heart, they also contain quercitin and other antioxidant flavonoids not found in garlic. The "pungency paradox" is another reason onions are Best of all alliums. As Dr. Irwin Goldman, associate professor of horticulture at the University of Wisconsin-Madison, succinctly puts it, "The more it stinks, the more it works."

Garlic stinks so much that it is hard to eat raw in enough quantity to be beneficial (heat destroys the health-promoting stinky stuff), but we can use raw onions all the time—in salsa and salads, on all kinds of sandwiches—in significant amounts.

Everyday Ways

Raw onions are ideal from a health standpoint. But using them sautéed, grilled, roasted, or boiled—any of which brings out a different aspect of their texture—still provides useful benefits. Have a heavy hand with onions. You can exceed the amount called for in most recipes without making them intrusive, especially if they're cooked.

KNOW YOUR OATS

Oats come in several forms, from the whole grain to thin, precooked flakes.

Whole oats: Called groats, they are the entire whole grain with just the hull removed.

Rolled oats (old-fashioned oats): Flat flakes made by passing whole groats through metal rollers. Table-cut is the thickest and chewiest.

Quick-cooking oats: Flakes rolled thinner to cook more rapidly.

Instant oats: Thin, precooked flakes.

Steel-cut oats (sometimes called Irish or Scotch oats): Whole groats chopped into pieces. Pinhead oats are cut finer.

Oat bran: The outer coating, milled off the whole grain in fine flakes. Higher in fiber and protein, it cooks quickly. Sometimes called oat bran cereal.

The Cook's Thesaurus (www.foodsubs.com/ GrainOats.html) explains more about the different kinds of oats for oatmeal.

DISCOVER
DEHYDRATED ONIONS

These tiny, crunchy onion "chips" sold in the spice section at the supermarket add a burst of flavor when toasted lightly in a dry pan and sprinkled on a spinach salad, pea and lentil soups, and on cottage cheese.

Use raw onions frequently for their aspirinlike effect of helping to prevent blood clots. Red and yellow onions also contain anti-inflammatory flavonoids, and red ones anthocyanins, which help prevent cancer.

Buying and Storing

Onions are divided into two major groups, based on when they are harvested.

Fall/Winter Storage Onions

These include the familiar, papery-skinned, pungent yellow, red, and white onions most often used in cooking.

Spanish onions are a larger, milder variety of yellow storage onion.

Pearl onions are usually 1 inch or less in diameter and come in red, yellow, and white. They are good in stews, with Brussels sprouts, chestnuts, and other vegetables, or pickled à la Grecque.

Creamers and boilers measure $1\frac{1}{4}$ to $1\frac{7}{8}$ inches and are frequently white but may be any color.

Storage onions should be hard, with no dusty mold, strong smell, or sprouting. Stored in one layer in a cool and airy, dry place, they keep for at least 4 to 5 weeks and up to several months.

BENEFITS AT A GLANCE

Serving size: 1 small, ½ cup chopped

Vitamins: C, folate

Minerals: Potassium, calcium

Phytonutrients: Thiosulfinates and fructooligosaccharides, flavonoids (red and yellow onions), anthocyanins (red onions)

Also provides: Fiber

- Sulfur compounds help combat heart disease by thinning the blood and helping to raise "good" HDL levels.

- Anti-inflammatory flavonoids, including quercetin, can help protect lungs against cancer and asthma, and are not destroyed by cooking.

- Antibacterial flavonoids protect against *Helicobacter pylori*, the bacteria that cause ulcers.

- May also promote bone strength, according to preliminary studies.

- Recommended servings: Eat onions and other alliums every day.

- Also eat: garlic, shallots, leeks, green onions, and chives.

Spring/Summer Fresh Onions

Harvested from May to September, these include sweet onions, bunching onions, scallions, and shallots.

Sweet onions, now available in stores year-round, have almost the same sugar content as storage onions, but we taste it far more because the high moisture content of spring onions dilutes their biting sulfur compounds.

Sweet onion varieties grown in the United States include: Vidalias from Georgia, Arizona's Grand Canyon Sweets, Texas Supersweet and 1015s, Walla-Wallas from Washington, Maui and Hawaiian Hula Sweets, NuMex and Carzalia from New Mexico, and Sweet Imperials from California. Sweet onions are also imported from Chile and Guatemala.

Sweet onions keep 2 weeks or longer, either wrapped loosely in newspaper and refrigerated or knotted one at a time in the legs of pantyhose and hung from a hook so air circulates around them and prevents them from turning moldy.

Bunching onions look like supersized scallions with a mature red, white, or yellow onion at the bottom. Milder in flavor than storage onions, they keep 1 to 2 weeks in the refrigerator with their green tops attached. They are sold mostly at farmers' markets.

Scallions or green onions are commonly called scallions in the eastern United States and green onions elsewhere. These immature onions should have a brush of roots at the tip of their thin, white bulbs and erect, succulent green tops with no yellowing, tears, or bruises.

Refrigerate unbanded in a plastic bag in the vegetable crisper; they should keep at least 3 to 4 days. (These are the only onions to store in a plastic bag.)

Shallots, a cousin to the onion, provide fair amounts of the same beneficial substances along with an onion's pungency and garlic's bite. Shallots should have papery skin and be quite firm and mold-free. Store them like storage onions.

WHAT ABOUT LEEKS?

Leeks are delicious but contain minimal amounts of the healthful compounds found in other alliums.

WHAT IS THE ORAC SCALE?

The ORAC scale was invented at the Jean Mayer USDA Human Nutrition Research Center on Aging at Tufts University in Boston to measure the antioxidant content in individual fruits, vegetables, and legumes, based on 100 grams or a 3½-ounce portion. ORAC stands for Oxygen Radical Absorbance Capacity. The Best Foods scored are:

Black beans:
4,181
Blueberries:
wild: 13,427
cultivated: 9,019
Broccoli:
890
Chocolate:
dark: 13,120
milk: 6,740
Onions (yellow):
450
Spinach:
1,260
Sweet potatoes:
301
Tomatoes:
189

Cooking Onions

Sauté onions in oil or butter over high heat until they soften, or continue to sauté until they caramelize and brown. Onions caramelize because they contain sugar. Bringing out their sweetness in a meltingly soft confit or onion marmalade without burning takes patience and frequent stirring.

When you sauté onions using oil or butter and high heat, they soften more quickly when you sprinkle them with a bit of salt right after they go into the pan; the salt draws out moisture. Use as little as ⅛ teaspoon. For fat-free sautéing, use broth in place of the fat, although the onions will not get as tender.

Gently cooking onions so they do not color brings out their sweetness, as in a meltingly soft confit. Browning onions caramelizes these sugars, which takes their flavor from sweet to something deeper and more earthy.

Sweating onions, a classic technique used in making onion soup, means cooking them, tightly covered, over gentle heat until they release their juices. Sweating brings out more flavor and mellows their pungency better than sautéing. Sweating onions with carrots and celery gives soups and stews a robust flavor base.

Salmon

America's favorite fresh fish, salmon is also the healthiest seafood choice because it contains an abundance of omega-3 essential fatty acids (EFAs). The human body needs these polyunsaturated fats to maintain overall balance and for a host of other reasons. Because we cannot generate them, we must get these vital fats from food. Cold-water fish are the best sources for two of the three EFAs, EPA and DHA, and salmon contains the most.

Everyday Ways

It's easy to eat salmon twice a week without doing any cooking—many supermarkets sell it already cooked or will steam fresh fish you buy on the spot. Smoked salmon is a first-rate convenience food, while canned salmon is an increasingly palatable choice.

If serving salmon a couple times a week seems costly, remember that the USDA's recommended portion size is just 3 ounces of cooked fish. Many of the recipes in this book demonstrate how satisfying this amount can be.

Smoked salmon may seem extravagant, but 6 ounces makes a meal for two. For making dips, inexpensive smoked salmon trimmings are downright budget friendly.

Canned salmon can be surprisingly delicious, especially using the skinless and boneless choices available at Trader Joe's and Costco, and in a tear-open pouch from supermarkets.

Buying and Storing

Atlantic salmon, which refers to the species and not where the fish is raised, is most common; wild Atlantic salmon are almost extinct. Virtually all Atlantic salmon is farmed in the United States, Canada, Chile, Scotland, and other European countries. Pacific salmon is mostly wild and includes five species:

King (Chinook). The aristocrat of salmon, with pink, moist flesh that is the fattiest and richest in omega-3s. Fish average 20 pounds, but some weigh 45 pounds or more.

Sockeye (red or blueback). Redder and firmer fleshed than king salmon, with each fish weighing in at about 6 pounds. It is sold fresh, canned, and smoked and has an assertive taste that some people prefer.

Coho (silver). With pink-orange flesh that is dry and firm, this midsize salmon, averaging 12 pounds, is increasingly common at fish counters during its fall run.

Pink. Used mostly for canning, this abundant species has soft flesh and mild flavor.

Chum (Keta). Used mainly in food service, it has little omega-3 content.

BENEFITS AT A GLANCE

Serving size: 3 ounces cooked or ¼ cup canned

Vitamins: A, B_6, B_{12}

Minerals: Potassium, phosphorus, selenium, calcium (with bones)

Micronutrients: Omega-3 fatty acids

Also provides: Protein

- Omega-3 fatty acids reduce the risk of heart disease and heart attacks by lowering triglycerides, "bad" LDL cholesterol, and blood pressure, and by helping to prevent blood from clotting.

- By reducing inflammation, omega-3 fatty acids may benefit people with rheumatoid arthritis and other autoimmune diseases.

- EFAs help reduce blood pressure and the risk of stroke.

- Recommended servings: Eat 12 ounces a week of salmon and other fish rich in EFAs (and low in mercury).

- Also eat: tuna, sardines, mackerel, walnuts, and flax.

Farmed fish accounts for 80 percent of the fresh salmon sold in the United States. Although wild salmon is less available, here are reasons why some prefer it.

• Wild salmon get their omega-3s and rich color from eating sea organisms, while farmed salmon get theirs from supplements in their feed. Farmed salmon are fed a colorant (a form of carotene).

• All salmon contain PCBs, dioxin, and pesticides, which collect mainly in the skin. Farmed fish get them from their feed, wild fish from pollution in our waters. Toxin levels have been found to be higher in farmed fish. Consensus has yet to be reached as to whether the higher amount of toxins in farmed fish has a significant effect on humans, particularly considering the benefits gained from eating any salmon, and what acceptable levels should be.

• Some farmed salmon, raised on organic feed and without antibiotics and hormones, in roomier pens and cleaner water, is labeled as organic. However, no government standards for organic salmon exist as of April 2005.

Wild salmon run from May to September but are available all year thanks to freezing. Most wild salmon is frozen, though fish departments selling it defrosted sometimes neglect to label it "previously frozen." Few consumers realize they are getting thawed frozen fish because today's techniques are so good; with the fish flash-frozen sometimes within 20 minutes of being caught, it is often fresher than never-frozen "fresh."

Fresh Salmon

Fresh salmon should be firm and not smell fishy. Steaks and fillets should be translucent.

Use fresh salmon within 24 hours or freeze it (unless it has been previously frozen).

As with all fish, get salmon home as quickly as possible. In hot weather, carry a cooler in the car. Before cooking, rinse and dry the fish, running your finger along the center of fillets where the thickest part starts to get thinner, to feel for bones. Pull them out with tweezers.

To store fresh salmon, cover it in plastic wrap and place in the coldest part of the refrigerator, ideally on a plate of ice, until you're ready to cook it. If marinating, always do so in the refrigerator.

To freeze fresh salmon, wrap individual portions first in plastic wrap or freezer paper, then in foil or a plastic freezer bag. Defrost it in the refrigerator.

Smoked Salmon

Whether it is produced in Norway, Iceland, Scotland, Ireland, Nova Scotia, or the Pacific coast, most smoked salmon is farmed Atlantic fish.

Cured with salt and sugar, then cold-smoked using wood chips for flavor, smoked salmon varies enormously in texture and taste—from soft, oily, and fishy to silky, dry, and smoky. At the deli counter, try to sample several kinds and see which you prefer.

Paper-thin hand-sliced fish tastes best, but most smoked salmon is sold presliced in vacuum-sealed packages. Unopened packages can be frozen for up to 3 months. Once opened, smoked salmon must be used within 3 days.

Nitrites, which are carcinogenic, are often used to preserve color, so check the label or ask the deli person.

Lox, a term used for smoked salmon, should refer only to salmon cured in brine. Extremely salty sometimes, it is an acquired taste.

Canned Salmon

Most canned salmon is wild Alaskan pink or red (also known as blueback or sockeye) salmon, though some farmed Atlantic fish is also canned.

When packed with bones, canned salmon is rich in calcium. If this notion turns you off, I suggest removing the larger bones but leaving the fine bones, which are so soft they disappear during cooking. Compared to fresh fish, water-packed canned salmon has roughly half the omega-3 content.

Cooking Salmon

Salmon is good grilled, broiled, baked, sautéed, steamed, poached, braised, and even stir-fried. Cook salmon just until it is translucent in the center to avoid drying it out. It will continue cooking to the perfect point after you remove it from the heat.

To avoid the fat near the skin where PCBs collect, remove the skin or slash it, and grill or broil on a rack to let the fat run off. Avoid using a skillet, where the fish sits in its fat.

To keep the fish moist when using dry heat (as in baking or grilling), brush it lightly with oil or teriyaki or other sauce, or coat it with cooking spray. When grilling, oil the rack so that steaks turn easily. Cook fillets until they get crusty to help them hold together when turned. Better yet, to retain moisture, cover fillets instead of turning them.

Soy

If one food is best of all, soy earns top spot as *the* Best Food because it offers so many benefits and delicious possibilities. The health benefits come from its protein, isoflavones (estrogenlike substances for which soy is the only major food source) and other bioactive elements, fiber, and omega-3 fatty acids. And soy comes in so many forms that you can include it in a nearly infinite variety of mouthwatering dishes.

DISCOVER KIPPERED SALMON

Flaky, moist, and buttery, kippered salmon is hot-smoked. Look for it packaged vacuum-sealed in slabs, canned, or in the deli section by the pound. Smoky-tasting kippered salmon is delicious on a bagel with a slice of tomato and a few thin rings of red onion and can be used as a healthy stand-in for bacon in some soups and pasta dishes.

Everyday Ways

Soy is the easiest Best Food to enjoy every day, in part because there are so many ready-to-eat possibilities.

For breakfast and snacks, you have soymilk, smoothies, yogurt, cereals, crisp chips, yummy bars like Luna and Kashi Go Lean, and edamame. For other meals, there are ready-to-heat entrées, from rice bowls with edamame to soy-topped pizza to dishes including soy meat alternatives or tofu. Many, though not all, veggie burgers also contain soy, so read the ingredients list.

To enjoy tofu, puree tofu to make creamy salad dressings and desserts. Make chilled soup with cultured soy yogurt, a butternut squash stew with black soybeans, and use soymilk in oatmeal or bread pudding. Try spicy Indonesian tofu, sunny Mediterranean dishes with edamame, or tempeh in a terrific sandwich. All of these options and many more are included in the 42 soy recipes in this book. You can easily use soymilk rather than dairy milk, as I do in Chocolate-Cherry Bread Pudding (page 264) and Chocolate Pancakes (page 302) and when making oatmeal or soups.

BENEFITS AT A GLANCE

Serving size: Varies depending on the form of soyfood (see chart, opposite page)

Vitamins: Folate, choline

Minerals: Calcium, potassium, selenium

Phytonutrients: Isoflavones, phytic acid, essential fatty acids, lignans

Also provides: Protein, fiber

- Soy provides the highest-quality cholesterol-free meatless protein.

- Soy protein reduces high blood cholesterol levels, provided you eat at least 25 grams a day in conjunction with a diet low in cholesterol and saturated fat. It also reduces blood pressure.

- Isoflavones help to protect and maintain bone strength (reducing the risk of osteoporosis). They also appear to help protect against cancers, including breast and prostate, and to stabilize blood sugar and reduce insulin resistance.

- Soy is a good source of choline, a vitamin B–like compound important for pregnant women to help ensure proper fetal brain development.

- Recommended servings: Eat one serving a day of soyfoods (authorities generally recommend eating whole soyfoods, including tofu, edamame, and canned soybeans, rather than taking soy supplements).

To consume the 25 grams of soy protein recommended for cholesterol reduction, here are three instant ways to get it:

- ¾ cup of canned black soybeans on a salad and ¼ cup of soynuts as a snack
- 1 cup of edamame as a snack and 8 ounces of soymilk on cereal
- A smoothie made with 1 ounce of soy protein powder and fruit

This chart shows more ways to get these 25 grams of soy protein.

SOY PROTEIN IN SELECTED FOODS

Product	What Is a Serving?	Soy Protein (grams/serving)
Tofu		
Regular	3 oz	6–8 g
Silken	3 oz	4–6 g
Baked and smoked	3 oz	10–18 g
Miso	1 Tbsp	1–3 g
Edamame, in pod and shelled	½ cup	8 g
Soybeans, canned, yellow and black	½ cup	11 g
Soynuts	¼ cup	11–14 g
Tempeh	4 oz	18–21 g
Soymilk		
Varies by brand, flavor, and fat content	8 oz	5–12 g
Cultured soy yogurt	6 oz	4–5 g
Soynut butter	2 Tbsp	7–8 g
Soy flour	¼ cup	8 g
Soy pasta	2 oz	6.4 g
Soy protein powder	1 oz	25 g
Soy drink mixes	1 oz mix	12–15 g

Note: Veggie burgers, meat alternatives, cereals, and soy cheeses contain protein from wheat (gluten) and other grains, egg, or casein. Their soy protein content is not specified.

A chicken breast is a chicken breast, but soyfoods are not standardized. The amount of protein and taste vary from one brand of soymilk, tofu, and soy yogurt to another. Protein content may vary among the flavors of one brand. In tofu, texture varies widely among brands. When trying a soyfood, sample a few brands to discover the one you will live with happily.

Guide to Soy Products

This guide will help you in buying and cooking the scores of soy products available.

Soymilk

Taste, including sweetness, is the main difference among the mind-boggling selection of soymilks, both in milk-carton packaging (which must be refrigerated) or in aseptic boxes that store on the shelf. Unless labeled as unsweetened, all soymilk, both plain and flavored, contains added sugar. Most also contain natural additives that make them feel more like cow's milk in your mouth. Pick your favorite based on taste, texture, and carb content.

Soymilk is usually calcium fortified to supply the same amount of calcium as dairy milk. And while the fat content in soymilk is the same as in reduced-fat (2%) milk, it is cholesterol-free and contains omega-3s. To reduce fat content, low-fat and fat-free soymilk are diluted with water. The fresh soymilk sold in Asian markets is water-thin and very beany tasting, reflecting a cultural preference.

Soymilk Cooking Secrets

Swap unsweetened soymilk for dairy in your favorite soups, baked goods, sauce recipes, and desserts so you can control the amount of sugar.

For baking, I recommend using soymilk made without texturizing natural gums. While these additives make soymilk more enjoyable to drink, they sometimes interfere with cooking results. It's also good to keep in mind that highly colored ingredients—including broccoli, spinach, sweet potatoes, winter squash, mushrooms, cinnamon, and chocolate—will conceal the fact that soymilk darkens when heated.

More Soy Dairy

The dairy and freezer case also offer:

Cultured soy yogurt. Made with soymilk and live cultures. Use it to make Blueberry-Lemon Trifle (page 252) and other desserts, dressings, and cold soups.

Soy cream cheese. Contains little soy protein but is excellent for dairy-free baking and cooking. Combined with silken tofu, it makes the exquisite cream filling in Key Lime Tartlets (page 250) and also superb cheesecakes.

Soy sour cream. Also contains little soy protein but is excellent for dairy-free baking and cooking as it does not break in heated sauces like dairy sour cream.

Soy cheese. Good only for cooking. Casein, a milk protein, may be added to help it melt. Avoid fat-free versions.

Soy creamer. Has no soy benefits but is useful for making cholesterol- and dairy-free drinks and in cooking. In Chocolate, Chocolate, Chocolate sauce (page 270), it lends a silkier texture than heavy cream.

Frozen dessert. Soy-based, dairy-free ice cream comes in many good flavors.

Terrific Tofu

Whether flavored or basic white, tofu can be as creamy as fresh mozzarella, hard as rubber, or grainy as plaster, depending on the brand you buy.

Regular tofu. Use the soft kind in desserts and thick dips; firm can be cubed or sliced for grilling, and in stir-fries and other dishes.

Silken tofu. Purees perfectly for creamy dressings, desserts, drinks, and soups. The firmer and lower in fat it is, the grainier it feels in your mouth.

Baked or smoked tofu. Marinated for flavor, this firm tofu is excellent in salads, stir-fries, and for grilling.

Avoid unpackaged tofu, except at Asian stores where high turnover reduces the risk of contamination. Refrigerate tofu unless aseptically packaged. Once opened, refrigerate tofu submerged in water that is changed every day. Stored this way, it can last several days.

To avoid cross-contamination from poultry, meat, or seafood, wash cutting boards with hot, soapy water before using them for tofu.

Tofu Cooking Secrets

Success with any tofu dish starts with using the right texture.

For grilled dishes and stir-fries: Firm tofu "steaks," or pressed slices, are ideal. Extra-firm tofu can be pasty and grainy and silken tofu can turn mushy.

For creamy desserts, dressings, and dips: Don't be tempted to use extra-firm tofu. Always use pureed soft silken tofu and add body with soy cream cheese or pureed veggies. Also, remember that these dishes thicken when chilled.

DISCOVER ORGANIC SOY

Organic soy products do not use genetically engineered soybeans and say so on the label.

DISCOVER ASIAN TOFU

Asian markets sell a mind-boggling array of tofu, from custard-soft *dofu* served warm with sugar syrup to chewy, five-spice-flavored slabs to dice into stews to bite-size golden puffs good in stir-fries.

If you cannot buy chewy
tofu steaks, create them by
pressing regular tofu.

To squeeze tofu: Cut the block of tofu into cubes and squeeze the pieces in your fist until they resemble cottage cheese. Note: Squeezing tofu eliminates one-third of its water, which makes a huge difference in a finished dish, so do not skip this step. Use immediately.

To press tofu: Cut a 16-ounce block of tofu horizontally into slabs and lay them side by side on a cutting board. Set another cutting board on top of the tofu. Add weight, such as 2 or 3 large cans of tomatoes or a cast-iron pot, on top of the cutting board. Set one side of the cutting boards at the edge of the sink, with a jar cap under the opposite side creating a slight tilt so the water from the tofu runs into the sink. Note: Covering the cutting board with plastic wrap will keep the tofu from picking up a taste from other foods.

Gives cubed tofu a chewy
crust and nutty flavor. Its
spongy texture soaks up
sauces. Use in stews and
stir-fries and to garnish
soups. Best made with
tofu steaks or pressed tofu.

To pan-crisp tofu: Coat a large nonstick skillet generously with cooking spray. Set the pan over medium-high heat and add 1 tablespoon oil. Arrange the cubed tofu in 1 layer in the pan, leaving some space between the pieces. When golden and slightly crusty, about 4 minutes, use tongs to turn the cubes. Keep searing and turning until the tofu is colored on all sides, about 8 minutes. Pan-crisped tofu keeps for 2 days, tightly covered in the refrigerator.

Other Soyfoods

Black and yellow soybeans. Exceptionally high in protein and fiber. Black soybeans have a nutty taste that is good in chili, soups, stews, and salads. They are good canned or dried. Yellow soybeans make creamy dips and spreads when pureed and seasoned with roasted peppers, sweet potato, tomato paste, mustard, barbecue sauce, chiles, or herbs. Use canned, as the dried ones take hours to cook. Drain. Rinse well before using.

Edamame. Picked when immature, these green vegetable soybeans resemble a tough little sugar snap or fuzzy-skinned snow pea. The shelled beans look like bright, plump baby limas and are delightful combined with other vegetables, tossed with pasta, or added to soups. Edamame are sold in the produce and deli departments and frozen in bags.

Most edamame sold at farmers' markets are immature regular soybeans. Their hairy pods are hard to clean, and the beans are usually tough and less sweet than true edamame.

The Japanese serve edamame as a bar snack, cooking them in salted water. Use 2 tablespoons kosher salt to 4 quarts water for 1 pound of beans. Drain but do not rinse the pods. Cool the beans on a baking sheet by fanning them with a piece of cardboard.

Meat analogs. Veggie burgers lead the herd of soy meat choices, which also include frozen entrées, chickenlike nuggets, meatballs, sausages and hot dogs, bacon, cold cuts, and crumbles resembling ground beef, which are excellent for quick chili and tacos. Fat-free soy meat crumbles make terrific chili, meat loaf, and pasta sauces with less fat and full flavor. If you like, substitute for a portion of chopped beef or turkey in your regular recipes. Coat veggie burgers lightly with oil before grilling so they do not dry out.

Soy meat alternatives frequently contain both soy protein and high-protein wheat gluten, making their soy protein content unclear unless the label spells it out.

Miso. One of the most ancient soyfoods, this peanut butter–like, fermented bean paste is used as a condiment and ranges from pale, creamy, and almost sweet to dark, crumbly, and meaty. Use light to medium-brown miso with poultry, seafood, and vegetables, and darker ones with grains and meat.

Unpasteurized miso contains beneficial enzymes created by fermentation. Boiling kills these live enzymes, so add it near the end of the cooking and heat briefly. It's also best to serve miso dishes the day they are made, as its complex flavors are volatile.

Always "cream" miso in a small amount of cool liquid until it dissolves, or you will fruitlessly pursue tiny balls of undissolved miso. Refrigerated in a tightly sealed glass jar, miso keeps for at least 1 year.

Soy flour. Also made from ground dried soybeans, it can be full-fat or defatted, though the latter is exceedingly dry and gritty. Store like other flours.

Soynuts. Loaded with fiber and protein, these dry-roasted soybeans are also high in fat. Sprinkle them on salads, use them in trail mix, and add them to cookie dough, but go lightly on eating them out of hand because they are calorie dense. Once opened, store packages in the refrigerator or freezer.

Soynut butter. Made from roasted soynuts ground to resemble peanut butter and available smooth or chunky, it is fine for sandwiches (orange marmalade goes with it particularly well), but it can feel gritty when used in cooking. Refrigerate after opening.

Soy protein powder and soy drink mixes. Isolated soy protein, a fluffy, bland powder that is 90 percent protein, provides 25 grams of soy protein per 1-ounce serving. Drink mixes may contain considerably less protein, so check the label.

Use the protein powder in baking as well as for drinks. Flavored soy drink mixes containing sweeteners and other ingredients to add body require more experimenting. Fresh or frozen fruit that turns a soy drink into a smoothie also helps cover their slightly grainy texture.

For a protein boost, add 1 or 2 tablespoons of soy protein powder to pancake batter, muffins, breads, pizza dough, cakes, and cookies, replacing part of the flour.

Soy sauce and **tamari (wheat-free soy sauce).** Neither of these traditional soyfoods contains enough soy protein or isoflavones to provide health benefits, but they add terrific flavor to soy dishes. The best, including Kikkoman, are naturally brewed.

Tempeh. Crammed with protein and fiber with a flavor similar to yeasty pizza dough, tempeh is excellent when marinated. It will absorb flavors better with heat, so bake it, covered, at 350°F in the marinade, then brush it lightly with oil and grill or sauté.

Baking with Soy

Soy flour, gritty and lacking gluten, should make up no more than one-third to one-quarter of the flour in recipes. However, used in these ratios, both soy flour and protein powder give baked goods a large, fluffy crumb that holds moisture so that they keep well and taste even better the next day.

Toasting gives soy flour a lovely nutty flavor. Place it in a dry skillet over medium heat, stirring constantly just until the flour starts to color, and spread immediately on a baking sheet to cool. It will keep for weeks in the pantry or the refrigerator.

Soy makes baked goods brown quickly, so they may look very dark without being burnt. *Never* use pureed tofu in baking. The result is heavy and flat-tasting.

Cooking with Soy

For great soy dishes, keep these tips in mind.

Be sneaky. Soy can easily disappear so completely that no one is aware of it. Asian dishes are the exception. Created for soy, their other ingredients harmonize and enhance its presence.

Make a perfect match. These culinary couples make exceptional soy-enriched dishes:

- Edamame + dark leafy spinach, kale, broccoli, collards, or watercress. Also pair them with red and green peppers, corn, radishes, carrots, zucchini, and red onion.
- Miso + tomatoes in soups, sauces, and chili.
- Miso + honey and/or mustard for a quick chicken, salmon, lean beef, or tofu marinade. Spread it on, cover with plastic wrap, and marinate in the refrigerator for 20 minutes. Wipe off and grill, broil, or sauté. The miso tenderizes while it flavors.

- Tofu + citrus, especially lemon. Lemon makes the flat taste of tofu vanish as if by magic, so add fresh lemon juice to salad dressings, dips, even desserts.
- Soymilk and tofu + chocolate. Again, add a touch of lemon.

Spinach

Spinach contains an abundance of antioxidants, including carotenoids, particularly beta-carotene and lutein (good for the eyes). It is so loaded with folate, important for women who are or might become pregnant, and for reducing the risk of heart disease that among vegetables only okra beats it. Possibly helping to protect against various cancers, it may also help in maintaining memory and reducing the risk of stroke.

Everyday Ways

Raw or cooked, spinach goes well in salads, dips, soups, pasta and rice dishes, and casseroles, as well as on top of pizza. It's even been known to appear in a few desserts, particularly strudel.

For a nutrition and flavor boost, use raw spinach on sandwiches in place of lettuce, or mix it into your next meat loaf, where it will cook as the meat loaf bakes.

BENEFITS AT A GLANCE

Serving size: 1 cup raw, ½ cup cooked

Vitamins: C, K, beta-carotene, folate, thiamine, riboflavin

Minerals: Iron, calcium, potassium, zinc

Phytonutrients: Lutein, zeaxanthin, polyphenols, alpha lipoic acid

Also provides: Fiber

- Folate in spinach may help protect against colon, breast, and other cancers and deep vein thrombosis. Consuming at least 400 micrograms a day may reduce the risk of stroke in adults over age 30.

- Eat spinach with lemon juice or other citrus to make the iron in it easier for your body to use.

- Recommended servings: Try to eat at least 1 cup of cooked spinach or other dark leafy greens (2 cups raw) a day.

- Also eat: romaine lettuce, watercress, Swiss chard, bok choy, kale, mustard greens, and turnip greens.

Also called lamb's quarters,
goosefoot, and pigweed, this
dark green weed grows in
country and suburban fields
and on city lots. You can
also buy it at some farmers'
markets. Its diamond-shaped
leaves, which taste like mild
spinach, are cooked and
used similarly. They are also
equally rich in beta-carotene,
vitamin C, calcium, and
other nutrients, but don't
leave your teeth "fuzzy."

Buying and Storing

Curly or Savoy spinach has thick, crinkly, very dark leaves and fibrous stems. Flat-leaf spinach has more tender leaves and stems. Semi-Savoy, which is somewhere between these two. Baby spinach, picked 1 to 2 weeks sooner than mature spinach, is one of the true convenience foods—all it needs is a quick rinse before using.

Consider buying organic spinach whenever possible, since conventionally grown spinach is one of the most heavily sprayed commercial crops, according to the Environmental Working Group.

Fresh Spinach

Spinach should be dark green, with no yellowed or wilted leaves or slimy spots. The stems should be crisp. Inspect bagged spinach to be sure there are no rotted leaves, which will degrade the rest of the bag. Avoid bunches with torn, tired-looking leaves or stems.

Cello bags usually contain 10 ounces; some bags are vented to cook in the microwave and will yield about 1½ cups cooked. A bunch weighs about 12 ounces, and the stemmed leaves make 1½ to 1¾ cups cooked. Keep spinach in the vegetable drawer of the refrigerator, storing it for up to 3 days.

Others advise washing spinach just before using it, but I find it holds up better when washed, whirled dry in a salad spinner, and stored in a resealable plastic bag.

To wash spinach, swish it in abundant cold water for a minute. Lift out the spinach and drain the sink, flushing away the dirt. Repeat at least twice more, paying particular attention to the small leaves where sand sticks in the wrinkles. For seriously dirty spinach, rinse off the worst dirt using the spray attachment on the sink, which gets into the wrinkles in smaller leaves. Shake lightly to remove excess water or spin the leaves dry in a salad spinner.

SHEAR MAGIC

To chop a bunch of spinach
in a blink, gather clusters or
loose leaves together into a
handful. With kitchen
shears, snip the leaves crosswise into ribbons or wider
strips, stopping at the base
of the leaves. Lengths of
stem that are mixed in will
be fine to eat.

Frozen Spinach

More than a time-saver, frozen spinach can be the preferred choice in many recipes. Chopped is better than whole leaf spinach, which tends to be mushy, with stringy stems. Trader Joe's brand, firm and flavorful, is the best I have had.

To thaw frozen spinach, use the microwave or leave it at room temperature, or place it in a colander, and pour at least 2 quarts of boiling water over it. When cool enough to handle, simply squeeze by the handful to remove its abundant moisture (it will reduce to about one-quarter of its volume). Fluff the compacted spinach by pulling the clumps apart with your fingers.

Cooking Spinach

Raw spinach provides more lutein, but cooking makes the beta-carotene in it more available. The more briefly it cooks, the more nutrients spinach retains, so blanching and steaming are the best methods. Here are the recommended times:

Blanching: 15 to 30 seconds.

Steaming: 2 minutes to wilt, 4 to 6 minutes to cook in a tightly covered pot using just the water clinging to washed leaves. The best choice nutritionally.

Boiling: 3 to 5 minutes. Not recommended because nutrients dissolve into the water.

Sautéing: 5 to 8 minutes in oil or a small amount of boiling liquid. My preference for taste and texture.

Sweet Potatoes

Packed with more beta-carotene than carrots and containing more than twice as much of this antioxidant as colorful winter squashes, sweet potatoes, particularly the deep orange–fleshed ones we call yams, are deliciously healthy. Beta-carotene, associated with boosting the immune

BENEFITS AT A GLANCE

Serving size: ½ cup cooked

Vitamins: C, E, beta-carotene, folate, thiamine, riboflavin

Minerals: Copper, magnesium, manganese, phosphorus, potassium

Phytonutrients: Quercetin, caffeic and chlorogenic acid

• Because they have a lower glycemic index, yams are a good choice for avoiding insulin resistance.

• 1 baked yam or a ½ cup of mashed has 3.2 grams of fiber.

• Recommended servings: Eat at least 1 serving a day of yams or other beta-carotene–rich produce.

• Also eat: carrots, butternut squash, pumpkin, and orange bell peppers.

Potatoes, true yams, and sweet potatoes are three totally different plants. Potatoes are tubers belonging to the nightshade family. They originated in the Andes in South America. True yams are a huge, hairy, starchy root that originated in Africa. Sweet potatoes, including the deep orange–fleshed varieties we call yams, are yet another root vegetable. They originated in the tropics and belong to the morning glory family.

Calling sweet potatoes yams began as a marketing ploy when, in the 1930s, Louisiana farmers decided to sell their orange-fleshed sweet potatoes as Louisiana yams to distinguish them from white sweet potatoes. Their plan succeeded so well that few people today know that what we call yams are simply darker, moister-fleshed sweet potatoes. To avoid confusion, recipes in this book tell which kind of sweet potatoes to use.

system and reducing oxidation of LDL cholesterol and cholesterol buildup in the arteries, also plays a role in fighting the formation of age-related cataracts and a number of cancers. Still, Americans consume roughly the same amount of sweet potatoes a year as we do celery—that is to say, very little.

Everyday Ways

Simply roasting yams brings out their natural sugars and makes them a treat to eat on their own. They are also good shredded, sliced, mashed, pureed, and even juiced, to use as an ingredient in all kinds of dishes from dips to desserts. I pair them with pork, black soybeans, broccoli, hot chiles, and more.

Buying and Storing

Not so long ago, supermarkets piled yams in a bin without distinguishing among varieties. Today, there may be several bins containing chubby, bright orange Beauregards from Louisiana, torpedo-shaped brownish to copper jewels from North Carolina, twisting purple garnets from California, and perhaps even an organically raised variety or two. Some stores also carry dry-fleshed sweet potatoes from New Jersey or Hayman's from North Carolina. Now and then you may find beige-skinned Okinawans or Japanese sweets, which are grown in Hawaii or California. Both have nearly off-white, dry flesh and a nutty flavor close to that of roasted chestnuts.

Unpredictability is a drawback with sweet potatoes of all varieties. The ones you buy one week may be woody and fibrous or pallid tasting; the following week, they might be the sweetest and velvetiest ever. Their fibrousness can be caused by dehydration during a dry season, poor nourishment at some point in the yam's development, or simply bad storage. It cannot reliably be spotted from the outside, but scaly, shrivelly skin is sometimes an indicator, so look for potatoes that are smooth, firm, and without blemishes or soft spots.

Store yams and sweet potatoes in a cool place with some humidity. Never refrigerate them.

Cooking Sweet Potatoes

When piping hot, the carroty side of yams is more noticeable. As they cool, their sweetness comes out more.

Dry heat methods like baking and roasting caramelize the sugar in sweet potatoes, bringing out their sweetness. Bake sweet potatoes whole, in wedges (with or without the skin), or sliced. Coat whole ones lightly with oil to make them easy to peel when done. Pierce them several times with a fork so steam can escape, and place on a rack in the center of a 400°F oven with a sheet of foil on the rack below to catch any juices.

Yams baked in their skin are so moist you can turn their flesh into a puree simply by mashing it vigorously with a fork. Sliced yams can be roasted on a baking sheet on their own or layered with fruits or vegetables. Brush the slices lightly with oil to keep them moist.

Stir-frying also concentrates the sugar in yams. To avoid burning, cut the raw yam into small dice or use an underbaked one, cubed.

Mashed yams are heavenly with a smidge of butter or a touch of oil, or just seasoned with aromatic spices, such as cinnamon, clove, and ginger. They can also be used as an ingredient in dips (Sweet Potato Butter, page 41), savory dishes (Turkey Tagine, page 130), waffles and pancakes, muffins and breads (Sweet Potato Muffins, page 216), and desserts (Sweet Potato Pudding, page 258).

When a recipe calls for boiled sweet potatoes, I steam or roast them. Steamed, they hold their shape, while boiling makes them taste watery and turns them to mush. Another alternative is to braise them in a flavorful liquid.

Sweet potatoes cook quickly, so add them after other, firmer ingredients—unless you want them to fall apart to give a dish body.

Tomatoes

Tomatoes stand above other fruits and vegetables for their abundance of lycopene, plus a wide range of other beneficial phytochemicals. Acting in synergy, these substances help protect us against cancers and heart attack and help us remain vigorous as we age.

Except for the first of the new crop sent to stores in October and those from small, local farmers, all sweet potatoes and yams are cured. This process makes their skin more durable, makes yams taste buttery and other sweet potatoes creamier, and converts starch to sugar. For kiln-curing, the potatoes are held in a hot, humid room for 3 to 5 days, after which they are cooled and stored. In California, some yams are field-cured by letting them bask in the hot sun. Uncured yams have paper-thin skin you can scratch with your nail.

Cooked tomatoes—including canned tomatoes and paste, juice, tomato soup, and ketchup—contain up to eight times more available lycopene than raw tomatoes. (Be especially generous with ketchup on charcoal-grilled burgers to benefit from substances in it that inhibit the formation of carcinogenic compounds associated with eating charred meat.) Fresh tomatoes are so loaded with other good substances that eating one or more servings a day of both raw and cooked or processed tomatoes is useful.

We must consume lycopene every day to maintain its benefits. Our bodies also need fat in order to absorb it. This makes pizza (with whole wheat crust) and whole grain pasta with red sauce smart choices.

To get lycopene, you must see red. Yellow and orange tomatoes don't have it.

Eating smaller tomatoes probably provides more lycopene. Since the skin of produce contains more antioxidants than the inner flesh. Servings of tiny currant and diminutive grape tomatoes contain more skin, so they likely include more antioxidants, too.

Everyday Ways

Here are some ideas to take you well beyond the tomato's usual uses. Grape, cherry, cocktail, and currant tomatoes are perfect in salad and *as* salad, such as Grape Tomato Salad with Fresh Herb Vinaigrette (page 94).

BENEFITS AT A GLANCE

Serving size: 1 medium raw, 5.5 ounces cherry tomatoes (about 1 cup), ½ cup chopped or sauce, ¼ cup puree, 2 tablespoons paste, or 6 ounces juice

Vitamins: A, C

Minerals: Potassium

Phytonutrients: Lycopene, quercetin, alpha lipoic acid, phytoene, and phytofluene

Also provides: Fiber

- This antioxidant carotenoid helps to protect against prostate and other cancers, heart disease, and perhaps age-related macular degeneration.

- In a study conducted at Harvard Medical School, eating at least 10 servings of tomatoes a week, including pasta sauce and tomato juice, reduced men's risk of prostate cancer 35 percent.

- Recommended servings: Eat cooked tomatoes every day, along with some fat to help in absorbing their lycopene.

- Also eat: watermelon, pink grapefruit, and guava.

Pack a handful of these small tomatoes in a plastic container to eat along with a sandwich at lunchtime (they have fewer calories than most other fruit, plus you get as much as 4 grams of fiber in a cup).

Toss, whole or halved, into spaghetti with garlic and oil, linguine with broccoli raab, and other simple dishes like Shrimp with Cherry Tomatoes and Feta (page 154). Add them on the side to accompany store-bought barbecued chicken and steamed broccoli. For a great side dish in 5 minutes, sizzle cherry tomatoes in a skillet with a drizzle of olive oil and garlic, rolling them around until their skins crack. Then sprinkle on fresh basil.

Tomato paste. Use this concentrated product to enlarge the flavor of minestrone and other soups and enhance meat loaf and even scrambled eggs (as in Ojja Tunisian Scrambled Eggs, page 182). And ketchup on scrambled eggs and cottage cheese may be retro, but it is also good for you.

Buying and Storing

Both fresh and canned tomatoes can produce excellent results depending on the dish and season.

Fresh Tomatoes

Tomatoes are best picked mildly red and allowed to ripen fully at room temperature. Don't be fooled by on-the-vine tomatoes—their fragrance comes from the vine, not the fruit, and does not translate into great tomato taste.

Supermarkets offer grape, cherry, plum, and slicing tomatoes. These usually include tomatoes on the vine and loose, grown both in the field and hydroponically. Depending on the season, you may see tomatoes grown in Holland, Israel, Canada, Mexico or Puerto Rico, Florida, and California, plus locally grown.

The following types of tomatoes are most common:

Slicing. Two inches in diameter and up, includes big beefsteaks and on-the-vine.

Plum. Egg-shaped, fleshy tomato also called Roma or Italian, used mostly for cooking and commercial canning.

Grape. One-inch oblong, sweet, thick-skinned, and fleshy.

Pear. One-inch teardrop-shaped, fleshier but tastes like a cherry tomato.

Cherry and cocktail. Three-quarter-inch to 1½-inch round, with more reliable flavor and a thicker skin than larger tomatoes.

Currant. One-half-inch round, sugar-sweet, and possibly related to the original South American tomato.

Most commercial tomatoes are picked as "mature green" and exposed to ethylene gas until they turn reddish. While vine-ripened supposedly means a tomato is picked when it just blushes with color, then comes to full color on its own, don't bet on it. No one keeps track, and some growers use the term vine-ripened loosely, if not inaccurately.

Heirloom generally refers to nonhybrid tomato varieties at least 50 to 100 years old. Now hothouse grown, they can be available year-round for $5 a pound and more. A few commercial growers, focusing on flavor over looks, are raising the Uglyripe, a 110-year-old heirloom variety with the juicy flavor, quirky shape, and fragility typical of heirlooms. They don't come cheap, but they do taste real.

Sun and heat make field-grown tomatoes better than hothouse grown—no commodity-farmed, hybridized, mechanically harvested, disease-resistant and travel-tolerant tomato can equal the taste of a locally grown one in season. But in my opinion, among commercially grown tomatoes, meaty beefsteaks (once grown only in New Jersey fields, but now cultivated elsewhere, too), with their paisley-shaped pockets of seeds, remain better than other slicing tomatoes with hard, tasteless, white core-and-spoke interiors.

Never refrigerate a tomato. Temperatures below 55°F destroy their flavor. Keep them on a kitchen counter, not a sunny windowsill, which is too warm.

Set tomatoes stem end up to avoid bruising their delicate shoulders.

Processed Tomatoes

The quality and flavor of canned tomatoes varies widely from brand to brand, particularly in imported plum tomatoes. It also varies from year to year within a brand, depending on growing conditions. Rather than shopping by price, which for a 28-ounce can ranges from $.49 for a store brand to $2.49 for organic brands, find the one you like and stick with it.

For whole tomatoes, those packed in juice are generally best overall. My favorite is Muir Glen. This organic producer offers almost every processed tomato product and maintains excellent consistency. I find that their tomatoes taste sweeter than other brands. Their unique fire-roasted tomatoes make fabulous sauces. I also like Bionaturae brand tomato paste.

Calcium citrate, a natural salt added to many canned tomato products, firms their texture and discourages microbes that can lead to spoilage.

Tubes of tomato paste or concentrate are convenient but pricey. Instead, freeze the unused portion in a snack-size resealable plastic bag, patted into a thin slab so you can break off pieces as needed.

Cooking with Tomatoes

When fresh tomatoes are good, just slice them thickly, add a touch of salt, a drizzle of good olive oil, and perhaps some herbs. Letting less-ideal tomatoes sit, seasoned, for 20 minutes before adding them to a salad significantly improves their flavor. When out of season, fresh tomatoes improve when they sit at room temperature until they are dark red.

Try plum tomatoes in salads and general cooking. Out of season, they have better flavor than slicing tomatoes. Even in season, their meaty texture is most appealing.

I almost never peel tomatoes, but seeds can be bitter, so scoop them out with your fingertip or gently squeeze the cut halves of slicing tomatoes like a lemon to get rid of them. For plum tomatoes, halve them lengthwise and slip a small knife under the rib down the center, scooping out the seeds along with the mealy pulp.

Walnuts

With experts acknowledging the importance of "good" fats, nuts are finally taking their rightful place as part of a healthy diet. The FDA supports eating 1½ ounces of nuts daily (as part of a diet low in saturated fat and cholesterol) to help reduce the risk of heart disease and to lower blood cholesterol. If you're still worried about fat and calories, consider this: In clinical studies where nuts replaced other foods, subjects lost weight and said they found the nuts helped them keep it off.

Everyday Ways

A 1-ounce serving of walnuts, about 14 halves or a modest handful, is the perfect satiating snack. Keeping to the recommended amount is easier with portion control, or what I call planned eating: Put the day's portion in a small bowl or plastic bag and store the rest away.

Eat walnuts raw because heat quickly diminishes their omega-3 content. Have them paired with a sliced apple or banana, a couple of dried figs, or other dried fruit; sprinkled on breakfast cereals; or whirled into smoothies.

Instead of GORP (the original trail mix that is an acronym for "good ol' raisins and peanuts"), I make wild blueberry trail mix with walnuts. You can also use walnuts instead of pine nuts in pesto, add them

TYPES OF CANNED TOMATOES

In cans, boxes, and tubes, these are all the types of processed tomatoes you will see:

• Whole: In juice or tomato puree, may contain a basil leaf.
• Plum: Meaty whole tomatoes. Imported San Marzano are considered best of all, especially for Mediterranean recipes.
• Diced: 1-inch pieces in juice. May be flavored with basil, chiles, or pizza seasoning.
• Chopped and ground: Finer than diced. Ground has bits of skin.
• Sauce and strained: Thinner than paste but thicker than juice.
• Paste and concentrate: Tomato sauce evaporated until thick. Sold in a can, jar, or tube.

DISCOVER THE ULTIMATE TOMATO PASTE

Sicilian tomatoes grown in the rich volcanic soil of Mount Etna have extraordinary, earthy flavor. Estratto is the concentrated, black-red tomato paste Sicilians make by pureeing and sun-drying these tomatoes. Italian specialty stores sell it.

Walnut oil, like the whole nut, is rich in omega-3 fatty acids. Good-quality walnut oil tastes voluptuously nutty; heating diminishes its aromatic flavor and benefits, so drizzle it directly onto salads and bean dishes. Whirl it with garlic, spinach, and walnuts for a great pesto.

to a stir-fry at the last minute, toss them into salads, and sprinkle them on cooked carrots, green beans, and other vegetables just before serving.

Buying and Storing

Walnuts taste sprightlier during and just after the harvest, which runs from September through November—conveniently timed for holiday baking and entertaining. Thanks to careful storage, you also get this experience almost any time you open a vacuum-sealed can or a new bag of walnuts, though less so with bags than with cans. For the freshest nuts, shop where there is good turnover, particularly if you're buying from bulk bins. Rancid walnuts smell like old paint and have a bitter taste.

Store bulk nuts in a sealed container and packaged nuts in their can or tightly sealed bag in the freezer or on the top shelf of the refrigerator (for lower humidity). Stored properly, shelled walnuts should be good for a year. Frozen, they can last up to 2 years.

BENEFITS AT A GLANCE

Serving size: 1 ounce, about 14 halves

Vitamins: E, folate, thiamine, and riboflavin

Minerals: Magnesium, manganese, potassium

Phytonutrients: Omega-3 fatty acids, arginine, sterols, ellagic acid, coenzyme Q_{10}

Also provides: Protein, fiber

• Only nut to contain a significant amount of ellagic acid, a cancer-fighting antioxidant.

• Walnuts are highest of all nuts in polyunsaturated fats, which help reduce LDL cholesterol and increase HDL cholesterol.

• Walnuts are one of the few plant sources of omega-3 fatty acids. These Essential Fatty Acids are antioxidant, anti-inflammatory nutrients that may even help combat depression.

• Arginine, an amino acid, helps to keep arteries relaxed, reducing the risk of blockages that can cause heart attack.

• Recommended servings: Eat 1½ ounces of walnuts or other nuts or seeds daily.

• Also eat: almonds, hazelnuts, peanuts, pecans, sesame seeds, sunflower seeds, pumpkin seeds.

Cooking with Walnuts

Toasting brings out the flavor in all nuts. For walnuts, preheat the oven to 350°F. Spread the shelled nuts evenly on a baking sheet or a foil pie plate and toast for 8 to 10 minutes. Set a timer and toss them after 3 minutes and again after 6 minutes. The nuts continue to cook and turn darker after they come out of the oven. Cooled and stored in a sealed container in the refrigerator, toasted walnuts keep for up to 3 days.

Unless the nuts are meant for decoration on a cake or cupcake, use the less-expensive combination of halves and pieces rather than top-grade halves.

Tools and Ingredients

The following guide will help ensure you have everything you need to prepare the recipes in this book. Because results may vary depending on the equipment and ingredients you choose, I've indicated my preferences where appropriate.

Tools

Pots. Good-quality cookware improves your cooking. Well-made pots heat evenly, so food is less likely to scorch, a frequent risk when cooking with minimal fat. Plus, it browns foods more evenly, which helps deepen flavors. And tight-fitting lids let you steam vegetables more quickly.

For saucepans and a skillet, use heavy-gauge stainless steel; I particularly like my All-Clad pots, which are made with special metal layers sandwiched inside the bottom so they conduct heat evenly.

I also keep a cast-iron skillet for making pancakes and a heavy cast-iron or anodized aluminum-ridged grill pan for cooking fish, poultry, and even vegetables and pizza indoors. I use an enameled cast-iron pot, such as those made by Le Creuset, that heats slowly and holds its heat evenly, for soups and stews.

Bakeware. Low-fat baked goods can take longer to finish baking. To avoid burning, use light-colored pans and baking sheets and baking sheets and cookie pans that are air cushioned. I prefer using baking parchment to a silicone pan liner, and I coat pans with cooking spray even when making meat loaf because it speeds cleanup.

SKIP THE NUTCRACKER

The best way to extract walnut halves intact is to use a hammer. Stand the nut on its pointy end and gently strike the top of the flat end, right on the seam. Then insert a knife into the seam and carefully work it around the nut, prying gently to pull apart the shell. No matter how you crack whole walnuts, be sure to discard the bitter papery membrane between the halves.

Other essential hardware. Besides a blender on the counter and a handheld immersion stick blender, these are four other items I cannot do without:

- A microplane grater for grating citrus peel, fresh ginger, and hard cheeses. It is faster, cleans more easily, and yields more than a regular grater, especially for Parmigiano-Reggiano, which comes out so fluffy that you can use less.
- A swivel-blade oxo vegetable peeler with a handle that is easy to grasp.
- A wooden citrus reamer that looks like a ridged darning egg (for anyone who recalls this sewing aid) to help wring the most fresh juice from a lemon or lime.
- A mini food processor for making creamy salad dressings, pureeing small amounts of tofu, and chopping nuts and fresh herbs. Do not use it for chopping vegetables; it will turn them into wet mush.

Ingredients

I prefer the most natural ingredients, including products that are the least processed and do not contain hydrogenated fats, preservatives, or monosodium glutamate (MSG). Many are organic—not just fresh produce but dairy products, eggs, meat and poultry, broth, canned beans, fruit spread, oils, and tomato products, too. I look for those natural and organic products I think taste best.

Broth. Many brands are loaded with MSG, preservatives or other undesirable ingredients, and too much sodium. I use only natural, preferably organic broths because they're most concentrated.

- Chicken broth: Pacific Foods, Trader Joe's, and Whole Foods Market 365 Organic have the best flavor and appearance.
- Vegetable broth: Avoid any that look like and taste strongly of carrots or garlic. The best choices are Health Valley Organic Vegetable Broth and Kitchen Basics Vegetable Stock.
- Beef broth: Health Valley Organic Beef-Flavored Broth and Kitchen Basics Beef Stock are my choices.

Dried fruit. Look for sulfite-free fruits, organic when possible. Trader Joe's is a good source. Check when buying dry-packed sun-dried tomatoes, as they, too, can contain sulfites.

Eggs. All the recipes here call for large eggs. If organic is expensive, select eggs from cage-free hens not fed antibiotics or feed containing animal products. Eggology's liquid egg whites whip up beautifully for baking and desserts.

Flour. Recipes here use unbleached all-purpose white flour. I tested them using all the major brands including King Arthur, Gold Medal, Arrowhead Mills, and Hecker's. For whole wheat flour, King Arthur's White Whole Wheat and Arrowhead Mills Whole Wheat Pastry Flour both taste milder than the red wheat used in other brands. I also prefer Arrowhead Mills Soy Flour.

Herbs and spices. Use fresh herbs as much as possible. For dried herbs and spices use brands that are not irradiated. Vann's Spices are excellent quality. I use organic Trader Joe's and Frontier Culinary Spices, too. My favorite vanilla is Flavorganics Vanilla Extract.

Honey. Wildflower honey has the most neutral flavor. I also use blueberry honey, which is medium-dark. (The darker the honey, the higher its level of antioxidants.)

Oil. I use extra-virgin olive oil and canola oil for cooking, extra-light olive oil in baking, and walnut and extra-virgin olive oils for dressing finished dishes. Look for cold-pressed oils, like those from Spectrum Organics. See page 169 for more about extra-virgin olive oils.

Salt. Kosher salt is my basic choice because it contains less sodium than others and I like its taste. I also use Sichuan sea salt, which tastes almost sweet.

CHAPTER TWO
DIPS, HORS D'OEUVRES, AND FIRST COURSES

These nibbles, finger foods, and starters are fun and full of health-promoting phytonutrients. Broccoli Pesto Dip, creamy with walnuts and crammed with the benefits of broccoli and garlic, packs a full serving of veggies into a few scoops with a carrot stick. Black Bean Hummus, both a dip and a spread, combines fiber-rich beans and cumin—both full of antioxidants that reduce the risk of cancer—with heart-protecting olive oil.

If you, too, are fed up with healthy dips that look delicious but disappoint when you taste them, one dollop of Curried Spinach Dip on a whole wheat pita chip will prove that I do more than cut fat and calories by just replacing sour cream and mayonnaise with fat-free versions or by substituting tofu. When I make a recipe leaner, I make sure to keep it just as good as the original. Hors d'oeuvres are an invitation to be imaginative with fillings for bite-size foods. Cherry tomatoes stuffed with pineapple cottage cheese are a little surprise with big nutritional benefits. For heat, try Finger-Lickin' Edamame tossed with Japanese shichimi, a red-hot pepper, or Jalapeño Poppers, fiery bites stuffed with salmon.

For more substantial openers, Smoked Salmon Carpaccio is a snap. The flavors and colors of Roasted Portobello Mushroom with Warm Avocado Salsa will make guests think you hired a chef for the evening, and Smoked Salmon Deviled Eggs replace cholesterol-laden egg yolks with cholesterol-reducing salmon.

CURRIED SPINACH DIP

I love the zip Indian spices add to this spinach dip. Serve it with celery sticks, zucchini spears, and carrot curls, or stuffed into cherry tomatoes.

1	teaspoon curry powder	1	large clove garlic, finely chopped
1	teaspoon ground cumin	1	(10-ounce) package frozen spinach,
¼	teaspoon ground turmeric		defrosted and squeezed dry
⅛	teaspoon cayenne pepper	2	tablespoons light cream cheese
1	vegetable bouillon cube	½	cup fat-free plain yogurt
2	teaspoons canola oil		Salt and freshly ground black pepper
1	small red onion, finely chopped		

1. Combine the curry, cumin, turmeric, and cayenne pepper in a small bowl. Dissolve the bouillon in ½ cup hot water and set aside.

2. Heat the oil in a medium skillet over medium-high heat. Sauté the onion until it is soft, 4 minutes. Mix in the garlic and continue cooking until the onion starts to brown, 3 to 4 minutes. Mix in the spices.

3. Add the spinach, pulling it apart with your fingers. Pour in the bouillon. Simmer until the spinach mixture is dry, 5 minutes.

4. Remove from the heat and mix in the cream cheese and yogurt. Season to taste with salt and pepper. Serve warm, accompanied by garlic-rubbed Whole Wheat Pita Chips (page 48).

Makes 1½ cups

Per serving (1 tablespoon): 13 calories, 1 g fat, 0 g saturated fat, 1 g protein, 1 g carbohydrates, 0 g fiber

SWEET POTATO BUTTER

Inspired by a velvet-smooth dip served at the vegetarian Sunflower Café in Boulder, Colorado, this butter is also thick enough to spread. You do not have to be precise with quantities, but the cooking time will be affected by the size of the onion and the potato. Serve Sweet Potato Butter with celery sticks, green pepper strips, and soy chips.

1	medium yellow onion	¼	teaspoon extra-virgin olive oil
2	medium Beauregard, Garnet, or Jewel	2	tablespoons tahini
	yams (about 1½ pounds)		Salt and freshly ground black pepper

FOOD FACT

Tahini, made from sesame seeds, is a good source of calcium and iron.

1. Preheat the oven to 400°F.

2. Remove the papery outer layer of the onion. Rub the onion and sweet potatoes with the oil, coating them lightly. Wrap the onion in a large square of aluminum foil. Wrap the yams in a second piece of foil.

3. Bake the onion and the sweet potatoes until the potatoes feel soft when squeezed while still wrapped in foil, 1 hour. Open the foil and let them sit until cool enough to handle.

4. With your fingers, peel away the 2 or 3 tough outer layers of onion. Halve the onion and coarsely chop 1 half. Set the other half aside for another use. Peel the yams.

5. In a food processor, puree the sweet potatoes and chopped onion. Add the tahini. Whirl until the mixture is creamy. Season to taste with salt and pepper. Sweet Potato Butter keeps for 3 days, tightly covered in the refrigerator.

Makes 1¾ cups

Per serving (1 tablespoon): 38 calories, 1 g fat, 0 g saturated fat, 1 g protein, 8 g carbohydrates, 1 g fiber

BROCCOLI PESTO DIP

Broccoli fits deliciously into this zesty dip. Serve it with red pepper strips and carrot sticks or as a spread on crostini. Also mix Broccoli Pesto into hot pasta, or mash it into a baked potato.

2	cups raw broccoli florets, cut with a minimal amount of stem	½	teaspoon salt
2	cloves garlic, coarsely chopped		Freshly ground black pepper
½	cup basil leaves, lightly packed	¼	cup extra-virgin olive oil
¼	cup walnuts	¼	cup grated Parmigiano-Reggiano cheese

1. Place the broccoli, garlic, basil, walnuts, and salt in a food processor. Add 4 or 5 grinds of pepper. Process until the broccoli is finely ground. (It will remain grainy.)

2. With the motor running, drizzle the oil through the feeder tube of the food processor. When it is blended, scrape down the sides of the bowl and puree 15 seconds longer. Turn the pesto into a bowl.

3. Mix in the grated cheese. Use immediately or cover tightly and refrigerate. This pesto keeps up to 2 days in the refrigerator.

Makes 1 cup

Per serving (1 tablespoon): 53 calories, 5 g fat, 1 g saturated fat, 1 g protein, 1 g carbohydrates, 0 g fiber

SMOKED SALMON DIP

Combining salmon with fromage blanc makes a light, creamy dip.

¼	pound smoked salmon, coarsely chopped	2	scallions, green part only, chopped
3	tablespoons light cream cheese		Pinch of cayenne pepper
½	cup fromage blanc		Freshly ground black pepper
2	teaspoons fresh lemon juice	1	tablespoon capers, rinsed and drained

Place the salmon, cream cheese, fromage blanc, lemon juice, scallions, and cayenne pepper in a food processor. Add 5 or 6 grinds of black pepper. Whirl until the mixture is creamy. Add the capers and pulse 4 or 5 times to distribute them evenly. Serve with celery stalks or cucumber spears, or spread on black bread.

Makes 1 cup

Per serving (1 tablespoon): 21 calories, 1 g fat, 0 g saturated fat, 3 g protein, 1 g carbohydrates, 0 g fiber

Using less-expensive packaged fish, or even smoked salmon trimmings, is fine in this dip.

Fromage blanc is a mild, fresh, fat-free cheese made from skim milk. Sold in a tub, it is easy to use in cooking and baking.

FOOD FACT
Scallions, which are alliums, contribute some of the same compounds as onions to this recipe.

FRESH GARDEN SALSA

Colorful as a fiesta, this mild salsa combines summer squash and sweet roasted red pepper with warmth from a poblano chile. Oregano adds an earthy note. This salsa goes well with grilled salmon or black beans, or spooned over steamed green beans. As an hors d'oeuvre, serve it with blue corn chips.

1 small zucchini squash	1 small red onion, finely chopped
1 small yellow squash	1 tablespoon chopped fresh oregano, or
4 medium plum tomatoes, seeded and chopped (about 1½ cups)	1 teaspoon dried
	Juice of ½ lime
1 small roasted red bell pepper, seeded and finely chopped	Salt and freshly ground black pepper
1 roasted poblano chile pepper, seeded and chopped	

1. Dice the zucchini and squash into uniform pieces by cutting off the bottom and standing each up on a cutting board. Vertically slice off a strip about ⅜" thick by about ¾" wide. Rotate the vegetable and cut off 3 more strips. Cut each strip lengthwise into ⅜"-wide strips. Stack these strips and cut them crosswise into ⅜" cubes. Transfer them to a bowl and combine with the tomatoes, bell and poblano peppers, and onion.

2. Mix in the oregano and lime juice. Season to taste with salt and black pepper. Let the salsa sit 15 minutes before serving to allow the flavors to meld.

Makes 2 cups

Per serving (1 tablespoon): 6 calories, 0 g fat, 0 g saturated fat, 0 g protein, 1 g carbohydrates, 0 g fiber

BLACK BEAN AND MANGO SALSA

While mango turns up in many of today's eclectic salsas, including a chopped orange is more unusual. It adds to the tropical flavors that give this salsa a Caribbean air.

1	(15-ounce) can black beans, drained	½	navel orange, peeled and chopped
1	medium tomato, seeded and chopped		Juice of ½ lime
1	jalapeño chile pepper, seeded and finely chopped	3	tablespoons chopped cilantro
½	cup finely chopped fresh mango		Salt and freshly ground pepper

Combine the beans, tomato, jalapeño, mango, and orange in a bowl. Add the lime juice and cilantro and toss to combine with the other ingredients. Season to taste with salt and pepper.

Makes 2 cups

Per serving (1 tablespoon): 14 calories, 0 g fat, 0 g saturated fat, 1 g protein, 3 g carbohydrates, 1 g fiber

For the most flavor, simply drain canned beans. Do not rinse them unless sodium is an issue for you.

To peel and chop an orange, slice off the top and bottom of the peel with a knife. Using your fingers, peel away the rest, leaving the white membrane, which is full of good nutrients, around the fruit. Cut the orange into thin slices, then chop. Add any juice from the cutting board to the salsa.

BROCCOLI PINZIMONIO

To Italians, *pinzimonio* means raw veggies dipped in seasoned olive oil. I prefer freshly steamed broccoli, served warm and accompanied by individual, shallow dishes so everyone can season their own oil.

1	*bunch broccoli*	*Sea salt and freshly ground black pepper*
	Extra-virgin olive oil	*Fresh lemon juice*

1. Cut the broccoli into long spears. Steam until spears are bright green but still crisp, 4 to 5 minutes. Drain the broccoli and arrange it on a serving platter.

2. For each person, pour 1 tablespoon oil into a small dish. Season to taste with salt, pepper, and a dash of lemon juice. Dip the warm broccoli in the oil.

Makes 8 servings

Per serving: 129 calories, 14 g fat, 2 g saturated fat, 1 g protein, 2 g carbohydrates, 1g fiber

WARM AVOCADO SALSA

Excellent with tostadas and other Tex-Mex dishes, this is the perfect cold weather salsa to serve with corn chips. Also serve it as an accompaniment to Roasted Portobello Mushroom (page 64) or Salmon Tacos (page 62).

4	plum tomatoes, seeded and chopped	1	ripe avocado, diced
2	scallions, white and green parts, chopped		Juice of 1 lime
1	small red onion, chopped	½	teaspoon salt
1	serrano or small jalapeño chile pepper,	3	grinds freshly ground black pepper
	seeded and finely chopped	½	cup chopped cilantro leaves

1. Coat a medium skillet with cooking spray. Sauté the tomatoes over medium-high heat until they soften, 2 to 3 minutes. Add the scallions, onion, and chile pepper, stirring to combine.

2. Reduce the heat to medium. Add the avocado, lime juice, salt, and black pepper. Mix gently until the avocado is just warm. Stir in the cilantro. Scoop the salsa into a bowl. Serve immediately with tortilla chips.

Makes about 2 cups

Per serving (1 tablespoon): 13 calories, 1 g fat, 0 g saturated fat, 0 g protein, 2 g carbohydrates, 1 g fiber

WHOLE WHEAT PITA CHIPS

You will enjoy the nutty taste of whole grain in these crisp chips, flavored either with garlic or Parmesan cheese. Serve them with soups and salads, as dippers with Black Bean Hummus (page 57) and Curried Spinach Dip (page 40), or as a snack all on their own.

1	8" whole wheat pita bread, quartered	1	tablespoon extra-virgin olive oil, or cooking spray
1	clove roasted garlic (opposite page), or 2 tablespoons grated Parmigiano-Reggiano cheese	⅛	teaspoon kosher or coarse sea salt, optional
			Freshly ground black pepper

1. Preheat the oven to 350°F.

2. Separate each pita wedge into 2 pieces. Arrange these wedges in 1 layer on a baking sheet.

3. Either: In a small bowl, mash the garlic in the oil using the back of a spoon, until just about dissolved, then brush the mixture on the pita, coating each piece lightly. Or: Coat the pita generously with the cooking spray, then sprinkle on the cheese. If desired, sprinkle a few grains of salt on each chip.

4. Bake 6 minutes, until the pita pieces curl at the edges and darken slightly in color. Cool them on the baking sheet. The chips crisp as they cool. Season the cold chips with some pepper. Store on a plate, covered with foil, for up to 8 hours. They are best served the day they are made.

Makes 8 chips

Per chip: 27 calories, 2 g fat, 0 g saturated fat, 1 g protein, 6 g carbohydrates, 1 g fiber

ROASTED GARLIC

Roasting the entire head of garlic whole produces softer, creamier cloves than if you separate the cloves before baking them. I also find that this makes it easier to get at the roasted garlic flesh.

1	*large head garlic*	¼	*teaspoon olive or canola oil*

1. Preheat the oven to 400°F.

2. Slice the top off the head of the garlic, about 1" below the tip, exposing the tops of all the cloves, so the head looks like a big flower. Coat the garlic with the oil, rubbing it on with your hands. Wrap the garlic in foil.

3. Bake the garlic in the center of the oven for 45 to 60 minutes, depending on the size of the head, until it is soft when pressed. To use, squeeze the head until individual cloves pop out. Wrapped in foil, roasted garlic keeps in the refrigerator for a week.

Makes 1 head

Per head: 46 calories, 1 g fat, 0 g saturated fat, 1 g protein, 9 g carbohydrates, 0 g fiber

FINGER-LICKIN' EDAMAME

I make 2 versions of this addictive nibble. Both use popular Japanese seasonings in an unorthodox way. *Togarashi shichimi*, or seven-flavor seasoning, includes ground red chile pepper, citrus zest, black sesame seeds, and poppy seeds. It is devilishly hot. *Furikake* is a mild, nutty-tasting blend of nori flakes, dried shiso leaf, and toasted sesame seeds. Sold ready-to-use at Japanese and Asian food stores, both are perfect for giving edamame a kick. They also cling to your fingers; hence the name.

¼ cup + 1 teaspoon kosher salt

8 ounces frozen edamame

1 teaspoon togarashi shichimi (seven-flavor seasoning) or 1 tablespoon furikake (sesame, nori, and shiso blend) and 1 teaspoon sea salt

1. Bring a large pot of water to a boil. Toss in the ¼ cup salt, add the edamame, and cook until the beans have the desired tenderness, 5 to 10 minutes. Drain in a colander.

2. Spread the beans in a single layer on a baking sheet covered with 3 layers of paper towels. Turn 2 or 3 times to help them cool. When the edamame are lukewarm, place them in a wide bowl.

3. Sprinkle on the togarashi or the furikake and the remaining 1 teaspoon salt, tossing lightly to distribute.

Makes 2 servings

Per serving: 192 calories, 10 g fat, 1 g saturated fat, 15 g protein, 14 g carbohydrates, 5 g fiber

---

Because edamame are cooked in salted water and cooled without rinsing, the salt clings to the outside of the pods.

For *furikake* without MSG, get the Urashima brand at Japanese and Asian food stores or Eden Shake at natural food stores.

FOOD FACT

Nori and sesame seeds are good sources of calcium.

CHOCOLATE-CHILE NUTS

Chocolate and chiles are notoriously good together. For this recipe, I combine them, then bake the coated nuts to crisp them. The flavor becomes most fully developed after these nuts sit overnight.

Natural cocoa powder has a milder flavor than Dutch processed. Hershey's is the most commonly available brand.

2	cups pecans	1	teaspoon ground cinnamon
1	cup walnuts	½	teaspoon ancho chile powder,
1	large egg white		optional
¼	cup brown sugar, firmly packed	⅓	teaspoon cayenne pepper
2	teaspoons natural cocoa powder	¼	teaspoon salt

1. Preheat the oven to 350°F. Generously coat a baking sheet with cooking spray. Place the nuts in a mixing bowl.

2. In a small, heavy saucepan, whisk the egg white until foamy. Set the pan over medium-low heat and whisk until the egg white is liquid, 1 minute. Whisk in the sugar, cocoa, cinnamon, chile powder (if using), and cayenne, until the mixture looks like grainy chocolate sauce. Take care not to cook the egg.

3. Scoop the chocolate mixture over the nuts. Mix with a fork until they are thoroughly coated, 3 minutes. Lift the nuts from the bowl with a slotted spoon to drain the excess coating. Spread the nuts in a single layer on the prepared baking sheet, turning each nut right side up.

4. Bake 20 minutes, until the nuts look shiny and feel dry. (They will be slightly soft.) When completely cool and crisp, break apart any nuts that are stuck together. Store in an airtight container at room temperature overnight to allow the flavors to meld. These nuts keep for 2 weeks.

Makes 14 servings

Per serving: 183 calories, 17 g fat, 2 g saturated fat, 3 g protein, 7 g carbohydrates, 2 g fiber

SMOKED SALMON DEVILED EGGS

Instead of yolks, these deviled eggs are stuffed with smoked salmon mousse that tastes as rich, although it contains significantly less fat and cholesterol.

¼	pound smoked salmon, coarsely chopped	2	teaspoons fresh lemon juice
			Freshly ground white or black pepper
2	tablespoons light cream cheese	4	large hard-cooked eggs, peeled and
2	tablespoons reduced-fat mayonnaise		halved lengthwise

1. Place the salmon, cream cheese, mayonnaise, and lemon juice in the bowl of a food processor. Whirl until the mixture is nubbly. Add 3 or 4 grinds of pepper and whirl to combine.

2. Remove and discard the egg yolks. Place the whites cut side up on a plate. With a spoon, scoop up enough salmon filling to make balls the size of yolks. Roll the filling between your fingers to form round balls. Set the filling into the whites. Serve chilled.

Makes 8 stuffed egg halves

Per serving (1 egg half): 80 calories, 5 g fat, 2 g saturated fat, 7 g protein, 1 g carbohydrates, 0 g fiber

HARD-COOKING EGGS THE EASY WAY

This method is recommended by Shirley O. Corriher in *Cookwise*, her primer on cooking techniques.

Use eggs you have had for a week or more. Fresh eggs are hard to peel.

Place the eggs in a pot that holds them in a single layer. Cover with water by 1½". Bring the water to a rolling boil. Cover the pot. Remove it from the heat. Let it sit for 15 minutes. Drain off the water.

Run cold water over the eggs for 5 minutes to prevent a green ring from forming around the yolk.

STUFFED CHERRY TOMATOES

For picture-perfect hors d'oeuvres, use large cherry tomatoes, like the ones sold in a 12-ounce net bag. Here are two different ways to fill them.

| 15 | large cherry tomatoes, about 1 pint | Cottage cheese filling or spinach and feta filling |

1. Using a sharp, small knife, cut off the top third of each tomato. Using a small melon scoop or demitasse-size teaspoon, scoop out the seeds and pulp. To keep the stuffed tomatoes standing upright, cut a very thin slice from the bottom. Prepare the tomatoes ahead, if you wish, and arrange them, cut side down, on a plate covered with a paper towel. Cover the plate with plastic wrap and refrigerate up to 8 hours.

2. Using a small spoon, fill the tomatoes, mounding the filling generously and spreading it out to the edge.

COTTAGE CHEESE FILLING
Cottage cheese containing bits of pineapple gives this filling a nice twist.

½	cup 1% cottage cheese with pineapple	¼	small green bell pepper, finely
1	large red radish, finely chopped		chopped
1	scallion, green part only, finely chopped		Salt and freshly ground black pepper

Combine the cottage cheese, radish, scallion, and bell pepper in a bowl. Season to taste with salt and pepper.

Makes enough filling for 15 large cherry tomatoes

Per tomato: 11 calories, 0 g fat, 0 g saturated fat, 1 g protein, 1 g carbohydrates, 0 g fiber

FOOD FACT

Radishes go from cool to hot because chewing releases isothiocyanate, a sharp-tasting, cancer-fighting phytochemical.

SPINACH AND FETA FILLING

Use only fresh spinach for this filling, as frozen tastes bland and gives the filling a pastelike texture.

4	cups fresh spinach leaves, packed	1	teaspoon finely chopped garlic
¼	cup crumbled feta cheese	½	teaspoon dried oregano
1	tablespoon fat-free plain yogurt		Salt and freshly ground black pepper

1. Coat a medium skillet with cooking spray. Rinse the spinach and add it to the skillet set over medium-high heat, leaving some water clinging to the leaves. Cook, stirring with a wooden spoon, until the leaves are wilted and bright green, 2 minutes. Transfer the spinach to a plate to cool.

2. When cool enough to handle, squeeze the moisture from the spinach and chop finely. Put the chopped spinach in a mixing bowl. Add the feta, yogurt, garlic, and oregano and mix thoroughly with a fork. Season to taste with salt and pepper.

Makes enough filling for 15 large cherry tomatoes

Per tomato: 13 calories, 1 g fat, 0 g saturated fat, 1 g protein, 1 g carbohydrates, 0 g fiber

The cottage cheese and spinach and feta fillings are also delicious spread on whole wheat toast.

JALAPEÑO POPPERS

If you love heat, these sassy bites are for you.

1	(7½-ounce) can pink salmon, drained	2	tablespoons very finely chopped red
2	tablespoons reduced-fat mayonnaise		onion
2	teaspoons fresh lemon juice	¼	teaspoon ground cumin
4	medium jalapeño chile peppers		

1. Remove the skin and bones, if desired, from the salmon, or use skinless and boneless canned salmon. Mix with the mayonnaise and lemon juice, mashing the fish with a fork until well combined and almost smooth.

2. Cut the top and tip off each jalapeño pepper, then cut each crosswise into ½" rings. Using your fingers or a small, thin knife, remove the seeded core from the pepper rings. Stuff 1 teaspoon of the salmon mixture into each ring, mounding it slightly on top.

3. In a small bowl, combine the onion and cumin, tossing to coat the onion evenly. Top each popper with about ⅛ teaspoon of the onion mixture. Serve, or cover with plastic wrap and refrigerate up to 8 hours.

Makes 16 pieces

Per serving (1 piece): 20 calories, 1 g fat, 0 g saturated fat, 2 g protein, 0 g carbohydrates, 0 g fiber

---

There will be filling left over. Use it to make up to 32 more poppers, or turn the filling into salad by mixing in some finely chopped celery, cucumber, and the jalapeño ends that you cut off plus any leftover cumin-coated onion and a dash more lemon juice.

FOOD FACT

Canned salmon from Alaska is wild.

PROTECT YOURSELF

When working with hotter chile peppers, like jalapeño and serrano, it's essential to protect your hands. Use plastic or rubber gloves, or slip your hands into thin plastic sandwich bags, the kind with fold-over tops.

BLACK BEAN HUMMUS

Middle Eastern and American southwestern ingredients meet brilliantly in this spreadable dip. Serve it with Whole Wheat Pita Chips (page 48), corn chips, or raw vegetables.

1	(15-ounce) can black beans, drained	1	tablespoon extra-virgin olive oil
1	clove garlic, minced		Juice of 1 small lime (about 1½
¼	cup soft silken tofu		tablespoons)
2	tablespoons tahini		Salt and freshly ground black pepper
1	teaspoon ground cumin		Ground sweet paprika, for garnish

Place the beans, garlic, tofu, tahini, cumin, oil, and lime juice in a food processor. Whirl until the mixture is smooth. Season to taste with salt and pepper. Serve the hummus in a bowl, garnished with a sprinkle of paprika. Black Bean Hummus keeps for 4 to 5 days, tightly covered in the refrigerator.

Makes 1⅓ cups

Per serving (1 tablespoon): 32 calories, 2 g fat, 0 g saturated fat, 1 g protein, 3 g carbohydrates, 2 g fiber

For a light meal, spread Black Bean Hummus inside a pita pocket, with sliced veggies and sprouts, or set a scoop of it beside summer-ripe sliced tomatoes on a plate.

SMOKED SALMON CARPACCIO

Europeans often serve smoked salmon on a plate, accompanied by buttered black bread. This requires the best smoked salmon, such as Irish or Scottish, hand-sliced impeccably paper-thin. It makes a most elegant and healthful first course.

6	ounces top-quality smoked salmon, thinly sliced	8	paper-thin lemon slices
			Freshly ground black pepper
2	tablespoons red onion, very finely chopped	6	teaspoons unsalted butter
		4	thin slices black bread
1	tablespoon snipped fresh dill, chives, or drained capers		

1. Set out 4 chilled salad plates. Arrange one-quarter of the salmon to cover each plate. Sprinkle one-quarter of the onion and dill, chives, or capers over each serving.

2. Halve the lemon slices. Arrange 4 halves on each plate. Season with a few grinds of pepper.

3. Butter the bread. Trim away the crusts and cut each slice into 4 triangles. Serve the bread on a separate plate.

Makes 4 servings

Per serving: 152 calories, 8 g fat, 4 g saturated fat, 10 g protein, 10 g carbohydrates, 1 g fiber

PROSCIUTTO WITH TOMATO TARTARE

Tomatoes and dates replace the usual melon or figs in this first course, sparkling with savory, sweet, and sharp acid flavors. Use a Spanish or Sicilian oil (sweeter) in the acidic tomato tartare, and a grassier, more assertive Tuscan oil on the sweet ham.

THE SKINNY ON PEELING TOMATOES

Removing the skin allows the soft flesh of a tomato to melt on your tongue. Some recipes, like this one, really demand this pleasure. Using a paring knife, cut a small "x" in the bottom. With the tip of the knife, cut out the stem end of the tomato. Plunge the tomato into boiling water for 15 seconds, then immediately drop it in a bowl of ice water. Slip off the loose skin with your fingers, or grasp a strip of the skin between your thumb and the blade of a small knife and lift it away.

2	ripe medium tomatoes (½ pound), peeled, seeded, and finely chopped
4	pitted dates, finely chopped
2	tablespoons Pan-Grilled Red Onion (page 243)
1	tablespoon finely chopped shallot
1	teaspoon Worcestershire sauce
¼	teaspoon salt
1	teaspoon Spanish or Sicilian extra-virgin olive oil
	Freshly ground black pepper
8	slices prosciutto or serrano ham
2	teaspoons Tuscan extra-virgin olive oil, for garnish

1. Place the tomatoes, dates, onion, shallot, Worcestershire sauce, and salt in a bowl. Combine with a fork and stir in the Spanish olive oil. Season with 3 or 4 grinds of pepper. Set aside 30 minutes to allow the flavors to meld. There will be ¾ cup tartare.

2. On each of 4 salad plates, lay out 2 slices of the ham. Mound one-quarter of Tomato Tartare on 1 side. Drizzle half a teaspoon of the Tuscan olive oil over the ham and serve.

Makes 4 servings

Per serving: 121 calories, 5 g fat, 1 g saturated fat, 6 g protein, 16 g carbohydrates, 2 g fiber

MUSHROOM CROSTINI

The meaty-tasting pâté topping these crostini is made with mushrooms, sage, white wine, and tempeh. It is also excellent served on a lettuce leaf, accompanied by crustless black bread and a garnish of little cornichon pickles.

1	tablespoon extra-virgin olive oil	1	teaspoon rubbed sage
1	medium red onion, finely chopped	2	tablespoons low-fat or fat-free cream
1	clove garlic, finely chopped		cheese
1	teaspoon finely chopped fresh	1	teaspoon fresh lemon juice
	rosemary, or 1 teaspoon dried	1	teaspoon salt
8	medium cremini mushrooms, stems		Freshly ground black pepper
	trimmed, finely chopped	8	(½"-thick) slices whole wheat Italian
4	ounces soy tempeh (½ package),		bread, grilled or toasted
	chopped	2	tablespoons chopped fresh parsley,
½	cup dry white wine		for garnish

1. Heat the oil in a medium skillet over medium-high heat. Sauté the onion until it is translucent, 3 minutes. Mix in the garlic and rosemary until aromatic. Add the mushrooms, cooking until they release their liquid and evaporate, 6 to 7 minutes. Add the tempeh, wine, and sage and cook, stirring occasionally, until the wine has evaporated, 8 minutes.

2. Off the heat, mix in the cream cheese, lemon juice, and salt. Season to taste with pepper. Using a wooden spoon, stir the mixture vigorously until it is a nubbly spread, about 1 minute.

3. Spread 2 tablespoons of the pâté on each slice of bread. Sprinkle on some parsley for garnish. The pâté keeps up to 1 week in the refrigerator.

Makes 8 crostini or 1 cup pâté

Per serving (1 crostini): 125 calories, 4 g fat, 1 g saturated fat, 6 g protein, 14 g carbohydrates, 2 g fiber

Tempeh, if you are not familiar with it, is one of the best-tasting forms of soy.

FOOD FACT
Mushrooms are a good source of selenium, which may reduce the risk of prostate cancer.

SALMON TACOS

Eating these fish tacos can be messy, so I serve them informally, letting everyone assemble their own. Just set out the ingredients on a big platter, and pass out the tortillas warm from the pan. The salmon can be either warm or at room temperature.

1	pound salmon fillet		Warm Avocado Salsa (page 47)
2	cups shredded romaine lettuce	8	corn tortillas
⅔	cup prepared salsa verde, lightly drained		

1. Poach or bake the salmon in a 400°F oven until it is opaque in the center (the time varies according to the thickness of the fish). Allow to cool to room temperature. Divide the salmon into 8 portions and arrange it on a platter.

2. Place the shredded lettuce, salsa verde, and Warm Avocado Salsa in serving bowls.

3. Heat the tortilla in a dry cast-iron skillet one at a time over medium-high heat for 1 minute. Turn and heat until the tortilla puffs, about 1 minute longer. Fill each tortilla as it is warmed or wrap in a dish towel until all are heated.

4. To assemble, place a warm tortilla on a plate. Top it with ¼ cup of the lettuce, salmon, 1 tablespoon salsa verde, and 2 tablespoons salsa. Fold 2 sides of the tortilla into the center and serve immediately.

Serves 8 as a first course, 4 as a main course

Per serving (1 taco): 230 calories, 11 g fat, 2 g saturated fat, 15 g protein, 20 g carbohydrates, 5 g fiber

SPINACH AND CORN QUESADILLA

This quesadilla makes a light meal that includes full servings of spinach, corn, and whole grain wheat. Using fresh spinach produces the best results, but using frozen is okay.

2	teaspoons canola oil	½	cup frozen white corn kernels
1	bunch spinach leaves cut in 1" ribbons, or 1 (10-ounce) package defrosted frozen chopped spinach, squeezed dry	2	(10") sprouted wheat or whole wheat tortillas
		¾	cup shredded Monterey Jack
1	jalapeño chile pepper, seeded and cut in thin rounds	¼	cup Pan-Grilled Red Onion (page 243), or sautéed thin-sliced onion

1. Heat the oil in a large, nonstick skillet over medium-high heat. Add the spinach (if using fresh, stir until it wilts). Add the jalapeño and corn. Cook, stirring, until the corn is warmed through, 3 minutes longer. Transfer the spinach and corn mixture to a bowl. Wipe out the pan and return it to the heat.

2. Coat a tortilla on 1 side with cooking spray and place it sprayed side down in the pan. Sprinkle half the cheese over the tortilla. Spread the spinach mixture over the cheese, leaving a ½" border around the edge. Sprinkle with the onions and top with the remaining cheese. Spray the second tortilla with cooking spray and place it coated side up over the filling. Cook until it is crisp and lightly browned on the bottom and the bottom layer of cheese is melted, 2 minutes.

3. Turn the quesadilla by sliding it onto the plate. Invert a second plate over it, press the plates together, and flip them. Slide the quesadilla, uncooked side down, back into the pan and crisp the second side. Place on a plate and cut the quesadilla into 8 wedges. Serve immediately, accompanied by your favorite salsa.

Makes 8 wedges

Per wedge: 83 calories, 5 g fat, 2 g saturated fat, 4 g protein, 8 g carbohydrates, 1 g fiber

Alvarado Street Bakery's organic sprouted wheat tortillas taste milder than other whole wheat tortillas. They crisp beautifully and have just 3.5 grams of fat per serving. Look for these burrito-size tortillas at natural food stores or visit www.alvaradostreetbakery.com.

FOOD FACT

Yellow corn contains lutein and zeaxanthin, carotenoids that help protect your eyes.

ROASTED PORTOBELLO MUSHROOM WITH WARM AVOCADO SALSA

Roasting portobellos concentrates their flavor while keeping them moist. Tart, chunky Warm Avocado Salsa is a perfect foil for their earthy, rich taste. Serve accompanied by focaccia or grilled slices of Italian country bread.

4   large (5-6 ounces each) portobello
        mushrooms, stems removed
1   tablespoon extra-virgin olive oil, or
        cooking spray

Salt and freshly ground black pepper
Warm Avocado Salsa (page 47)

1. Preheat the oven to 400°F.

2. Brush the mushroom caps with the oil or coat them with cooking spray. Set them, gills facing up, on a baking sheet. Sprinkle each mushroom with a pinch of salt and a couple grinds of pepper. Roast the mushrooms for 10 minutes. Turn them over and continue roasting until they are tender when pierced in the center with a knife, 10 minutes. Set the mushrooms on a plate, gills facing up.

3. When mushrooms are lukewarm or room temperature, place each in the center of a salad plate. Mound about ½ cup salsa in the center.

Makes 4 servings

Per serving: 77 calories, 4 g fat, 0 g saturated fat, 3 g protein, 7 g carbohydrates, 0 g fiber

VIETNAMESE SWEET POTATO AND SHRIMP PANCAKES WITH LIME DIPPING SAUCE

Lightly fried food is fine, I believe, provided it is nutritionally sound in other ways and served only occasionally. These crisp ovals of shredded sweet potato and shrimp qualify. I call them Asian latkes and serve them as finger food at parties, accompanied by a sweet and sour dipping sauce flavored with ginger, red chile pepper, fish sauce, and lime.

PANCAKES

1   medium Beauregard, Garnet, or Jewel
     yam (about ¾ pound)

¼   cup + 1 tablespoon unbleached
     all-purpose flour

½   teaspoon salt

½   pound medium shrimp, peeled and
     cut in 2 or 3 pieces each

⅓   cup oil, divided

1. Peel the yam. Halve it crosswise, then halve each piece lengthwise. Using a coarse grater, shred the sweet potato the long way. There will be about 3½ cups. Place the shredded sweet potato in a bowl.

2. Using a fork, mix ¼ cup of the flour and the salt into the yam until the mixture feels sticky, 1 minute. In another bowl, toss the shrimp with the remaining 1 tablespoon of flour to coat it. For each pancake, press about 2 tablespoons of the sweet potato into the palm of your hand, making a 2" oval. Press 2 or 3 pieces of shrimp on the potato, and press, folding any long pieces of the potato so they don't burn. Set on a plate. Repeat, using waxed paper between the layers to make 16 pancakes.

3. Heat ¼ cup of the oil in a medium nonstick skillet over medium-high heat until it is almost smoking. Add 5 of the pancakes and cook until they potatoes start to brown at the edges, 1 minute. Turn, using tongs, and cook until the shrimp are pink and the pancakes are dark brown around the edges, 2 minutes. Be careful as the oil will spatter while the second side cooks. Drain the pancakes on paper towels. Repeat until all the

pancakes are cooked, adding the remaining oil when needed. Serve immediately, accompanied by Lime Dipping Sauce.

Makes 16 pancakes

Per pancake: 61 calories, 2 g fat, 0 g saturated fat, 3 g protein, 8 g carbohydrates, 1 g fiber

LIME DIPPING SAUCE

Ginger-Chile Dressing (page 114)
1 *tablespoon fish sauce*
1 *lime*

Combine the dressing with the fish sauce. Peel the lime by cutting off the ends, standing the lime on a cutting board, and slicing off the skin in strips, as you would an orange. Release half the lime sections from their membranes by working the knife down either side of each section. Chop them into 3 or 4 pieces and add to the dressing. Let sit 10 minutes for the flavors to meld before serving. Lime Dipping Sauce keeps, covered in the refrigerator, for up to 3 days. Reserve the remaining lime for another use.

Makes ½ cup

Per serving (1 tablespoon): 40 calories, 0 g fat, 0 g saturated fat, 0 g protein, 11 g carbohydrates, 0 g fiber

CHAPTER THREE
SOUPS

I like robust soups crammed with stuff. Besides Scotch Oatmeal Soup, Black Bean Minestrone, and other soups so chunky they are almost stews, my favorites include pureed Sweet Potato–Carrot and Red Velvet Soups—both of which are thick and satisfying. Even my clear Mushroom Consommé with Sake and Double Miso Soup are intensely flavorful.

All these soups provide vegetables in such abundance that they effortlessly help your total of daily servings mount toward the recommended three to five a day. You get an entire bunch of broccoli in the vichyssoise and more than half a pound of tomatoes in one serving of spicy Indian Tomato Soup. Based on the USDA's ½-cup serving size for cooked vegetables, you get three servings of veggies in each bowl of Sweet and Sour Cabbage Soup.

Many of these soups actually contain less than a teaspoon of beneficial extra-virgin olive or canola oil per serving. Others, including Italian Lentil Soup and Broccoli Vichyssoise, have no added fat at all. When I switch to a bit of butter, as in Spinach Cappuccino, or some preservative-free bacon, it is well worth the flavor and reasonable when you eat sensibly overall.

At lunchtime, I frequently have a bowl of soup (or a Thermos-full, if I'm brown-bagging it) made a day or two earlier. While the soup provides solid servings of the 12 Best Foods, whole grain bread and a piece of fruit complete the meal.

For dinner, I recommend eating a cup of soup the minute you walk in the door. Then get comfortable and get the rest of dinner ready. Do this even when you bring home take-out. With the edge off your appetite and in a better mood, you'll eat smaller portions and enjoy putting a balanced meal together—instead of grabbing the first thing you see.

BLACK BEAN MINESTRONE

Black beans, although not typically used in Italian cooking, are perfect in this hearty vegetable soup. A rind from Parmigiano-Reggiano cheese makes an excellent addition.

1	tablespoon extra-virgin olive oil	1	medium potato, peeled and cut in ½" cubes
1	medium carrot, thinly sliced		
1	rib celery, thinly sliced	6	plum tomatoes, seeded and diced
1	medium leek, white part only, halved and sliced	1	tablespoon tomato paste
		1	(3") piece Parmigiano-Reggiano rind, optional
1	medium onion, chopped		
1	clove garlic, minced	1	cup canned black beans, drained
4	cups fat-free, reduced-sodium chicken broth or vegetable broth		Salt and freshly ground black pepper
		⅓	cup grated Parmigiano-Reggiano cheese
3	cups coarsely chopped Swiss chard leaves		

RELISH THE RIND

The rind of Parmigiano-Reggiano cheese, which is totally edible, adds beautiful flavor to soups. A 3" square is enough to enhance a good-size pot of soup like this one. When serving, break up the supple rind and include a piece in each bowl.

1. Heat the oil in a medium Dutch oven over medium-high heat. Sauté the carrot, celery, leek, and onion until the onion is translucent, 4 minutes. Mix in the garlic. Cook until the onion is soft, 3 minutes longer, stirring often.

2. Add the broth, chard, potato, tomatoes, tomato paste, and the cheese rind, if using. Simmer until the potatoes are almost tender, 10 minutes. Add the beans, cooking until they are heated through, 5 minutes. Season the soup to taste with salt and pepper. Ladle it into deep bowls. Top with a generous sprinkling of grated cheese and serve. This soup keeps up to 3 days, tightly covered in the refrigerator. It reheats well in a covered pot.

Makes 6 servings

Per serving: 156 calories, 6 g fat, 2 g saturated fat, 7 g protein, 21 g carbohydrates, 5 g fiber

INDIAN TOMATO SOUP

A kitchen disaster can produce a great new dish. I was making chutney one day, when I used the wrong kind of tomatoes and cooked it in a pot that was too deep. Instead of thick chutney, I ended up with this sensational red-hot soup. Serve it hot but not steaming, so you can taste all the spices. Even if you omit the curry leaves, you will enjoy it.

2	tablespoons canola oil	½	teaspoon cayenne pepper
2	teaspoons black or yellow mustard seeds	½	teaspoon turmeric
1	teaspoon cumin seeds	4	pounds ripe tomatoes, seeded and coarsely chopped
6	curry leaves, optional	1	tablespoon sugar
2	teaspoons ground coriander	¼	cup tomato paste
1	teaspoon sweet paprika	2	teaspoons salt
1	teaspoon curry powder	¾	cup low-fat or fat-free plain yogurt

1. Heat the oil in a deep saucepan over medium-high heat. Add the mustard seeds, cumin seeds, and curry leaves, if using. When the mustard seeds start to pop, 1 to 2 minutes, stir in the coriander, paprika, curry powder, cayenne, and turmeric. As soon as the ground spices start to darken, 30 seconds, add the tomatoes, sugar, tomato paste, and salt. Cook until the tomatoes are soft and their skin separates from the flesh, 20 minutes.

2. Divide the soup among 6 bowls. Dollop 2 tablespoons of the yogurt into the center of each bowl.

Makes 6 servings

Per serving: 154 calories, 7 g fat, 1 g saturated fat, 5 g protein, 22 g carbohydrates, 5 g fiber

SWIFTLY SEEDED

To quickly seed a tomato, stand it stem end up. Holding the blade of a sharp knife at 90 degrees to the tomato's top, vertically slice off 1 side. Rotate the tomato 90 degrees and cut off the second side. Repeat, cutting off the 4 sides and leaving the seedy center as a square core. Lay this on 1 side and slice off the bottom. Discard the core and chop the 5 pieces into the desired size.

FOOD FACT

In addition to lycopene, an antioxidant, tomatoes are abundant in vitamin C.

GREEK WHITE BEAN SOUP

This is one of the best dishes at Molyvos, an exceptional Greek restaurant in New York City that features less-familiar regional dishes. For a completely fat-free soup, you can skip the feta and olive oil garnish.

1	cup dried giant lima beans		Salt and freshly ground black pepper
1	large red onion, chopped	2	cups baby spinach, packed
1	leek, white part only	⅓	cup crumbled feta cheese, for garnish
2	cups fat-free, reduced-sodium chicken broth or vegetable broth	4	teaspoons extra-virgin olive oil, optional, for garnish

1. Soak the beans in cold water until their skins are wrinkled and most of the beans have split open, 2 to 4 hours. Drain the beans.

2. Place the beans in a small Dutch oven or deep, heavy saucepan. Add the onion, leek, and broth. Pour in 2 cups cold water. Bring to a boil over high heat. Reduce the heat, cover, and simmer until the beans are soft, about 1 hour. Season the soup to taste with salt and pepper.

3. Off the heat, using an immersion blender, whirl until half the beans are pureed. Or puree half the soup in a blender and pour the pureed soup back into the pot. At this point, the soup may be cooled and refrigerated up to 4 days.

4. To serve, heat the soup until it is almost boiling. Mix in the spinach until it wilts, 3 to 4 minutes. Divide the soup among 4 bowls. Spoon 1 table-spoon of the feta cheese into the center of each bowl. If using, drizzle 1 teaspoon of the oil over the soup.

Makes 4 servings

Per serving: 278 calories, 8 g fat, 3 g saturated fat, 15 g protein, 38 g carbohydrates, 12 g fiber

ITALIAN LENTIL SOUP

Soaking lentils is unusual. It helps this soup cook in just half an hour.

FOOD FACT

Lentils, like other legumes, are loaded with fiber; they contain lots of folate, too.

Several kinds of Italian lentils are becoming increasingly available in the United States. Their distinctive flavors seem related more to their color than the region of Italy they come from. When I buy either Umbrian Castelluccio lentils or those from Pantelleria, an island off the coast of Sicily, I find that when they are dark, they taste earthy and spicy. When they are paler, their taste is usually sweeter and milder.

3	*cups Italian brown lentils (1 pound)*	1	*(4") sprig rosemary, or 4 thyme sprigs*
1	*small red onion, halved*	1	*(15-ounce) can beef broth*
1	*bay leaf*	½	*bunch Swiss chard, stemmed, cut in*
1	*(3") cinnamon stick*		*½" ribbons (about 4 cups)*
1	*clove garlic, chopped*		*Salt and freshly ground black pepper*

1. Soak the lentils in cold water for 2 hours, then drain.

2. Place the lentils in a large, deep saucepan. Add the onion, bay leaf, cinnamon stick, garlic, and rosemary or thyme. Pour in cold water to cover the lentils to a depth of 2". Bring to a boil, reduce the heat, and simmer for 30 minutes. Drain the lentils. Remove and discard the onion, bay leaf, cinnamon stick, and rosemary or thyme. Rinse out the pot.

3. Return the lentils to the pot and pour in the beef broth. Add 2 cups cold water. Bring the soup to a boil. Mix in the chard, reduce the heat, and simmer until the chard is tender, 10 minutes. Season the soup to taste with salt and pepper.

Makes 6 servings

Per serving: 338 calories, 1 g fat, 0 g saturated fat, 28 g protein, 57 g carbohydrates, 30 g fiber

SCOTCH OATMEAL SOUP

The nutty taste of oats is a revelation in this country soup. Cabbage, leek, onion, tomatoes, and thyme combine to add to a rustic flavor. After 1 steaming bowl, you will feel ready to toss the caber, a Scottish test of strength.

1	tablespoon canola oil	4	cups vegetable broth
1	medium carrot, thinly sliced	½	cup steel-cut oats
1	leek, white part only, chopped	1	teaspoon dried thyme
1	medium onion, chopped	½	teaspoon sugar
½	small cabbage, halved, cored, and sliced crosswise into ½" strips	1	bay leaf
		½	teaspoon salt
1	(15-ounce) can diced tomatoes, with their liquid		Freshly ground black pepper

FOOD FACT

In dried herbs, fragrance is an indication of potency: the more aromatic, the more effective—for health as well as seasoning. When opening a tightly closed jar, if you are not hit with the herb's fragrance, replace it.

1. Heat the oil in a large Dutch oven over medium-high heat. Add the carrot, leek, and onion and stir to coat with the oil. Cover tightly, reduce the heat to medium, and cook until the vegetables release their juices, about 10 minutes. Mix in the cabbage, cover the pot, and cook until the cabbage is wilted, 8 to 10 minutes.

2. Add the tomatoes, broth, oats, thyme, sugar, bay leaf, and salt. Season the soup to taste with pepper. Simmer uncovered until the oats are cooked and the cabbage is tender, about 30 minutes. Remove the bay leaf. This soup keeps for 3 to 4 days, tightly covered in the refrigerator. When re-heating, you may need to add some more vegetable broth if it is too thick.

Makes 6 servings

Per serving: 135 calories, 4 g fat, 0 g saturated fat, 5 g protein, 23 g carbohydrates, 5 g fiber

SWEET AND SOUR CABBAGE SOUP

I combine tender Savoy cabbage and sturdy Tuscan kale along with tomatoes and other vegetables in this tangy soup. Tuscan kale, an heirloom variety with long, plume-shaped leaves, is also called lacinato, dinosaur, black, or *cavalo nero*.

2	tablespoons extra-virgin olive oil	½	bunch lacinato kale, stemmed and cut
1	large rib celery, sliced		crosswise in ½" ribbons
1	medium carrot, sliced	1	teaspoon salt, divided
1	medium leek, white part only, chopped	1	(14-ounce) can plum tomatoes
1	medium red onion, chopped	2	large cloves garlic, chopped
1	small Savoy cabbage (2 pounds), quartered, cored, and cut crosswise in ¾" strips	1	bay leaf
		2	teaspoons sugar
		⅓	cup chopped flat-leaf parsley
			Juice of ½ lemon

1. Heat the oil in a large Dutch oven over medium-high heat. Sauté the celery, carrot, leek, and onion until the onion starts to soften, 3 minutes.

2. Mix in the cabbage, kale, and ½ teaspoon of the salt. Stir until the cabbage is bright green and the kale is limp, 2 minutes. Cover tightly, reduce the heat to medium-low, and cook until the vegetables have given up their juices, 5 minutes.

3. Meanwhile, work a knife up and down in the can of tomatoes to coarsely chop them. Add the tomatoes, with their liquid, to the pot. Toss in the garlic, bay leaf, and the remaining ½ teaspoon salt. Pour in 5 cups cold water. Raise the heat until the liquid boils. Reduce the heat and simmer for 20 minutes. Mix in the sugar, parsley, and lemon juice. Cook until the cabbage is tender, 20 minutes longer. Remove the bay leaf and serve.

Makes 6 servings

Per serving: 143 calories, 5 g fat, 1 g saturated fat, 6 g protein, 23 g carbohydrates, 7 g fiber

MAKE 'EM SWEAT

Chefs sweat vegetables to intensify their flavor. First, coat the vegetables lightly with oil or butter, then cook tightly covered over low heat until the vegetables give up their juice and look moist.

HANDY TRICK

To separate kale leaves from the tough center stalk, hold the stem with the leaf pointing down. With the other hand, fold the sides as if closing a book. Starting near the top, pull the leaves away from the stem.

GREEN BORSCHT

Borscht, although commonly associated with beets, is usually a hearty beef soup. This one is full of greens, too. When fresh sorrel is available, add half a bunch in place of the lemon juice. For a Russian feast, serve with lightly buttered black bread, the kind that is thin and sour.

1	pound lean chuck, well-trimmed, cut in 1" cubes	1	bunch curly spinach, stemmed
4	cups fat-free beef broth	2	medium yellow-fleshed potatoes, diced
2	ribs celery, chopped		Juice of 1 lemon
1	carrot, chopped	1	tablespoon sugar
1	large leek, white part only, chopped		Salt
½	cup chopped flat-leaf parsley	8	hard-cooked eggs, peeled
10	whole black peppercorns		Sour cream (optional), for garnish

1. Place the meat in a deep soup pot. Add the broth and 2 quarts cold water. Bring the liquid to a boil, reduce the heat, and simmer, skimming off the foam until the liquid is clear, 20 minutes.

2. Add the celery, carrot, leek, parsley, and peppercorns. Simmer, covered, for 1½ hours.

3. Cut the spinach leaves in ½" ribbons and add them to the soup. Add the potatoes, lemon juice, and sugar. Cover and simmer until the potatoes are tender, 20 minutes. Season to taste with salt.

4. To serve, place an egg, quartered lengthwise into wedges, in each of 8 bowls. Ladle the hot soup over the egg. If desired, top with sour cream.

Makes 8 servings

Per serving: 278 calories, 13 g fat, 4 g saturated fat, 28 g protein, 13 g carbohydrates, 2 g fiber

BLACK BEAN BISQUE

This almost-instant soup takes advantage of the creaminess of Refried Black Beans (page 186). When you make them specifically for this soup, add the broth to them in the skillet and proceed. This is a perfect introduction to Roasted Salmon with Fresh Garden Salsa (page 148) for dinner or Green Eggs and Ham (page 183) for brunch.

Refried Black Beans (page 186)
1½ cups fat-free, reduced-sodium chicken broth, or vegetable broth
⅓ cup finely chopped sweet or red onion
1 tablespoon sherry vinegar, or juice of ½ lime
4 tablespoons snipped dill, for garnish

In a medium saucepan, heat the refried beans with the broth. Pour the mixture into a blender. Add the onions and vinegar or lime juice and puree. Divide the hot soup among 4 bowls. Garnish with dill and serve.

Makes 4 servings

Per serving: 369 calories, 8 g fat, 1 g saturated fat, 20 g protein, 48 g carbohydrates, 20 g fiber

BLACK BEANS SOUP

NOT a misspelling, this soup is made using 2 kinds of black beans—the usual black turtle beans plus black soybeans. This combination of beans increases the soup's protein content, plus the black soybeans add isoflavones.

1½	cups dried black turtle beans (¾ pound)	2	sprigs flat-leaf parsley
½	cup dried black soybeans	2	cloves garlic, finely chopped
2	strips preservative-free bacon, cut in ½" pieces	1	large bay leaf
		1	teaspoon salt
1	small carrot, thinly sliced		Freshly ground black pepper
1	rib celery, thinly sliced	¼	cup dry Madeira or sherry
1	small parsnip, thinly sliced		Thin lemon slices, for garnish

1. Soak the black turtle beans and soybeans together overnight or use the quick-soak method (page 2). Drain the beans.

2. Place the soaked beans in a deep saucepan. Add 8 cups cold water. Bring to a gentle boil, reduce the heat, cover, and simmer 90 minutes.

3. Place the bacon in a large Dutch oven over medium heat. When the bacon is translucent, mix in the carrot and celery. Sauté until the celery starts to soften, 4 minutes. Add the beans with their cooking liquid, the parsnip, parsley, garlic, bay leaf, salt, and a few grinds of the pepper. Bring to a boil. Reduce the heat, cover, and simmer until the beans are very soft, 40 minutes. Remove the parsley and bay leaf.

4. Puree 2 cups of the soup in a blender. Return the pureed soup to the pot. Mix in the Madeira. To serve, ladle the soup into 8 deep soup bowls and float a lemon slice on top.

Makes 8 servings

Per serving: 193 calories, 1 g fat, 0 g saturated fat, 11 g protein, 35 g carbohydrates, 13 g fiber

BACON, CLEAN AND LEAN

Uncured bacon is made without added nitrites, nitrates, or other preservatives. Some brands are also antibiotic-free and may contain as little as 3 grams of fat and 1.5 grams of saturated fat in 2 slices.

Select the package with the meatiest slices by taking time to look at the window or the back of the package.

When the ends of a slice are mostly fat, trim them away, to make bacon even leaner.

FOOD FACT

Nitrites, a preservative used in curing bacon, form nitrosamines, powerful, cancer-causing agents. This is why I use only preservative-free bacon.

SWEET POTATO–CARROT SOUP

Roasting brings out the sweetness in the potatoes and carrots, enhancing the flavor of this thick puree. Each special garnish gives the soup a different personality.

Cutting the vegetables and apple to different sizes lets them roast to the proper point at the same time.

FOOD FACT
Shallots, like garlic and onions, add heart-protecting sulfur compounds to dishes.

1	tablespoon canola oil
1¼	pounds Beauregard, Garnet, or Jewel yam, cut in 2" pieces
1	large carrot, cut in 1" pieces
1	Fuji apple, peeled, cored, and cut into 8 pieces
1	tablespoon unsalted butter or canola oil
1	shallot, chopped
3	cups fat-free, reduced-sodium chicken broth

Salt and freshly ground black pepper
Garnish each serving with
   1 tablespoon, choosing from:
Cranberries—Homemade or canned
   chunky relish, adds tangy contrast
Sautéed sliced mushrooms—Bring
   out the root vegetables' earthy flavor
Flaked hot smoked salmon—Also
   called kippered salmon (page 17);
   adds richness

1. Preheat the oven to 400°F. Rub the oil over the yam, carrot, and apple to coat them. Spread them in 1 layer on a baking sheet and roast for 30 minutes. When cool enough to handle, lift the peels off the sweet potato pieces.

2. Heat the butter in a large, heavy saucepan over medium-high heat. Sauté the shallot until soft, 5 minutes. Add the roasted vegetables, apple, and broth. When the liquid boils, reduce the heat, cover, and simmer until the carrot is soft, 20 minutes.

3. Puree the soup in a blender. Season it to taste with salt and pepper. Ladle into 4 deep soup bowls, garnish as preferred, and serve.

Makes 4 servings

Per serving: 269 calories, 7 g fat, 2 g saturated fat, 5 g protein, 48 g carbohydrates, 8 g fiber

SPINACH CAPPUCCINO WITH PARMESAN FOAM

Broccoli and leek deepen the flavor of the spinach in this layered soup that features a topping of frothy milk steamed with Parmigiano-Reggiano cheese. Serve it in clear bowls to show this ivory foam floating over the dark soup.

FOOD FACT
Spinach plus broccoli makes a bowlful of potent antioxidants.

1	tablespoon unsalted butter
2	teaspoons canola oil
1	medium leek, white part only, chopped
1	clove garlic, chopped
2	cups fat-free, reduced-sodium chicken broth
3	cups broccoli florets
1½	cups chopped, peeled broccoli stems
1	small russet potato, peeled and chopped
2	cups spinach leaves, firmly packed
	Pinch of cayenne pepper
¾	cup cold whole milk
⅓	cup grated Parmigiano-Reggiano cheese
	Fresh nutmeg, for garnish

1. Heat the butter and oil in a large saucepan over medium-high heat. When the butter melts, add the leek and garlic. Cook until the leek is soft, 10 minutes. Pour in the broth and 2 cups cold water. Add the broccoli and potato. When the liquid boils, reduce the heat, cover, and simmer 15 minutes. Add the spinach and cayenne. Cover and simmer 10 minutes. Set the soup aside, uncovered, to cool slightly.

2. Puree the soup in a blender and divide it among 4 deep bowls.

3. Combine the milk and cheese in a deep, heatproof cup. Using a cappuccino maker, foam the milk. Spoon enough foam over each serving to cover the soup. (Discard the remaining milk and cheese mixture). Serve immediately with a garnish of nutmeg.

Makes 4 servings

Per serving: 133 calories, 7 g fat, 3 g saturated fat, 7 g protein, 14 g carbohydrates, 4 g fiber

RED VELVET SOUP

This colorful, Moosewood-inspired soup gets its elusive flavor from a combination of beans, tomatoes, and beets. Cooking the beets is messy, but worth it.

1	medium beet, peeled and diced (about 1 cup)	⅛	teaspoon red-pepper flakes
1	(15-ounce) can kidney beans, drained		Salt and freshly ground black pepper
1	tablespoon canola oil	¼	cup plain yogurt or low-fat sour cream, optional, for garnish
½	Spanish onion, chopped		
1	(28-ounce) can diced tomatoes, with their liquid	2	tablespoons snipped chives, optional, for garnish

1. In a medium saucepan, boil the beet in 4 cups cold water for 30 minutes. Add the beans and cook until the beets and beans are very soft, 20 minutes. Set them aside.

2. In a small Dutch oven or a large saucepan, heat the oil over medium-high heat. Sauté the onion until soft, 5 minutes. Add the tomatoes and red-pepper flakes. Cook until the onion is very soft, 15 minutes.

3. Drain the beets and beans in a colander set over a bowl to reserve their liquid. Add the beets and beans to the tomato mixture. Remove the pot from the heat and cool 10 minutes.

4. Puree the soup in a blender or use an immersion blender in the pot. If the soup is too thick, add some of the reserved beet liquid. Season the soup to taste with salt and pepper. Divide it among 4 bowls and serve hot, garnished with a dollop of yogurt or sour cream, plus snipped chives, if desired.

Makes 4 servings

Per serving: 141 calories, 4 g fat, 0 g saturated fat, 7 g protein, 21 g carbohydrates, 7 g fiber

FOR NEATER BEETS

Cover your work surface with waxed paper when chopping beets to avoid staining it. Wash your hands after peeling each beet and again after chopping them to keep stained fingers to a minimum.

FOOD FACT

Beets contain folic acid, a B vitamin which helps the body get rid of homocysteine. High homocysteine levels are associated with heart disease.

BROCCOLI VICHYSSOISE

The silken texture of this chilled dairy-free soup comes from pureed potatoes.

1	bunch broccoli	2	potatoes, peeled and diced
2	leeks, white parts only, coarsely chopped	½–1	teaspoon salt
1	medium onion, coarsely chopped	2	Freshly ground black pepper tablespoons snipped chives, for
1	shallot, chopped		garnish

1. Chop the broccoli florets, including the thinner stems just below the florets. Reserve the lower stems for another use.

2. Place the broccoli in a large saucepan or a small Dutch oven. Add the leeks, onion, shallot, potatoes, salt, and a few grinds of pepper. Pour in 4 cups water and bring the liquid to a boil over medium-high heat. Reduce the heat, cover, and simmer until the vegetables are very tender, 30 to 35 minutes. Let the soup sit for 10 minutes to cool slightly.

3. Puree the soup in a blender until it is smooth or use an immersion blender in the pot. Chill thoroughly, 3 hours to overnight. Adjust the seasoning. Divide the cold soup among 4 bowls and garnish each with one-quarter of the chives.

Makes 4 servings

Per serving: 103 calories, 0 g fat, 0 g saturated fat, 4 g protein, 22 g carbohydrates, 4 g fiber

SALMON AND
CREAMED CORN CHOWDER

Buttery hot-smoked salmon gives this chowder the flavor that usually comes from bacon or pork. Hot-smoking also firms the fish so it flakes easily. Creamed corn contributes richness without adding fat and keeps the soup dairy-free. Serve with crackers made without trans fat.

FOOD FACT
Green bell peppers are a good source of vitamin A.

1	small russet potato, peeled and diced	1	cup fat-free, reduced-sodium chicken broth
1	tablespoon canola oil	2	teaspoons fresh thyme leaves, or ½ teaspoon dried
1	small red onion, chopped		Pinch of cayenne pepper
1	small green bell pepper, seeded and chopped	4	ounces hot-smoked salmon, flaked (see page 17)
1	(14-ounce) can creamed corn		Salt and freshly ground black pepper
½	cup frozen corn kernels		

1. Place the potato in a medium saucepan. Cover it to a depth of 2" with cold water and set the pot over medium-high heat. Boil until the potato resists slightly when pierced with a knife, 10 minutes.

2. Meanwhile, heat the oil in another saucepan. Sauté the onion and bell pepper until the onion is soft, 4 minutes. Add the creamed corn, frozen corn, broth, thyme, and cayenne. Bring the soup just to a boil. Add the cooked potato, remove the pot from the heat, and stir in the salmon. Season the soup to taste with salt and pepper, divide among 4 bowls, and serve immediately.

Makes 4 servings

Per serving: 251 calories, 13 g fat, 1 g saturated fat, 12 g protein, 35 g carbohydrates, 5 g fiber

CHICKEN TORTILLA SOUP
WITH CORN AND SPINACH

Baby spinach, frozen corn, store-bought roast chicken, and canned broth are healthy convenience foods. Combined, they make a soup with flavor that tastes like it took more than 15 minutes to make.

2	teaspoons canola oil	2	cups diced cooked chicken breast
1	onion, chopped	½	cup salsa
3	cups fat-free, reduced-sodium chicken broth		Juice of 1 lime
			Salt and freshly ground black pepper
1	cup frozen or canned corn kernels	¼	cup coarsely chopped cilantro leaves
4	cups lightly packed baby spinach (4 ounces)	1	ounce unsalted tortilla chips

1. Heat the oil in a deep medium saucepan over medium-high heat. Sauté the onion until it is translucent.

2. Pour in the chicken broth. Add the corn and spinach. Reduce the heat to medium and cook until the corn is heated through and the spinach is bright green, 3 minutes. Mix in the chicken, salsa, and lime juice. Season the soup to taste with salt and pepper.

3. To serve, divide the soup among 4 deep bowls. Top each bowl with one-quarter of the cilantro. Coarsely crush the tortilla chips and stir one-quarter of them into each bowl. Serve immediately.

Makes 4 servings

Per serving: 260 calories, 7 g fat, 1 g saturated fat, 27 g protein, 22 g carbohydrates, 4 g fiber

---

If you do not have leftover cooked chicken, poach a ¾ pound boneless, skinless breast in a saucepan in 1¾ cups (one 14.5-ounce can) chicken broth over medium-high heat until bubbles form around the edges of the pot, 4 to 5 minutes. Reduce the heat and simmer gently until the chicken is white in the center, about 8 minutes. Skim off any foam from the cooking liquid. Cool the chicken in the broth. Tear the chicken into ½" strips. Strain and reuse the poaching liquid in other dishes.

FOOD FACT

Corn and spinach are rich sources of lutein and zeaxanthin, 2 carotenoids helpful for your eyes.

MUSHROOM CONSOMMÉ WITH SAKE

The intensely flavored liquid created by soaking dried mushrooms is the base for this clear, vegetarian soup. A fusion of East and West techniques and flavors, it makes a refined first course. It is also comforting sipped from a mug if you omit the garnishes.

If not using all the broth for this soup immediately, refrigerate for 3 days, or freeze for up to 2 months.

2	teaspoons canola oil	½	teaspoon whole black peppercorns
1	cup diced yellow onion	1	cup diced soft regular tofu (4 ounces)
10	ounces white mushrooms, with stems, thinly sliced	¼	cup fresh spinach, cut in ¼" ribbons
		¼	cup sake
3	medium dried shiitake mushrooms	2	teaspoons tamari
⅓	cup dried porcini mushrooms (¼ ounce)	1	teaspoon salt
2	ribs celery, chopped	¼	cup enoki mushrooms, for garnish
3	sprigs parsley	4	paper-thin slices daikon radish, for garnish
¼	teaspoon rubbed sage		

1. Heat the oil in a deep saucepan over medium-high heat. Sauté the onion until it is well-browned, 10 minutes. Pour in 10 cups cold water. Add the mushrooms, celery, parsley, sage, and peppercorns. When the liquid boils, reduce the heat and simmer uncovered for 40 minutes.

2. Set the broth aside to steep for 30 minutes. Strain it into a large bowl. Press lightly on the solids before discarding them. There will be about 8 cups mushroom broth.

3. To serve, set out 4 small, deep bowls. Place one-quarter of the tofu and spinach in each bowl. Heat 4 cups of the broth in a saucepan over medium-high heat. When the soup starts bubbling around the edges, add the sake, tamari, and salt. Divide among the 4 bowls. Add in the enoki and daikon slices, and serve.

Makes 4 servings

Per serving: 110 calories, 4 g fat, 0 g saturated fat, 7 g protein, 10 g carbohydrates, 3 g fiber

DOUBLE MISO SOUP

Using 2 kinds of miso and 2 kinds of sea vegetables makes this a nutritionally powerful, sustaining soup. Pale misos are lower in sodium than the darker varieties. Dashi, the traditional base for miso soup, is made with kombu, a sea vegetable.

1	tablespoon dried wakame	1	tablespoon sweet rice miso
1	(2" × 5") strip dried kombu	½	teaspoon fresh ginger, cut in fine
2	tablespoons frozen shelled edamame		julienne, for garnish
1	tablespoon light yellow miso		

1. In a small bowl, soak the wakame in ½ cup cold water until it rehydrates, 6 minutes. Drain and squeeze out the excess moisture. Set aside.

2. For the dashi, wipe the kombu with a damp paper towel. Place it in a small saucepan and pour in 1¾ cups cold water. Set the pot over medium-high heat until tiny bubbles cover the bottom of the pot, 4 minutes. Off the heat, steep the dashi 2 minutes. Discard the kombu.

3. In another small pot, boil the edamame until tender, 5 minutes. Drain, cool briefly, and squeeze each bean gently between your thumb and first finger to pop it out of its skin.

4. Place the 2 misos and 2 tablespoons of the dashi in a small bowl. With the back of a spoon, mix and mash until the miso mixture resembles gravy. Mix the miso into the pot of dashi. Heat the soup until the surface shimmers. Do not let it boil.

5. Divide the wakame between 2 small soup bowls. Pour in the soup, add the edamame and ginger to each bowl, and serve.

Makes 2 servings

Per serving: 55 calories, 2 g fat, 0 g saturated fat, 4 g protein, 7 g carbohydrates, 1 g fiber

I like Cold Mountain Light Yellow Miso and South River Miso Company's Sweet-Tasting Brown Rice Miso for this soup. If you double the recipe, steep the kombu for 4 minutes, and use 2½ tablespoons of each miso.

IN A MERMAID'S GARDEN

Dried sea vegetables, a.k.a. seaweed, range from mild-tasting, green wakame and kombu, to black-brown hijiki that has a strong, iodine flavor. They are always soaked before using. Asian markets and natural food stores sell a variety of them.

ICED GREEN CHILE
AND YOGURT SOUP

FOOD FACT

Cilantro, used in Ayurvedic medicine to aid digestion, is rich in beta-carotene.

You will welcome this refreshing, pale green soup on a hot day. It is equally good made with dairy yogurt or dairy-free cultured soy, a.k.a. soy yogurt.

2	cups plain low-fat yogurt or cultured soy	1	jalapeño chile pepper, seeded and chopped
1	cup mint leaves, divided	½	cup chopped scallions, green and white parts
¾	cup cilantro leaves, lightly packed, divided	3	tablespoons fresh lime juice
1	large clove garlic, chopped		Salt and freshly ground black pepper

1. Place the yogurt, ½ cup mint, ½ cup cilantro, the garlic, jalapeño pepper, scallions, and lime juice in a food processor or blender. Whirl until the soup is smooth. Season with salt and pepper. Chill the soup for 1 to 8 hours.

2. Finely chop the remaining mint and cilantro leaves. Divide the soup among 4 small bowls and garnish with the chopped herbs. Serve immediately.

Makes 4 servings

Per serving: 96 calories, 2 g fat, 1 g saturated fat, 7 g protein, 13 g carbohydrates, 2 g fiber

BLUEBERRY SOUP

Usually fruit soups are chilled, but I serve this one warm, as a starter or for dessert. It is best made with fresh or frozen cultivated berries; wild ones make it gritty. The pectin in the fruit thickens it slightly, and a touch of spice balances its concentrated fruit flavor.

1	pint fresh blueberries, or 2 cups frozen	2 or 3	tablespoons maple syrup
3	tablespoons frozen apple juice concentrate	⅛	teaspoon ground allspice

Place the blueberries, apple juice concentrate, maple syrup, and allspice in a medium saucepan. Set the pot over medium-high heat. When the liquid boils, reduce the heat. Simmer until the berries burst and give up their liquid, 15 minutes for fresh blueberries, 12 minutes for frozen. Serve warm, not hot.

Makes 4 servings

Per serving: 89 calories, 0 g fat, 0 g saturated fat, 1 g protein, 22 g carbohydrates, 2 g fiber

FOOD FACT

Besides containing antioxidants that help to ward off cancer, blueberries contain a compound to help fight cholesterol.

CHAPTER FOUR
SALADS AND DRESSINGS

Eating a generous salad a day can provide three or more servings of vegetables. Salads are also perfect for adding beans, fruit, nuts, and soy to your day. Of course, salad every day can get boring and might be overly caloric if you douse it with dressing. But I think the biggest obstacle to eating at least one salad a day is needing time to prepare them.

Are you nodding agreement? Then check out Tomato and Watermelon Salad and Gazpacho Salad, which you can put together in a snap. Luscious, thick, and creamy Blue Cheese, Cracked Mustard, and Pepper Ranch Dressings are lean enough to use lavishly, and they provide soy benefits. To avoid boredom toss together Canned Salmon Salad—yes, canned salmon, but more about that later on.

Here are nearly a month's worth of salads. Some feature spinach, including citrus-dressed Napa and Spinach Slaw; tomatoes, in speedy Grape Tomato Salad with Fresh Herb Vinaigrette; salmon, including smoked; and walnuts. Then there's mischievous Kaleslaw with Red Pepper, finely shredded cabbage and raw kale in an old-fashioned creamy dressing with a touch of curry powder. Serve this delicious powerhouse and have fun watching family and friends take seconds.

Salads, homemade or from a salad bar, provide the perfect place to include a serving of soy, such as cubes of the flavorful baked or smoked tofu, a scattering of fiber-rich edamame, or crunchy soynuts. Southwestern Three-Bean Salad also uses soy, in the form of convenient canned black soybeans.

Even if your spinach or leafy green salads always come out of a bag, the week's worth of dressings here will keep them fresh and interesting.

GRAPE TOMATO SALAD WITH FRESH HERB VINAIGRETTE

Firm, sweet grape tomatoes, crisp watercress, plus a light dressing make an ideal trio. If fresh spearmint is available, it is the perfect choice in the vinaigrette. Serve with grilled tuna, salmon, or chicken.

2	teaspoons minced red onion	1	pint grape or red cherry tomatoes, halved lengthwise
2	tablespoons Champagne vinegar		
1	tablespoon fresh lemon juice	2	tablespoons snipped chives
1	teaspoon salt	1	tablespoon chopped mint, preferably spearmint
	Freshly ground black pepper		
1	tablespoon extra-virgin olive oil	½	bunch watercress, trimmed into sprigs

1. In a small bowl, combine the onion, vinegar, lemon juice, salt, and 3 or 4 grinds of pepper to taste. Whisk in the oil. This dressing can be made up to 4 hours in advance, covered, and refrigerated.

2. Place the tomatoes in a mixing bowl. Add the chives and mint. Remix the dressing and pour it over the tomatoes, tossing with a fork to coat. Divide the tomatoes equally among 4 salad plates and place a portion of the watercress to 1 side. Serve immediately.

Makes 4 servings

Per serving: 54 calories, 4 g fat, 1 g saturated fat, 1 g protein, 5 g carbohydrates, 1 g fiber

Save the dressing left in the bowl to use on a green salad.

FOOD FACT

Watercress is a cruciferous vegetable related to cabbage and Brussels sprouts.

BROCCOLI SALAD
WITH SHERRY VINAIGRETTE

Broccoli florets, chunky carrot slices, and toasted almonds make this a crunchy and bright salad. To save time, make the sherry vinaigrette dressing in your salad bowl, then add everything else and toss.

4	cups large broccoli florets	½	teaspoon salt
1	large carrot, cut diagonally into ½"-thick slices	1	tablespoon extra-virgin olive oil Freshly ground black pepper
2	teaspoons sherry vinegar	2	tablespoons toasted sliced almonds, optional, for garnish
1	tablespoon finely chopped shallot		
½	teaspoon dried oregano		

FOOD FACT

A meal that provides a small amount of fat along with cooked carrots helps the body to absorb more than half of the beta-carotene present.

1. Steam the broccoli and carrot slices together until they are bright but still crisp, 2 minutes. Drain, and drop the vegetables into a bowl of ice water until chilled. Drain them well. You can do this up to 24 hours ahead, storing the vegetables tightly covered in the refrigerator.

2. For the dressing, combine the vinegar, shallot, oregano, and salt in a large mixing bowl. Whisk in the oil. Season the dressing to taste with pepper.

3. Add the broccoli and carrots to the bowl and toss to coat with the dressing. Garnish with almonds, if using. This salad is best served the day it is made.

Makes 4 servings

Per serving: 63 calories, 4 g fat, 1 g saturated fat, 2 g protein, 7 g carbohydrates, 3 g fiber

SPINACH SALAD WITH NECTARINE, BLUEBERRIES, AND LIME BALSAMIC VINAIGRETTE

With nectarines available nearly all year long, you can enjoy this salad almost anytime. I actually like it best in the winter, when the tartness of imported nectarines seems to make it even more refreshing. Tossing fresh mint with the spinach adds an unexpected flavor.

4	cups baby spinach (4 ounces)	½	teaspoon salt
¼	cup mint leaves	1	tablespoon extra-virgin olive oil
	Juice of ½ lime		Freshly ground black pepper
2	teaspoons balsamic vinegar	1	nectarine, thinly sliced
1	teaspoon chopped shallot	½	cup fresh blueberries, or ¼ cup dried

1. Place the spinach in a large mixing bowl. Stack the mint leaves and cut them crosswise into thin strips. Toss the mint with the spinach.

2. For the dressing, combine the lime juice, vinegar, shallot, and salt in a small bowl. Whisk in the oil. Season the dressing to taste with pepper.

3. Pour the dressing over the greens, tossing to coat lightly. Divide the dressed spinach among 4 salad plates. Fan one-quarter of the nectarine slices on 1 side of each plate. Sprinkle the blueberries over the spinach. Serve immediately.

Makes 4 servings

Per serving: 72 calories, 4 g fat, 0 g saturated fat, 1 g protein, 10 g carbohydrates, 2 g fiber

BABY SPINACH, WATERCRESS, AND APPLE SALAD

To enjoy the contrast of sliced apple against dark greens in this salad, I suggest serving it in a clear bowl and tossing it at the table. Serve it with Pork Medallions with Wild Mushrooms (page 138) or roast or grilled chicken.

⅓	cup coarsely chopped walnuts	½	bunch watercress, tough stems removed
1	small red onion, cut vertically into thin slices	1	Granny Smith apple, peeled, cored, and thinly sliced
4	cups baby spinach (4 ounces)		Cracked Mustard Dressing (page 119)

FOOD FACT

Apples, particularly the skin, contain quercetin, a potent inflammation-fighter.

1. Preheat the oven to 350°F. Spread the nuts in 1 layer on a baking sheet and roast until fragrant, 10 minutes, stirring once so they toast evenly. Set the nuts aside to cool.

2. Place the onion in a small bowl. Cover with cold water and soak for 20 minutes. Drain and pat dry by pressing the slices in paper towels. Set aside.

3. In a salad bowl, combine the spinach and watercress. Arrange the apple slices over the greens. Sprinkle the onion slices and nuts over the apples.

4. To serve, pour the dressing over the salad and toss.

Makes 4 servings

Per serving: 102 calories, 7 g fat, 1 g saturated fat, 3 g protein, 10 g carbohydrates, 3 g fiber

TOMATO AND WATERMELON SALAD

Sun-kissed summer-ripe tomatoes are essential for this red-on-red salad. When good local tomatoes are not in season, just use 3 watermelon slices.

2	*medium beefsteak tomatoes, each cut into ½" slices*		*Ginger-Chile Dressing (page 114)*
8	*(3" × 1" thick) seedless watermelon triangles, chilled*	4	*mint sprigs, for garnish*

Alternate 2 tomato slices and 2 watermelon slices on each of 4 salad plates, starting with the tomato. Spoon one-quarter of the dressing over each salad. Garnish with the mint and serve.

Makes 4 servings

Per serving: 190 calories, 3 g fat, 0 g saturated fat, 4 g protein, 43 g carbohydrates, 3 g fiber

FOOD FACT
Watermelon is rich in both vitamin A and lycopene.

NINE-A-DAY SALAD

A powerhouse made with 9 vegetables, beans, and soynuts, this meal-size salad was inspired by the USDA's Nine-A-Day program. Some salad bars conveniently offer all of its healthy ingredients. Serve it with grilled salmon and Blueberry Turtles (page 280) and you have nearly all the Best Foods in 1 meal.

DRESSING

2	tablespoons cider vinegar
1	teaspoon fresh lemon juice
½	teaspoon dried basil
½	teaspoon dried oregano
1	clove garlic, finely chopped
1	teaspoon salt
1	tablespoon + 1 teaspoon canola oil
	Freshly ground black pepper

SALAD

1	cup broccoli or cauliflower florets
4	green bell pepper rings
4	red bell pepper rings
2 or 3	thin slices onion, separated into rings
½	cup black beans or chickpeas
½	cup sliced carrots
½	cup sliced zucchini
1	large mushroom, thinly sliced (¼ cup)
8	whole cherry tomatoes, or 1 cup halved
2	cups curly spinach torn in bite-size pieces and packed
2	tablespoons whole soynuts

1. For the dressing, in a 10-cup plastic container, combine the vinegar, lemon juice, basil, oregano, garlic, and salt. Shake gently to combine, then add the oil and several grinds of the pepper. Cover tightly and shake vigorously to blend. Set aside for an hour so the flavors can meld.

2. In layers, add the broccoli, green and red pepper rings, onion, beans, carrots, zucchini, mushroom, tomatoes, and spinach. Cover and shake vigorously to coat the salad with the dressing. Serve immediately or marinate in the refrigerator for 2 to 24 hours. Garnish with soynuts and serve.

Makes 4 servings

Per serving: 125 calories, 6 g fat, 1 g saturated fat, 6 g protein, 14 g carbohydrates, 5 g fiber

To boost protein and cut carbs, salmon, tuna, or hard-cooked egg can replace the beans.

Looking at the ingredients used in many commercial salad dressings, I prefer to make this pungent vinaigrette.

MEDITERRANEAN CHOPPED SALAD

I serve this combination of raw vegetables mixed with hummus as a quick lunch. In summer, I like it for breakfast, too. The dressing perks up even bland tomatoes and ho-hum green pepper. Few salads are more convenient when you are cooking for one. Serve with Whole Wheat Pita Chips (page 48) or pile the salad into a whole pita, along with some chopped lettuce.

1	ripe medium tomato, preferably on-the-vine	½	small red onion, finely chopped
1	small green bell pepper, seeded and chopped	⅓	cup prepared hummus
			Juice of ½ lemon
1	rib celery, sliced crosswise		Salt and freshly ground black pepper
1	large scallion, white and green parts, chopped	¼	cup chopped flat-leaf parsley
⅓	cucumber, preferably unwaxed, seeded and diced	4	oil-cured black olives

To double the recipe for the dressing, increase the hummus to ½ cup and the lemon juice to 3 tablespoons.

An organic cucumber with the peel on, or partially removed in strips, adds fiber and looks colorful.

1. On a cutting board, vertically slice off 1 side of the tomato. Turn it 90 degrees and cut off another side. Repeat, leaving a square core. Turn the core on its side and slice off the bottom. Discard the core. Chop the remaining tomato and scoop it into a bowl, including the juice and seeds. Add the bell pepper, celery, scallion, cucumber, and onion.

2. For the dressing, add the hummus and lemon juice to the chopped vegetables and mix with a fork to combine. Season the salad to taste with salt and pepper. Mix in the parsley, add the olives, and serve.

Makes 1 serving

Per serving: 310 calories, 13 g fat, 2 g saturated fat, 11 g protein, 44 g carbohydrates, 13 g fiber

GAZPACHO SALAD

In this layered salad, even the spicy dressing is a lovely red, so show it off in a clear bowl, if possible. Serve with grilled halibut, salmon, or tuna salad sandwiches.

DRESSING

½ cup tomato juice

1 tablespoon distilled white vinegar

1 clove garlic, chopped

¼ teaspoon dry mustard

¼ teaspoon sweet paprika

½ slice white bread, crust removed

Salt and freshly ground black pepper

SALAD

1 large beefsteak tomato, cut in ½" slices

1 large Kirby cucumber, peeled in strips and cut in ½" slices

3 large white mushrooms, sliced

1 medium green bell pepper, seeded and cut in ½" rings

2 thin slices red onion, separated into rings

8 green or red leaf lettuce leaves

8 pitted kalamata olives, halved lengthwise, for garnish

1. For the dressing, in a mini food processor, whirl the tomato juice with the vinegar, garlic, mustard, paprika, and bread. Season the dressing to taste with salt and pepper.

2. In a wide bowl, layer the tomato, cucumber, mushrooms, pepper, and onion. Pour the dressing over the layered salad, cover with plastic wrap, and refrigerate overnight.

3. To serve, arrange 2 of the lettuce leaves on each of 4 salad plates. Divide the chilled salad equally over the lettuce. Spoon on some of the dressing and garnish with the olives.

Makes 4 servings

Per serving: 64 calories, 2 g fat, 0 g saturated fat, 2 g protein, 9 g carbohydrates, 2 g fiber

NAPA AND SPINACH SLAW

Asian ingredients give this succulent salad a special flavor. It is best served soon after the dressing is added, but you can prepare all the vegetables ahead and refrigerate them overnight. Serve with Salmon Paillard (page 150) and other salmon dishes, or with grilled flank steak.

1	teaspoon Sichuan peppercorns, or ¼ teaspoon freshly ground white pepper		Juice of ½ lemon
6	cups Napa cabbage, cut crosswise into ½" strips	1	tablespoon rice wine vinegar
		1	teaspoon salt
4	cups spinach leaves, shredded into ¼" strips	⅛	teaspoon freshly ground black pepper
		2	teaspoons canola oil
1	medium yellow bell pepper, seeded and julienned	1	teaspoon roasted sesame oil

1. If using white pepper, skip this step. Roast the Sichuan peppercorns in a dry skillet over medium-high heat until they are fragrant, 3 minutes, shaking the pan frequently. Cool the peppercorns on a plate. Crush them to a powder using a mortar and pestle, a spice grinder, or a clean coffee mill. Or, place the peppercorns in a medium, dry skillet and crush them with a smaller skillet. Measure ½ teaspoon, reserving the rest for another use.

2. In a large bowl, combine the Napa cabbage, spinach, and bell pepper, using your hands to toss them. Add the lemon juice, vinegar, salt, black pepper, and the Sichuan or white pepper. Toss to mix. Drizzle on the canola and sesame oils. Toss, using 2 forks or your hands. Serve within an hour of adding the lemon juice and oils.

Makes 8 servings

Per serving: 43 calories, 2 g fat, 0 g saturated fat, 2 g protein, 6 g carbohydrates, 2 g fiber

KALESLAW WITH RED PEPPER

Under its traditional creamy dressing, this is a subversive salad, combining finely shredded green cabbage with raw kale. Once they get over the shock, every kale-hater I know has asked for seconds. Any type of kale will do, but the tender Tuscan heirloom variety known by several names, including lacinato, dinosaur, and *cavalo nero*, or black kale, is best.

½	bunch lacinato kale, stemmed (page 76)	½	cup buttermilk
½	small head green cabbage, finely shredded (about 4 cups)	2	tablespoons low-fat whipped dressing or low-fat mayonnaise
2	medium red bell peppers, cut in ¼" strips	½	teaspoon curry powder
1	medium red onion, halved and cut vertically in ¼" crescents		Juice of ½ small lemon (about 1 tablespoon)
		½	teaspoon salt
			Freshly ground black pepper

1. Stack 3 or 4 kale leaves. Cut the stacked leaves horizontally into ¼" strips, making about 3 cups. Place the kale in a large bowl. Add the cabbage and red pepper.

2. Rinse the sliced onion under cold running water for 30 seconds. Drain well and pat dry with paper towels. Add the onion to the other vegetables.

3. For the dressing, in a small bowl whisk the buttermilk with the whipped dressing or mayonnaise, curry powder, lemon juice, and salt. Season to taste with pepper. Pour the dressing over the kaleslaw, tossing with a fork until it is well coated. Cover and refrigerate at least 4 hours or overnight. This salad keeps 3 to 4 days, tightly covered in the refrigerator.

Makes 6 servings

Per serving: 80 calories, 2 g fat, 0 g saturated fat, 4 g protein, 13 g carbohydrates, 3 g fiber

MACARONI SALAD

This would be a classic macaroni salad, creamy dressing and all, except that chopped broccoli replaces the usual green pepper.

Using the same boiling water to blanch the vegetables and then cook the macaroni saves time.

FOOD FACT

Chopping broccoli releases its beneficial compounds.

2	cups small broccoli florets	½	teaspoon dry mustard
1	medium carrot, halved lengthwise and thinly sliced crosswise	½	teaspoon sugar
1	cup elbow macaroni	1	teaspoon distilled white vinegar
1	medium red onion, finely chopped	½	teaspoon salt
2	tablespoons low-fat whipped salad dressing or low-fat mayonnaise		Freshly ground black pepper
		2	tablespoons chopped flat-leaf parsley

1. Drop the broccoli and carrot into a large pot of boiling water and cook for 30 seconds. Scoop them out, using a slotted spoon, drop them into a colander, and run cold water over them until they are cool. Drain well and place them in a large mixing bowl.

2. Using the same boiling water, cook the macaroni according to package directions. Drain the pasta thoroughly and add it to the broccoli and carrots. Add the onion.

3. For the dressing, in a small bowl whisk together the whipped dressing or mayonnaise, mustard, sugar, vinegar, and salt. Season to taste with pepper. Pour the dressing over the pasta and vegetables, mixing with a wooden spoon to coat evenly. Let the salad sit 15 to 20 minutes to allow the flavors to meld. Just before serving, mix in the parsley. This salad will keep for 2 days, tightly covered in the refrigerator.

Makes 4 servings

Per serving: 161 calories, 3 g fat, 0 g saturated fat, 5 g protein, 28 g carbohydrates, 3 g fiber

SOUTHWESTERN THREE-BEAN SALAD

The citrus flavor from lime plus the tangy tomatillos in salsa verde make my version of this salad different from the cloying sweetness you expect. In fact, it is sugar-free. Nutty-tasting black soybeans boost both its protein and fiber.

1	(15-ounce) can black-eyed peas, rinsed and drained, or 1¾ cups cooked	½	cup prepared salsa verde
			Juice of ½ lime
1	cup frozen cut green beans, defrosted	¼	teaspoon onion powder
1	cup canned black soybeans, rinsed and drained	1	teaspoon salt
		1	tablespoon canola oil
2	scallions, white part only, thinly sliced		Freshly ground black pepper
½	small red onion, finely chopped		

Canned black-eyed peas often contain sulfites. To avoid them, use a brand that is organic.

Place all the beans, the scallions, and the onion in a mixing bowl. Add the salsa, lime juice, onion powder, salt, and oil. Using a fork, mix to combine the salad. Season to taste with pepper. Cover and refrigerate 1 to 4 hours to allow the flavors to meld. This salad keeps 3 days, tightly covered in the refrigerator. The onion flavor becomes more assertive as the salad sits.

Makes 6 servings

Per serving: 111 calories, 3 g fat, 0 g saturated fat, 7 g protein, 15 g carbohydrates, 5 g fiber

BLACK BEAN AND WALNUT SALAD

Toasting the nuts enhances their flavor in this toss-together salad. If you do not have fresh basil, using a teaspoon of dried is fine. Serve with Ojja Tunisian Scrambled Eggs (page 182), roast chicken, or as an accompaniment to sliced ripe tomatoes.

SALAD

⅓ cup walnuts

1 (15-ounce) can black beans, drained

1 scallion, white and green parts, chopped

1 small clove garlic, finely chopped

2 tablespoons chopped flat-leaf parsley

3 large basil leaves, rolled and cut into
thin strips

DRESSING

4 teaspoons red wine vinegar

1 teaspoon Creole or Dijon mustard

1 teaspoon salt

Freshly ground black pepper

1 tablespoon extra-virgin olive oil

1. Preheat the oven to 350°F.

2. Toast the nuts in a shallow pan for 10 minutes, until they are fragrant, stirring 2 or 3 times. Set them aside. When they are cool, use your fingers to break them into small pieces. Place the nuts in a medium mixing bowl.

3. Add the beans, scallion, garlic, parsley, and basil to the nuts. Using a fork, toss to combine.

4. For the dressing, combine the vinegar, mustard, and salt in a small bowl. Season to taste with the pepper. Whisk in the oil. Pour the dressing over the bean mixture and stir with a fork to coat evenly. Let it sit 30 minutes before serving, to allow the flavors to meld. Check the seasoning and serve.

Makes 4 servings as a side dish, 2 as a main dish

Per side dish serving: 180 calories, 11 g fat, 1 g saturated fat, 7 g protein, 15 g carbohydrates, 6 g fiber

TUNA AND VEGETABLE SALAD

It is hard to believe lemon juice is the only dressing on this fat-free salad, or that 1 serving includes nearly 3 USDA-size servings of raw vegetables. Do not use a food processor for chopping the veggies. It tears them, making the salad too wet. Chopping them by hand also gives you time to appreciate their bright colors.

1	small carrot, thinly sliced and chopped	½	small red onion, finely chopped
1	small rib celery, finely chopped	1	(6-ounce) can water-packed light tuna, drained
½	medium green bell pepper, seeded and finely chopped		Juice of 1 large lemon
½	medium red bell pepper, seeded and finely chopped		Salt and freshly ground black pepper
½	cup finely chopped broccoli florets	½	cup chopped flat-leaf parsley

In a mixing bowl, combine the carrot, celery, green and red bell peppers, broccoli, and onion. Add the tuna and lemon juice and mix with a fork, breaking up the tuna into small flakes. Season to taste with salt and pepper. Mix in the parsley. Serve immediately or refrigerate for up to 2 days.

Makes 3 servings

Per serving: 229 calories, 0 g fat, 0 g saturated fat, 3 g protein, 54 g carbohydrates, 7 g fiber

Use only the topmost part of the broccoli florets.

SPEED CHOPPING

To quickly cut bell peppers, carrot, celery, cucumber, and other firm vegetables into fine pieces, cut them length-wise into strips, then halve them crosswise. Holding them together in a bunch, cut the strips crosswise.

FOOD FACT

Although albacore tuna is richer than light tuna in omega-3 essential fatty acids, it is also high in mercury, making light tuna a safer choice.

CANNED SALMON SALAD

On a hot day, this light, protein-rich salad is just right. Serve it accompanied by long, oval cucumber slices or Whole Wheat Pita Chips (page 48).

FOOD FACT

Dill contains the antioxidants beta carotene, lutein, and zeaxanthin.

1	(7.5-ounce) can pink or red salmon, drained, skin removed, or use skinless and boneless cooked salmon	1	small cucumber, seeded and chopped
		⅓	cup chopped dill
		⅓	cup chopped flat-leaf parsley
			Juice of ½ lemon
3	scallions, white and green parts, chopped	1	tablespoon canola oil
			Salt and freshly ground black pepper

Place the salmon in a mixing bowl. Add the scallions, cucumber, dill, and parsley. Using a fork, mix to combine. Mix in the lemon juice and oil. Season to taste with salt and pepper. Let it sit 15 minutes so the flavors can meld.

Makes 2 servings

Per serving: 216 calories, 14 g fat, 2 g saturated fat, 18 g protein, 5 g carbohydrates, 2 g fiber

SALMON AND
WHITE BEAN SALAD

No oil or fat is added to this almost-instant salad. Navy beans are best because they taste sweeter than great Northern or other small white beans.

1	(14.75-ounce) can pink or red salmon, drained and skin removed	1	tablespoon tarragon vinegar
		½	teaspoon salt
1	(15-ounce) can navy beans, drained		Freshly ground black pepper
⅓	cup finely chopped red onion	¼	cup chopped flat-leaf parsley

Combine the salmon, beans, onion, vinegar, and salt in a bowl and toss together using a fork. Season the salad with ground pepper and additional salt if desired. You can refrigerate the salad at this point. Just before serving, mix in the parsley.

Makes 2 servings

Per serving: 420 calories, 15 g fat, 3 g saturated fat, 44 g protein, 31 g carbohydrates, 10 g fiber

FOOD FACT

Navy beans are a good source of calcium.

SPARKLING MOLDED BERRY SALAD

FOOD FACT

The berries in this salad provide 3 grams of fiber in a serving, as much as in ½ cup of raw carrots.

You may think serving Jell-O is uncool, but watch everyone's guilty pleasure as they make this salad disappear. As with the fresh berries, cranberry juice also adds valuable phytonutrients. Use juice with sugar-free sweetener to reduce the carbs if you wish.

2	cups cranberry juice cocktail	1½	cups sliced fresh strawberries
2	(4-ounce) packages dark cherry gelatin dessert, regular or sugar-free	1	cup mixed fresh blueberries and raspberries, for garnish
1½	cups cold seltzer or club soda	6	large strawberries, for garnish
1	teaspoon fresh lemon juice		
1½	cups fresh or unsweetened frozen blueberries		

1. Bring the cranberry juice to a boil. Place the gelatin in a large heatproof bowl. Pour in the hot juice, stirring until the gelatin dissolves, 2 minutes. Add the cold seltzer or soda and lemon juice. Refrigerate until the gelatin mixture has the consistency of unbeaten egg whites, 1½ hours. Or, set the mixing bowl in a large bowl filled with ice water and cool 30 minutes, stirring occasionally so it does not set at the edges.

2. Mix in the 1½ cups blueberries and the sliced strawberries. Rinse a 5-cup ring mold in cold water. Shake out the excess water but do not dry the mold. Pour in the fruited gelatin. Cover with plastic wrap and refrigerate until firm, at least 4 hours. Unmold the salad onto a serving plate. Arrange the mixed blueberries and raspberries and the 6 strawberries in a ring around the molded salad, and serve.

Makes 8 servings

Per serving: 177 calories, 0 g fat, 0 g saturated fat, 3 g protein, 43 g carbohydrates, 3 g fiber

SPICED SWEET POTATO SALAD

Indian cooks boil the potatoes for this dish, but roasting them brings out more sweetness to play off the tart tamarind in the dressing. The finished salad of chunky potatoes streaked with dark brown from the tamarind tastes so good you will not mind how it looks.

2	medium Beauregard, Garnet, or Jewel yams (1½ pounds)	1	teaspoon grated fresh ginger
1	teaspoon cumin seeds	1	tablespoon defrosted apple juice concentrate
1	long green chile pepper, thinly sliced, seeding optional	¼	teaspoon ground coriander
1	tablespoon brown sugar	½	teaspoon salt
1	tablespoon tamarind paste	⅓	cup chopped cilantro

1. Preheat the oven to 400°F. Roast the yams 30 minutes. (They should still have slight resistance when pressed at the widest point.)

2. Toast the cumin seeds in a small skillet over medium-high heat until they are fragrant and slightly colored. Spread them on a plate to cool. Crush the toasted cumin in a mortar.

3. When cool enough to handle, peel the yams. Cut them into ¾" cubes and place in a mixing bowl. In another bowl, combine the crushed cumin, chile pepper, brown sugar, tamarind paste, ginger, apple juice concentrate, coriander, and salt. Pour the dressing over the warm potatoes and set aside until ready to serve, or cover and refrigerate. Garnish with the chopped cilantro just before serving. This salad keeps for up to 3 days, covered, in the refrigerator. Bring it to room temperature before serving.

Makes 4 servings

Per serving: 229 calories, 0 g fat, 0 g saturated fat, 3 g protein, 54 g carbohydrates, 7 g fiber

If you do not have a mortar and pestle, crush the spices in a skillet by pressing on them with the bottom of a smaller skillet.

GINGER-CHILE DRESSING

Use this sweet-tart dressing as a dipping sauce for Smoked Salmon Summer Roll (page 146) as well as for Tomato and Watermelon Salad (page 99) and on crisp romaine lettuce or spinach salad.

| 1 | lime | 6 | (¼") slices fresh red chile pepper |
| ⅓ | cup sugar | 1 | teaspoon grated fresh ginger |

1. Cut four ½" × 1" strips of zest from the lime. Squeeze the juice into a small saucepan. Add the zest, sugar, chile pepper, and ginger. Pour in ½ cup cold water.

2. Place the saucepan over medium-high heat and boil vigorously until the dressing is pale gold, about 3 minutes. Set aside and cool to room temperature.

3. Before serving, remove the lime zest and chile pepper from the dressing.

Makes ⅓ cup

Per serving (2 tablespoons): 104 calories, 0 g fat, 0 g saturated fat, 1 g protein, 27 g carbohydrates, 1 g fiber

CURRY DRESSING

For this golden dressing, the curry powder sold in Asian or Caribbean food stores has just the right flavor. Use this dressing, warm or chilled, on watercress, spinach, or cottage cheese topped with fresh fruit.

2	tablespoons light coconut milk	2	tablespoons low-fat yogurt or pureed
1	teaspoon mild curry powder		soft silken tofu
1	teaspoon honey		Juice of ½ lime
½	teaspoon salt		

1. Combine the coconut milk, curry powder, honey, and salt in a small microwaveable bowl. Partially cover the bowl and microwave for 1 minute.

2. Whisk the yogurt or tofu and lime juice into the dressing. Use warm or refrigerate to chill. This dressing keeps, refrigerated in a sealed container, for up to 3 days.

Makes ⅓ cup

Per serving (2 rounded tablespoons): 19 calories, 1 g fat, 0 g saturated fat, 1 g protein, 4 g carbohydrates, 0 g fiber

Thai Kitchen Lite Coconut Milk is creamy and sulfite-free. They make an organic version, too.

FOOD FACT

Curry powder's golden color comes from turmeric, a potent anti-inflammatory.

Clockwise from left: Creamy Herb Dressing (page 118), Curry Dressing (page 115), Pepper Ranch Dressing (opposite page)

PEPPER RANCH DRESSING

Some packaged foods are appealing until you read the list of ingredients. That is what made me create this low-fat ranch dressing. Serve it on salads or as a dip.

1	scallion, white and green parts		9–10	ounces soft silken or regular tofu
2	large cloves garlic		1	teaspoon dried oregano
2	teaspoons fresh lemon juice		½	teaspoon cracked black pepper
1	tablespoon rice vinegar		1	tablespoon canola oil
½	teaspoon sugar			Salt

1. In a food processor, place the scallion, garlic, lemon juice, rice vinegar, and sugar. Pulse 5 to 6 times, then let the blade run 10 seconds, until all the ingredients are finely chopped. Stop and scrape down the sides of the bowl.

2. Add the tofu and process until the dressing is a smooth puree. Add the oregano, pepper, and oil. Whirl briefly to blend. Season to taste with salt. Let the dressing sit at least 10 minutes or up to 1 hour to let the flavors meld before using. This dressing keeps up to 3 days, tightly covered in the refrigerator.

Makes 1 cup

Per serving (2 tablespoons): 39 calories, 3 g fat, 0 g saturated fat, 2 g protein, 2 g carbohydrates, 0 g fiber

Soft regular tofu makes a thicker dressing.

FOOD FACT

Using 9 ounces of tofu instead of ½ cup reduced-fat mayonnaise cuts about 32 grams of fat from this dressing.

BLUE CHEESE DRESSING

Cheese lovers flip for this thick, creamy, low-fat dressing.

1	ounce blue cheese	2	teaspoons fresh lemon juice
2	tablespoons soft silken tofu		Salt and freshly ground black pepper
¼	cup buttermilk		

Place the blue cheese, tofu, buttermilk, and lemon juice in a mini food processor or blender. Whirl until the dressing is creamy. Season to taste with salt and pepper. This dressing keeps 3 to 4 days, tightly covered in the refrigerator.

Makes ½ cup

Per serving (2 tablespoons): 36 calories, 2 g fat, 1 g saturated fat, 2 g protein, 1 g carbohydrates, 0 g fiber

CREAMY HERB DRESSING

Here is proof that tofu helps salad lovers enjoy lean, creamy dressings.

½	cup soft silken tofu	½	cup buttermilk
2	cloves garlic, sliced	1	tablespoon fresh lemon juice
¼	cup flat-leaf parsley leaves	½	teaspoon salt
2	tablespoons fresh oregano leaves	¼	teaspoon freshly ground black pepper

Puree the tofu in a mini food processor or blender, scraping down the sides of the bowl as needed. Add the garlic, parsley, and oregano and whirl. Add the buttermilk, lemon juice, salt, and pepper. Whirl to blend. This dressing keeps for 2 days, tightly covered in the refrigerator.

Makes 1 cup

Per serving (2 tablespoons): 17 calories, 1 g fat, 0 g saturated fat, 1 g protein, 2 g carbohydrates, 0 g fiber

CRACKED MUSTARD DRESSING

Perfect on spinach salad, this dressing can also replace mayonnaise on sandwiches with ham, smoked turkey, or Swiss cheese.

2	tablespoons coarse-grain mustard	1	tablespoon reduced-fat mayonnaise
2	tablespoons soft silken tofu		Freshly ground black pepper

In a mini food processor or blender, combine the mustard, tofu, mayonnaise, and a few grinds of pepper, whirling until they are well blended. This dressing keeps for 3 days, tightly covered in the refrigerator.

Makes ⅓ cup

Per serving (2 rounded tablespoons): 35 calories, 3 g fat, 0 g saturated fat, 1 g protein, 2 g carbohydrates, 0 g fiber

CITRUS MISO SPLASH

Use this sharp dressing on dark greens, watercress, romaine, or steamed spinach.

1	tablespoon shiro or sweet white miso	1	teaspoon sugar
¼	cup rice wine vinegar, divided	¼	teaspoon roasted sesame oil
2	teaspoons fresh lemon juice	2	tablespoons canola oil

1. Place the miso in a small mixing bowl. Add 1 tablespoon of the vinegar. With the back of a teaspoon, cream the miso into the liquid to dissolve it.

2. Whisk in the lemon juice, sugar, and the remaining vinegar, until the sugar dissolves. Whisk in the two oils. Use the dressing within an hour.

Makes ⅓ cup

Per serving (2 tablespoons): 112 calories, 10 g fat, 1 g saturated fat, 0 g protein, 6 g carbohydrates, 0 g fiber

Japanese markets have both these types of light miso.

CHAPTER FIVE

POULTRY AND MEAT

Most of my cooking has ethnic roots that provide exuberant ways to enjoy a 3- to 5-ounce serving of protein together with lots of vegetables. I eat mostly chicken, turkey, and lean pork, including the many wonderful, lean sausages now available. I also eat beef when I feel like it—which is more often, as good tasting, responsibly raised meat has become more available.

Using poultry and meat that is antibiotic-free and, preferably, organic is important to me. In addition to appreciating what is not in them and the humane, ecologically sound way in which they were raised, I find that they taste better and are more succulent. If you find heirloom pork, it will really show what I mean. It may be costly, but it's worth every penny.

For days when cooking is not part of your program, many of these dishes can be made ahead. Even on special occasions, the pork tenderloin and stuffed pork chops can be made in advance so you have less to deal with on the day when you are entertaining. These dishes, including Pork Medallions with Wild Mushrooms, are festive but will not force a choice between memorable food and your health.

ROAST CHICKEN WALDORF SALAD

Wild fennel bulbs are long and slim. You can find them at an increasing number of supermarkets as well as farmers' markets, particularly during the summer and fall. They should be thinly sliced, as they are crunchier (some would say tougher) than the bulbous fennel we are used to. They also have a more pronounced anise flavor.

Fennel and toasted nuts give a new twist to this salad with creamy dressing. Instead of waiting for leftovers from a roast chicken, you can make it using a barbecued breast from the store.

SALAD

⅔ cup coarsely chopped walnuts

2 cups diced roast chicken breast (8 ounces)

1 Granny Smith apple, peeled, cored, and cut in ¾" cubes

2 wild fennel bulbs, or ¼ medium fennel bulb, chopped

6 cups shredded red leaf, romaine, or Boston lettuce, or any combination

DRESSING

2 tablespoons low-fat whipped dressing

Juice of 1 lemon

½ teaspoon salt

⅛ teaspoon ground black pepper

Pinch of cayenne pepper

1. Preheat the oven to 350°F. Spread the nuts in 1 layer on a baking sheet. Toast until they are fragrant and lightly colored, 10 minutes, stirring after 3 minutes and again after 6 minutes so they toast evenly. Set the nuts aside to cool.

2. In a mixing bowl, combine the chicken, apple, fennel, and nuts.

3. For the dressing, in a small bowl, whisk together the whipped dressing, lemon juice, salt, black pepper, and red pepper, adjusting the seasoning to taste. Pour the dressing over the chicken mixture, tossing until the salad is evenly coated.

4. To serve, divide the lettuce among 4 dinner plates and mound the chicken salad equally over the greens.

Makes 4 servings

Per serving: 279 calories, 16 g fat, 2 g saturated fat, 22 g protein, 16 g carbohydrates, 5 g fiber

SESAME-OAT CHICKEN FINGERS

Oats and sesame seeds form a crisp coating on this oven-fried chicken. Because it is so lean, careful timing is important to avoid drying out the chicken. Serve with Cracked Mustard Dressing (page 119) or barbecue sauce for dipping.

8	ounces boneless, skinless chicken breast	1	teaspoon dried oregano
¾	cup quick-cooking oats	½	teaspoon salt
2	tablespoons hulled sesame seeds		Freshly ground black pepper
		1	egg white, beaten until foamy

1. Set a rack in the center of the oven. Preheat the oven to 450°F. Coat a baking sheet with cooking spray and set it aside.

2. Slice the chicken on the diagonal, with the grain, into ¾"-wide strips.

3. In a shallow bowl combine the oats, sesame seeds, oregano, salt, and a few grinds of the pepper. Place the egg white in a wide shallow bowl and set it next to the oat mixture. Roll each chicken strip in the egg white, lift and shake gently, then drop it into the oat mixture. Roll the chicken 3 or 4 times in the coating until completely covered. Holding it at both ends, gently place the coated chicken on the baking sheet.

4. Coat the chicken generously with cooking spray. Bake 3½ to 4 minutes, until lightly browned on the bottom. Using tongs, turn the chicken, and coat again with cooking spray. Bake 3 to 4 minutes longer, or until the chicken is white when cut crosswise at the thickest point. Serve immediately.

Makes 4 servings

Per serving: 149 calories, 4 g fat, 1 g saturated fat, 17 g protein, 12 g carbohydrates, 2 g fiber

FOOD FACT

Oregano is rich in antioxidants; fresh oregano contains more of them than dried.

SENEGALESE LEMON CHICKEN

Cooking chicken breast with the ribs tends to keep it moister.

In Senegal, where this is called Yassa Chicken, cooks first stew, then marinate the chicken. Then they simmer it with an abundance of onions. I prefer to marinate skinless chicken breast, then brown and stew it in its marinade. Serve with Kaleslaw with Red Pepper (page 105) or steamed broccoli and brown rice to soak up the mouthwatering sauce.

2	large white onions, thinly sliced	6	grinds black pepper
¼	cup chopped flat-leaf parsley		Juice of 2 lemons
4–5	fresh thyme sprigs, or ½ teaspoon dried	2	tablespoons canola oil
1	bay leaf	1	large skinless whole chicken breast
1	small clove garlic, smashed		with ribs, cut in 4 pieces (1½
½	teaspoon salt		pounds)

1. Place the onions in a large, resealable plastic bag. Add the parsley, thyme, bay leaf, garlic, salt, and pepper. Pour in the lemon juice and oil. Seal the bag and shake to coat the onions with the marinade. Add the chicken, re-seal, and shake the bag. Refrigerate for 2 to 3 hours.

2. Remove the chicken from the marinade and pat dry. Coat a deep, medium skillet, with a tight-fitting lid, with cooking spray. Over medium-high heat, brown the chicken on both sides, turning it once, 8 minutes. Remove the chicken to a plate.

3. Lift the onions from the marinade and add them to the skillet. Cook, stirring occasionally, until they are limp and brown, but not soft, 10 minutes. Return the chicken to the pan. Pour in the reserved marinade, including the solids. Cover the pan and simmer for 20 minutes. Turn the chicken, cover, and continue cooking until the meat is white near the bone, 15 to 20 minutes. Remove bay leaf before serving.

Makes 4 servings

Per serving: 212 calories, 8 g fat, 1 g saturated fat, 21 g protein, 14 g carbohydrates, 3 g fiber

MEXICAN CHICKEN STEW
WITH BLACK BEANS

Just 20 minutes gets this dish going, then you can prepare a salad while it cooks, making it a perfect weekday recipe. Or prepare it ahead. While its ingredients are everyday, the final flavor, with paprika and cilantro enhancing the flavor of canned tomatoes, definitely is not. Serve with Jalapeño Spinach (page 224).

4	teaspoons canola oil, divided	1	clove garlic, chopped
1	large skinless whole chicken breast with ribs (1½ pounds), cut in 4 pieces	½	cup chopped cilantro leaves
		1	teaspoon paprika
		½	teaspoon dried oregano
1	medium onion, chopped	1	(15-ounce) can diced tomatoes
1	medium green bell pepper, seeded and chopped	1	(15-ounce) can black beans, drained

1. Heat 2 teaspoons of the oil in a medium nonstick skillet over medium-high heat. Brown the chicken pieces 12 minutes, turning them once. Remove the chicken to a plate.

2. Add the remaining oil to the pan and sauté the onion, pepper, and garlic until the onion is soft, 5 minutes. Mix in the cilantro, paprika, and oregano just until they are fragrant. Add the tomatoes with their liquid and the beans. When the liquid starts to boil, return the chicken to the skillet. Reduce the heat and simmer uncovered until the chicken is cooked through, 20 minutes.

Makes 4 servings

Per serving: 182 calories, 6 g fat, 0 g saturated fat, 12 g protein, 21 g carbohydrates, 8 g fiber

CHICKEN WITH RHUBARB SAUCE

The rosy sauce for this dish is enhanced by layers of flavor created by reducing wine with aromatics, then blueberry juice, and finishing it with butter.

2	tablespoons cold unsalted butter, divided	⅓	cup dry white wine
		1	cup blueberry juice
2	thin rhubarb stalks, peeled and thinly sliced	1¼	pounds boneless, skinless chicken breast
			Salt and freshly ground black pepper
1	small carrot, thinly sliced	2	cups steamed spinach, optional
1	small red onion, finely chopped	¼	cup defrosted frozen wild blueberries, for garnish
1	shallot, finely chopped		

FOOD FACT

Rhubarb, a vegetable eaten as a fruit, is a good source of vitamin C.

1. Preheat the grill or a grill pan on top of the stove.

2. In a medium, deep saucepan, heat 1 tablespoon of the butter over medium-high heat. Stir in the rhubarb, carrot, onion, and shallot and cook until they are soft and moist, 5 minutes. Add the wine and boil until the liquid is reduced by half, about 8 minutes. Pour in the blueberry juice. Boil until the vegetables are soft and there is 1 cup of sauce, about 10 minutes.

3. Meanwhile, season the chicken with salt and pepper and grill it. Set the grilled chicken on a plate and cover it loosely with foil to keep warm.

4. In a blender, purée the rhubarb mixture. Whirl in the remaining butter, cut in pieces. Season to taste with salt and pepper.

5. To serve, cover the centers of 4 dinner plates with equal amounts of the sauce. If using, make a bed of spinach on each plate. Slice the chicken and arrange equal portions of chicken over the spinach or on the sauce on each plate. Sprinkle on the wild blueberries and serve.

Makes 4 servings

Per serving: 260 calories, 8 g fat, 4 g saturated fat, 34 g protein, 10 g carbohydrates, 2 g fiber

TURKEY SAUSAGE WITH RED PEPPERS

Roasted sweet peppers and onions, tangy tomatoes, plus a touch of wine give this dish more flavor than the usual sausage and peppers.

Cover the broiler pan with foil for easy cleanup.

To reheat: Use a covered skillet over medium heat, stirring occasionally, or place in a covered baking dish at 350°F for 20 minutes.

FOOD FACT

Italian turkey sausage, sold in packages, contributes 3 grams of fat per serving in this dish.

2	large red bell peppers, halved and seeded		1	Spanish onion, halved and cut crosswise into ½" slices
4	teaspoons extra-virgin olive oil, divided		½	cup dry white wine
3	links fresh Italian-style turkey sausage (about ¾ pound)		1	(15-ounce) can diced tomatoes
			¼	teaspoon ground fennel
				Salt and freshly ground black pepper

1. Preheat the broiler.

2. Broil the peppers, cut side down, until the skin blisters and blackens, about 4 minutes. Transfer to a small bowl, cover with plastic wrap, and steam the peppers for 20 minutes. Peel off their skin. Cut into ¾" strips.

3. Heat 2 teaspoons of the oil in a deep, medium skillet over medium-high heat. Brown the sausages on all sides for 8 minutes, turning as needed. They will not be cooked through. Transfer the sausages to a plate.

4. Add the remaining oil to the skillet and sauté the onion until it is translucent (parts of it will brown). Pour in the wine. Using a wooden spoon, scrape the browned bits from the bottom of the pan.

5. Add the tomatoes with their liquid and then the fennel to the pan. Add the bell peppers, browned onions, and sausages cut into 1" slices to the pan. Reduce the heat, cover, and simmer 20 minutes. Uncover and cook until half the liquid evaporates, 10 minutes longer. Season to taste with salt and pepper. Serve immediately, or cool and refrigerate for up to 2 days.

Makes 4 servings

Per serving: 219 calories, 8 g fat, 2 g saturated fat, 16 g protein, 21 g carbohydrates, 4 g fiber

TURKEY STEW WITH COLLARD GREENS AND HEIRLOOM BEANS

I like one-pot dishes—especially this moist stew that I first made using heirloom trout beans and a quince. Then I found that using pink beans and a tart Granny Smith apple works well, too. If you are handy with a knife, everything for this country-style dish can be ready in 15 minutes, with dinner on the table in 40 minutes flat. Slices of black bread go well with it.

1	tablespoon extra-virgin olive oil	½	quince or Granny Smith apple, peeled, cored, and diced
1	large onion, diced		
¾	pound fresh Italian-style turkey sausage	1	cup fat-free, reduced-sodium chicken broth
½	bunch collard greens, cut crosswise into ¾" strips	1	(15-ounce) can trout or pink beans, drained
1	large carrot, cut in ½" pieces		Salt and freshly ground black pepper
1	medium Beauregard, Garnet, or Jewel yam, peeled and cut in 1" pieces	1	lemon, quartered, for garnish

1. Heat the oil in a large Dutch oven over medium-high heat. Sauté the onion until it is translucent, 4 minutes.

2. Squeeze the sausage meat from its casing and form it into 1" balls. Add the sausage to the onion, turning the balls until they start to brown.

3. Add the collards, carrot, sweet potato, quince or Granny Smith apple, and broth. Pour in 1 cup cold water, bring to a boil, reduce the heat, and simmer 15 minutes.

4. Add the beans, season to taste with salt and pepper, and cook until the beans are heated through, 10 minutes.

5. Serve this stew in wide shallow bowls, garnished with a wedge of lemon.

Makes 6 servings

Per serving: 269 calories, 5 g fat, 1 g saturated fat, 17 g protein, 42 g carbohydrates, 7 g fiber

Westbrae sells a selection of canned heirloom beans, including trout beans, at natural food stores and some supermarkets.

FOOD FACT
Fresh and frozen collard greens are good sources of fiber and beta-carotene.

TURKEY TAGINE

This dish is based on tagines I ate in Morocco, where fruit is included in savory dishes and citrus is a frequent seasoning. Because its flavor improves when made ahead, it is a good dish to serve when entertaining.

This dish reheats well, covered, on top of the stove or in a 350°F oven. It keeps in the refrigerator for a week.

1	tablespoon canola oil	1	large tomato, seeded and diced
1	large red onion, diced	1	(15-ounce) can chickpeas, drained
1	leek, white part only, coarsely chopped	4	kumquats, sliced and seeded, or
1	pound boneless turkey breast, cut in 1" pieces		1 teaspoon orange zest
1	Fuji apple, peeled, cored, and diced	2	cups vegetable broth
1	carrot, peeled and cut in 1" pieces	1	teaspoon ground cumin
1	parsnip, peeled and cut in 1" pieces	1	teaspoon ground ginger
1	red bell pepper, seeded and diced	½	teaspoon dried basil
1	large Beauregard, Garnet, or Jewel yam, peeled and cut in 1" pieces	½	teaspoon ground cinnamon
		4	chopped dates
			Chopped fresh parsley, for garnish

1. In a large Dutch oven or a heavy pot with a tight-fitting lid, heat the oil over medium-high heat. Sauté the onion and leek until lightly brown, 5 to 6 minutes. Push them to 1 side of the pot.

2. Add the turkey and brown the pieces on all sides, about 6 minutes.

3. Add the apple, carrot, parsnip, bell pepper, sweet potato, tomato, chickpeas, kumquats or orange zest, and broth. Stir in the cumin, ginger, basil, cinnamon, and dates. Bring to a boil and reduce the heat. Cover and simmer until the turkey and vegetables are tender, about 40 minutes. Serve garnished with parsley, if desired.

Makes 8 servings

Per serving: 274 calories, 7 g fat, 1 g saturated fat, 17 g protein, 38 g carbohydrates, 7 g fiber

TURKEY MEATBALLS IN PORCINI SAUCE

Making great meatballs is an art. Using milk-soaked bread is part of the secret for keeping them light. Here, mushrooms, a trio of alliums, and balsamic vinegar give the chunky sauce big flavor. If you like, serve this sauce over spaghetti, including 3 meatballs per serving. Save the extras for a sandwich.

GREAT CRUMB

For the best dry bread crumbs, whirl dried-out Italian or French bread in the food processor. These taste much better and have a better texture than commercial bread crumbs. They will keep for at least 1 month in an airtight container in the freezer.

½	cup dried porcini mushrooms		1	teaspoon salt
4	teaspoons extra-virgin olive oil, divided		⅛	teaspoon freshly ground black pepper
1	small red onion, finely chopped			
1	clove garlic, finely chopped			**SAUCE**
½	cup + ¾ cup fine, dry bread crumbs		1	(28-ounce) can plum tomatoes, with their liquid
3	tablespoons low-fat milk		1	cup tomato sauce
1	pound ground turkey breast		1	medium yellow onion, chopped
¼	cup chopped flat-leaf parsley		1	clove garlic, finely chopped
1	large egg		1	teaspoon dried thyme
1	large egg white		2	teaspoons balsamic vinegar
3	tablespoons grated pecorino cheese			Salt and freshly ground pepper

1. Place the mushrooms in a small bowl. Add ½ cup hot tap water and set aside to soak until soft, 20 minutes.

2. Coat a large, nonstick skillet with cooking spray and set the pan over medium-high heat. Add 1 teaspoon of the oil. Sauté the onion until it starts to soften, 3 minutes. Mix in the garlic and cook 1 minute longer. Scoop the mixture into a large mixing bowl to cool.

3. In a small bowl, combine ½ cup of the bread crumbs with the milk.

4. Add the ground turkey, parsley, egg, egg white, cheese, salt, pepper, and bread crumb mixture to the onion. Work the mixture with the fork until well combined.

5. Spread the remaining ¾ cup bread crumbs on a dinner plate. Form the turkey into sixteen 2" meatballs and roll them in the bread crumbs until coated.

6. Add 2 teaspoons of the oil to the skillet and return the pan to medium-high heat. To avoid overloading the pan, brown half the meatballs for about 8 minutes, using tongs to turn them. Remove them to another plate. Add the remaining oil and brown the remaining meatballs. Do not clean the pan.

7. For the sauce, coarsely chop the tomatoes by working a knife up and down in the can. Pour the tomatoes with their liquid into the skillet. Add the tomato sauce, onion, garlic, and thyme. Squeeze the liquid from the mushrooms, reserving it for another use. Chop the mushrooms and add them to the sauce. Set the skillet over medium-high heat. When the sauce boils, add the browned meatballs. Reduce the heat and simmer 15 minutes. Turn the meatballs and cook until they are white in the center, 10 to 15 minutes longer. Divide the meatballs among 4 plates. Stir the balsamic vinegar into the sauce. Season it to taste with salt and pepper. Spoon the sauce equally over the meatballs.

Makes 4 servings

Per serving: 580 calories, 20 g fat, 5 g saturated fat, 35 g protein, 63 g carbohydrates, 9 g fiber

VARIATION: Form the turkey mixture into an oval meat loaf on a baking sheet, cover with foil, and bake at 375°F. Make the sauce to serve over the sliced meat loaf.

TURKEY-WALNUT MEAT LOAF

Cooking ground turkey breast with a lavish amount of chopped raw vegetables plus finely ground walnuts instead of the usual bread filler, produces a beautifully flavorful and moist meat loaf. The vegetables add moisture as the meat loaf bakes, which the walnuts help it retain. Bacon strips on top enhance the flavor even more.

1	pound ground turkey breast		1	teaspoon dried thyme
1	clove garlic, finely chopped		½	teaspoon salt
½	medium onion, finely chopped			Freshly ground black pepper
1	small carrot, shredded		1	cup chopped tomatoes
1	rib celery, finely chopped		2	bay leaves
⅓	cup chopped flat-leaf parsley		2	slices preservative-free bacon
½	cup walnuts			
1	large egg			

1. Preheat the oven to 350°F.

2. Place the turkey, garlic, onion, carrot, celery, and parsley in a mixing bowl. In a food processor, pulse the walnuts until they are finely ground. Add the nuts, egg, thyme, salt, and 5 or 6 grinds of pepper to the bowl. Mix with a fork until well combined. Pack the mixture firmly into an 8½" × 4½" × ½" loaf pan. Spread the tomatoes over the top. Lay the bay leaves on top of the tomatoes. Arrange the bacon slices to cover the bay leaves.

3. Bake 50 minutes, or until an instant-read thermometer inserted into the center registers 160°F and the meat loaf has pulled away from the edges of the pan. Cool for 20 minutes. Remove the bay leaves before serving.

Makes 6 slices

Per slice: 224 calories, 15 g fat, 3 g saturated fat, 17 g protein, 6 g carbohydrates, 2 g fiber

LEAN MEAN CHOCOLATE CHILI

Seemingly odd combinations are fun, provided they work. Chocolate and chili make a great pair in this thick, intense chili. Normally, I use chili powder that does not contain garlic powder, but Trader Joe's makes a fabulous one with it. Serve accompanied with black beans, cooked brown rice, and a cold beer.

1	tablespoon + 1 teaspoon canola oil	1	teaspoon dried oregano
1	pound lean stewing beef, such as	1	(28-ounce) can whole tomatoes
	round, hand-chopped into ½" cubes	2	ounces unsweetened chocolate,
1	large onion, chopped		coarsely chopped
1	small green bell pepper, chopped	1	tablespoon cider vinegar
3	cloves garlic, chopped	1	teaspoon salt
2	tablespoons chili powder	⅛	teaspoon freshly ground black pepper
1	tablespoon ground cumin		

Small cubes of meat (¼" is even better than ½") make the best chili. Using responsibly raised natural or organic beef makes it even better.

1. In a medium Dutch oven, heat 1 tablespoon of the oil over medium-high heat. Add the meat and brown it on all sides, 5 minutes. Transfer the meat to a plate.

2. Add the remaining 1 teaspoon oil to the pot. Sauté the onion and green pepper for 3 minutes, mix in the garlic, and sauté 2 minutes longer, until the onion is soft. Stir in the chili powder, cumin, and oregano.

3. Return the meat to the pot, including any juices on the plate. Add the tomatoes with their liquid, using a wooden spoon to break them up. When the liquid boils, stir in the chocolate. Reduce the heat and simmer uncovered for 30 minutes. Add the vinegar, salt, and pepper. Cook until the meat is tender, 40 to 45 minutes longer.

Makes 4 servings

Per serving: 339 calories, 17 g fat, 6 g saturated fat, 31 g protein, 22 g carbohydrates, 7 g fiber

ITALIAN POT ROAST WITH ONION SAUCE

This Neapolitan-style pot roast produces an intense, brown onion "gravy" that is the true goal of the recipe since the meat gives its all to flavor the sauce. Good enough to spoon from a bowl, it is the ultimate extravagance served on rigatoni. I use top round, so the sauce is lavish but lean. The meat, too dry to serve on its own, is perfect served with the pasta or in Pot Roast Hash (opposite page).

1	(2-pound) piece top round	¼	teaspoon white peppercorns
8	large onions, thinly sliced (about 12 cups)	1	cup dry white wine
1	carrot, finely chopped	1	teaspoon salt
½	rib celery, finely chopped	2	teaspoons tomato paste
2	tablespoons chopped flat-leaf parsley	1	pound rigatoni pasta
1	teaspoon rubbed sage		Grated Parmesan cheese

1. Place the meat in a large, deep saucepan or a small Dutch oven. Arrange the onions, carrot, and celery over the meat. Add the parsley, sage, and peppercorns. Pour in the wine. Add 8 cups cold water and the salt. Bring the liquid just to a boil, reduce the heat, and simmer gently, uncovered, until strands of meat pull away when lifted with a fork, 3 to 3½ hours. As the liquid evaporates, turn the meat every 20 minutes so it cooks evenly. Remove the meat and set it aside. Mix the tomato paste into the sauce that remains in the pot. (You will have about 4 cups of sauce.)

2. Cook the pasta according to package directions. Divide it among 8 wide shallow bowls. Reheat the sauce if necessary and ladle it over the pasta, Serve accompanied by grated Parmesan cheese. Serve the pot roast, very thinly sliced, on the side.

Makes 8 servings

Per serving: 524 calories, 12 g fat, 4 g saturated fat, 35 g protein, 65 g carbohydrates, 6 g fiber

POT ROAST HASH

I make Italian Pot Roast (opposite page) just to use it in this comforting yet lean hash. However, any leftover long-grained meat, including brisket or lean stewing beef, can be used.

1	slice preservative-free bacon, or 1 tablespoon canola oil	¾	cup beef broth, or ¾ cup water
½	medium onion, chopped	2	(1½") slices Italian Pot Roast (opposite page), pulled into thin strips (2 cups shredded meat)
1	rib celery, finely chopped		
1	small green bell pepper, finely chopped	1	teaspoon Worcestershire sauce
4	plum tomatoes, seeded and chopped	¼	cup chopped flat-leaf parsley
1	Yukon Gold or other yellow-fleshed potato, peeled and finely chopped		Salt and freshly ground black pepper

1. Cook the bacon, if using, in a medium skillet over medium-high heat until it is crisp. Drain it on a paper towel and set aside. Using the fat remaining in the pan, sauté the onion, celery, and bell pepper until the onion is translucent, 4 minutes. Or heat the canola oil in a medium skillet and sauté the vegetables.

2. Add the tomatoes and cook until they start to soften, 3 minutes. Add the potato and beef broth or water. Simmer until the tomatoes break down and the potato is almost soft, 6 minutes. Mix in the shredded meat, Worcestershire sauce, and parsley and cook 2 minutes, until the meat is heated through and most of the liquid has evaporated. Season to taste with salt and pepper, and serve.

Makes 4 servings

Per serving: 216 calories, 7 g fat, 3 g saturated fat, 23 g protein, 15 g carbohydrates, 3 g fiber

PORK MEDALLIONS
WITH WILD MUSHROOMS

Not so long ago, only chefs could get exotic mushrooms like black trumpet and hen's foot. Now you find them even at some supermarkets. They quickly add flavor to this wine sauce and turn seared pork chops into a sophisticated dish worthy of using great pork like Niman Ranch or SallyJoe's organic. Serve with Miso Mashed Potatoes (page 241), followed by a mesclun salad with Cracked Mustard Dressing (page 119).

4	(¾"-thick) pork medallions (about 6 ounces each)	¼	pound hen's foot mushrooms
		¼	cup dry Marsala or Madeira wine
4	teaspoons unbleached all-purpose flour	½	cup fat-free, reduced-sodium chicken broth
1	tablespoon olive oil	½	cup canned black beans, drained and rinsed
¼	pound black trumpet mushrooms		
1	shallot, finely chopped		Salt and freshly ground black pepper

1. Rub the pork with the flour, coating the medallions lightly on both sides.

2. Heat the oil in a medium skillet over medium-high heat. Brown the pork on both sides, turning the medallions once, 5 minutes total. Remove them to a plate.

3. In the same pan, sauté the trumpet mushrooms and shallot until most of the mushrooms are wilted, 3 minutes. Mix in the hen's foot mushrooms and cook 1 minute longer.

4. Pour in the wine and boil until the pan is almost dry, 3 minutes. Pour in the broth, bring to a boil, and scrape up all the browned bits from the bottom of the skillet. Add the beans and season to taste with salt and pepper.

5. Return the pork to the pan. Reduce the heat to medium and cook until the meat is just slightly pink in the center, 6 minutes, or white all the way through, 7 minutes, turning the medallions once.

6. To serve, place a medallion on each of 4 dinner plates. Spoon the mushrooms and beans over the chops. Spoon the remaining pan juices around them.

Makes 4 servings

Per serving: 461 calories, 22 g fat, 7 g saturated fat, 51 g protein, 9 g carbohydrates, 2 g fiber

PORK CHOPS WITH SWEET POTATO GRAVY

These overstuffed chops will have friends and family talking for weeks. The idea came from watching a cooking show on television. That recipe, however, was seriously loaded with butter and cream, while I use just enough to make velvety potatoes and moist chops. I also replaced a long list of Cajun spices with Thai chili paste, making this a down-home dish with melting-pot flavors.

3	medium Beauregard, Garnet, or Jewel yams (about 1½ pounds)	½	Golden Delicious apple, peeled, cored, and finely chopped
1	tablespoon unsalted butter	⅓	cup dry breadcrumbs
¼	teaspoon Thai red chili paste	4	(1½"-thick) boneless center cut pork chops (5–6 ounces each)
3	tablespoons half-and-half		
	Salt and freshly ground black pepper	1	teaspoon sweet paprika
1	small red onion, finely chopped	¼	teaspoon onion powder

1. Preheat the oven to 400°F. Roast the sweet potatoes. Peel and mash them. There should be 3 cups. Reduce the oven to 350°F.

2. For the gravy, in a bowl combine 2⅓ cups of the sweet potatoes with the butter, chili paste, and half-and-half. Season it to taste with salt and pepper. Spread the creamy potatoes to cover the bottom of an 8" square baking dish. Set aside.

3. For the stuffing, in a second bowl, combine the remaining sweet potato with the onion, apple, and breadcrumbs. Season to taste with salt and pepper.

4. Make a 3½" × 2½" pocket in each chop. Pack the stuffing generously into the pockets. Combine the paprika, ¼ teaspoon salt, and onion powder in a small bowl. Rub 1 side of each chop with this mixture and set them seasoned side down on top of the sweet potatoes in the baking dish. Rub the remaining seasoning on top of each chop. Cover the pan with foil.

5. Bake for 35 minutes. Uncover and bake the chops 10 minutes longer, until they are nicely browned on top. Serve immediately.

Makes 4 servings

Per serving: 474 calories, 12 g fat, 5 g saturated fat, 32 g protein, 60 g carbohydrates, 9 g fiber

PORK TENDERLOIN IN CHIPOTLE MOLE

Pork tenderloin, because it is so lean, requires tying in order to roast evenly. For this recipe, have your butcher tie the 2 tenderloins together. After cooking, they will make nice, round slices.

Serve leftover mole with turkey cutlets or sautéed chicken breasts, or spoon it over a plate of brown rice, black beans, and corn for a meatless dinner.

FOOD FACT

Tenderloin, with just 5 grams of fat in a 3½-ounce serving, cooked, is the leanest cut of pork.

Mole is famous as the Mexican chocolate sauce though these complex blends use many other ingredients, as well. This streamlined version still has an unforgettable blend of heat, sweet, and darker flavors, thanks to chile peppers, nuts, fruit, and a touch of chocolate. In place of the pork, substitute a boneless turkey breast, tied as a roast, if you like.

1	tablespoon canola oil	1	tablespoon sugar
2	large cloves garlic, coarsely chopped	½	teaspoon ground cinnamon
½	cup sliced almonds	¼	teaspoon ground black pepper
1	cup canned tomatoes, with their liquid	¼	teaspoon ground clove
1	slice whole wheat bread, darkly toasted	1	(14.5-ounce) can fat-free, reduced-sodium chicken broth, divided
1	canned chipotle chile in adobo sauce	1	whole pork tenderloin (1½ pounds), tied
½	cup golden raisins		
1	tablespoon unsweetened cocoa powder (not Dutch-process)	2	tablespoons unhulled sesame seeds, for garnish

1. Preheat the oven to 325°F.

2. For the mole, heat the oil in a medium skillet over medium-high heat. Add the garlic and sauté 1 minute. Stir in the nuts, spreading them in an even layer, and cook until they are light gold, 2 minutes, stirring several times so they color evenly. Transfer the mixture to a blender. Wipe out the pan and set aside.

3. Pour the tomatoes and liquid into a blender, taking care, as they will splatter. Add the toasted bread, torn in 8 pieces, the chipotle chile, raisins, cocoa, sugar, cinnamon, black pepper, and clove and whirl to chop finely. Pour in ½ cup of the broth and whirl until the sauce is a pulpy puree.

4. Pour the sauce into the skillet and add 1 cup of the remaining broth. Bring the sauce to a gentle boil over medium-high heat. Reduce the heat and simmer until the mole has the thickness of medium cream soup, stirring occasionally to prevent sticking.

5. Coat a small Dutch oven with cooking spray and set it over medium-high heat. Add the pork, browning it on all sides, about 12 minutes total. Pour in the mole and the remaining broth, scraping the bottom of the pot to incorporate any browned bits into the sauce.

6. Cover the pot, place it in the oven, and bake 20 to 25 minutes, or until an instant-read thermometer inserted into the thickest part of the meat registers 155°F. Transfer the meat to a cutting board and let it rest 10 minutes.

7. In a small, dry skillet over medium-high heat, toast the sesame seeds until fragrant, 3 minutes, stirring frequently.

8. To serve, remove the strings and cut the pork into ½" slices. Arrange the meat on a serving platter. Spoon the mole generously over it and garnish with the toasted sesame seeds. Pour the remaining mole into a sauceboat to pass separately.

Makes 6 servings

Per serving: 314 calories, 13 g fat, 2 g saturated fat, 29 g protein, 21 g carbohydrates, 3 g fiber

CHAPTER SIX
FISH

Not so long ago, fish was scornfully labeled brain food and only chefs knew how to poach salmon. Except for "gourmet" cooks or those whose ethnic heritage made cooking fish and shellfish second nature, at home most people served only tuna salad, hot tuna noodle casserole, and frozen fish sticks. Everyone else waited until they dined out to eat fish.

Today, most of us broil, steam, and bake salmon, grill tuna, and prepare other seafood without thinking much about it. Perhaps the only place we err is by disdaining canned salmon. To entice you into discovering how enjoyable canned salmon can be, I hope you will try Salmon, Corn, and Mint on a Tomato Star and some of the salads in chapter 4.

The fish dishes fall into one of four categories—quick and convenient, special occasions, ethnic recipes, and comfort food. Often these overlap. Smoked Salmon Summer Roll is my take on Vietnamese summer rolls. Greek-accented Shrimp with Cherry Tomatoes and Feta makes a company dinner that takes less than 15 minutes from a standing start. Salmon Paillard with Napa and Spinach Slaw dresses up dinner for two even more, while Sake-Poached Salmon with Ginger Gremolata is positively elegant. Salmon Hash and Broccoli-Stuffed Baked Potato with Salmon are comforting and perfect to eat in front of the TV. For convenience, some recipes can be made using cooked salmon, which you may have on hand from planned leftovers or is easy to pick up at the supermarket.

While salmon gets top billing as *the* superfish these days, tuna, halibut, and shrimp are good, too. Pan-Roasted Halibut with Caramelized Onions is, in fact, one example of seafood dishes that provide an opportunity to include other Best Foods.

The USDA's recommended 3-ounce portion size for cooked fish, which seems skimpy to most people when the fish is served in one piece, is comfortable in salmon kebabs. And even less is fine in a generous portion of the hash or Salmon Fried Rice, while some of the following recipes do offer a 6-ounce serving.

SMOKED SALMON SUMMER ROLL

Using leaf lettuce for the wrapper in place of rice paper makes them simple to assemble: In these Vietnamese-inspired hand rolls, smoked salmon takes the place of shrimp.

1	cup fine rice noodles	24	mint leaves
3 or 4	scallions, green part only	8	cilantro sprigs, coarse lower stems
1	(4") section European cucumber		removed
8	leaves green leaf lettuce	¼	cup shredded Thai or Italian basil
8	thin slices smoked salmon (about		Ginger-Chile Dressing (page 114)
	4 ounces)	¼	cup finely chopped shallot

1. Cook the noodles according to package directions. Drain and rinse the noodles under cold water. Drain well and set aside. Cut the scallion into 4" lengths. Peel the cucumber, halve it lengthwise, seed it, and cut into strips.

2. Tear off the lower part of the lettuce leaves, keeping the upper, fan-shaped green portion. Lay out the leaves on a work surface, with the narrow end toward you. Cover most of the leaf with a slice of smoked salmon. Divide the noodles equally on top of the salmon, placing them horizontally on top of the salmon, halfway between the top and bottom of the leaf. Place 2 or 3 pieces of scallion and 3 cucumber strips on top of the noodles. Add 3 mint leaves and a cilantro sprig. Sprinkle on some basil. Starting at the end nearest you, roll up the lettuce, enclosing the filling. Arrange the hand rolls on a serving platter.

3. For dipping sauce, divide the dressing among 4 small bowls. Add 1 table-spoon cold water and 1 tablespoon shallots to each bowl. Place a bowl of dipping sauce in front of each person and pass the platter of hand rolls.

Makes 4 servings

Per serving: 185 calories, 1 g fat, 0 g saturated fat, 8 g protein, 34 g carbohydrates, 2 g fiber

---

One hand roll makes a good starter, while 2 are a light meal.

For entertaining, set out a platter of salmon-covered lettuce leaves and another heaped with the noodles, vegetables, and other ingredients, arranged in separate piles. Let your guests assemble their own hand rolls.

FOOD FACT

Mint, basil, and parsley all contain terpenes, cancer-fighting antioxidants.

SALMON, CORN, AND MINT ON A TOMATO STAR

Stars, in Hollywood's heyday, loved to pick at health-guru Gaylord Hauser's tomato stuffed with chopped vegetables. I prefer using solid salmon or tuna salad. And instead of scooping out the tomato, I make a Tomato Star. Use either leftover roasted corn and baked salmon or frozen corn and canned fish for this eye-filling dish. Serve it for a late brunch or as a light dinner. The salad alone packs well if you want to brown-bag it.

2	cups leftover roasted corn, cut off the cob, or 1 (10-ounce) package defrosted frozen corn
2	cups (6 ounces) baked or poached fish, or 1 (6-ounce) can skinless and boneless pink or red salmon
1	green bell pepper, seeded and chopped
1	large shallot, finely chopped

1	teaspoon crumbled dried mint
½	cup chopped cilantro leaves
2	tablespoons basil oil
	Juice of 1 lime
	Salt and freshly ground black pepper
4	red leaf lettuce leaves, for garnish
4	Tomato Stars, optional

1. Combine the corn, salmon, bell pepper, and shallot in a bowl, tossing them together with a fork. Add the mint, cilantro, basil oil, and lime juice. Toss until the salad is evenly coated. Season it to taste with salt and pepper.

2. Arrange a lettuce leaf on each of 4 salad plates. If using, set a Tomato Star on each plate. Spoon one-quarter of the salad over the tomato, or onto the lettuce, and serve.

Makes 4 servings

Per serving: 149 calories, 4 g fat, g saturated fat, 1 g protein, 21 g carbohydrates, 3 g fiber

You can buy basil-flavored oil at specialty stores and some supermarkets.

A STAR IS BORN

To make a Tomato Star, place a vine tomato, blossom end down, on a cutting board. Hold a knife vertically and cut it in half, stopping before the knife goes all the way through. Make 2 more vertical cuts, so that 6 even wedges are formed, and spread out the points to form a star. Spoon about 1 cup of your favorite salad over the Tomato Star, leaving its points showing.

FOOD FACT

The red tips on red-leafed lettuce indicate the presence of plant pigments called anthocyanins, which are antioxidants.

ROASTED SALMON
WITH FRESH GARDEN SALSA

Elegantly simple, roasted salmon topped with juicy salsa makes a perfect dish. This is a technique for cooking fish that chefs often use. Searing the surface, then finishing the fish in a hot oven gives it good color and keeps it succulent. Just remember that the pan will be very hot when it comes out of the oven — and make sure that it doesn't have a rubber or plastic handle.

1 teaspoon canola, grapeseed, or olive oil	1½ pounds salmon fillet with skin, cut in 4 pieces
Salt and freshly ground black pepper	Fresh Garden Salsa (page 44)

1. Preheat the oven to 425°F. Season each piece of fish with a pinch of salt and a few grinds of black pepper.

2. Heat the oil in an ovenproof medium skillet. When a drop of water dances on the surface of the pan, add the pieces of fish skin side up. Cook until they are seared and have a golden crust, 3 minutes. Using tongs, turn the fish skin side down. Slip the skillet into the oven and roast until the fish is pearlescent in the center, 8 minutes for a 1"-thick fillet. Transfer the salmon to a serving platter or individual plates. Add ½ cup of the salsa to each plate and serve.

Makes 4 servings

Per serving: 228 calories, 15 g fat, 3 g saturated fat, 23 g protein, 0 g carbohydrates, 0 g fiber

SALMON PAILLARD WITH NAPA CABBAGE AND SPINACH SLAW AND SOY AND HONEY DRIZZLE

Halving the thick part of a salmon fillet creates thin "steak" that sears quickly. A bed of crisp vegetables and the pungent Asian flavors in this dish let you enjoy 4 ounces of salmon as a satisfying portion. You can make the sauce and slaw ahead, then serve the dish to company with minimal time in the kitchen after your guests arrive.

2 teaspoons light olive or canola oil	½ teaspoon Sichuan peppercorn powder,
2 (8-ounce) skinless salmon fillets	or freshly ground white pepper, for
Salt and freshly ground black	garnish
pepper	Soy and Honey Drizzle
Napa and Spinach Slaw (page 104)	(opposite page)

1. Coat a grill or ridged grill-pan with the oil.

2. Lay the salmon on a flat work surface, and place your palm on top to hold it securely. Use a thin, sharp knife to slice each fillet horizontally into 2 slabs. Season each piece of fish with ¼ teaspoon salt and 2 grinds of black pepper.

3. Grill the salmon until well-marked, 2 minutes. Turn and grill until the other side is marked, 2 minutes longer.

4. Make a bed with 1 cup of slaw on each of 4 dinner plates. Top each with a piece of salmon. Sprinkle each with a pinch of peppercorn powder or white pepper and spoon 2 tablespoons Soy and Honey Drizzle around the plate and on the fish. Serve immediately.

Makes 4 servings

Per serving: 228 calories, 15 g fat, 3 g saturated fat, 23 g protein, 0 g carbohydrates, 0 g fiber

SOY AND HONEY DRIZZLE

This is the kind of high-flavor sauce chefs squirt from a bottle to accent a dish. Just a little bit adds a big flavor boost to grilled halibut or shrimp or sliced grilled flank steak, as well as to the salmon.

2	tablespoons wildflower or mesquite honey		Juice of ½ lime
1	tablespoon reduced-sodium soy sauce	¼	teaspoon red-pepper flakes

Place the honey, soy sauce, lime juice, and pepper flakes in a small saucepan. Pour in ½ cup water and boil over medium-high heat until reduced to ½ cup, about 2 minutes. Use warm.

Makes ½ cup

Per serving (1 tablespoon): 20 calories, 0 g fat, 0 g saturated fat, 0 g protein, 5 g carbohydrates, 0 g fiber

SAKE-POACHED SALMON WITH GINGER GREMOLATA

This dish is as elegantly spare and surprising as Japanese haiku. The gremolata, an Italian condiment, here uses Japanese ingredients.

1	rib celery, sliced	2	cups cilantro leaves, lightly packed
2	scallions, white and green parts, chopped	1	shallot
1	(2") piece fresh ginger, peeled and thinly sliced		Grated zest of 1 lime (about 1 tablespoon)
2	cups sake, preferably dry	1	teaspoon finely grated ginger
1	teaspoon salt	¼	teaspoon salt
		4	(6-ounce) pieces salmon filet with skin

1. In a deep pot with a tight-fitting lid large enough to hold the salmon in 1 layer, combine the celery, scallions, sliced ginger, sake, and salt. Bring to a boil, reduce the heat, simmer very gently for 30 minutes.

2. For the gremolata, finely chop the cilantro and shallots (see note) and place them in a small bowl. Mix in the grated lime zest, grated ginger, and salt. Set aside.

3. Remove the pot with the cooking liquid from the heat and add the salmon fillets, leaving at least ½" between them. The liquid will come ¼" to ½" up the sides of the fish. Return the pot to the heat. When the liquid is barely boiling, cover the pot. Cook until the fish is opaque, except for a slightly translucent spot in the center. Divide the fish among 4 dinner plates and spread one-quarter of the gremolata on top of each piece. Serve immediately.

Makes 4 servings

Per serving: 483 calories, 19 g fat, 4 g saturated fat, 35 g protein, 8 g carbohydrates, 1 g fiber

PAN-ROASTED HALIBUT WITH CARAMELIZED ONIONS

Creamy caramelized onions contrast nicely with this firm, meaty fish. Searing the fish on top of the stove to give it a brown crust, then finishing it in the oven, is how chefs keep a thick fillet crisp outside and moist inside.

2	tablespoons unsalted butter	1½	pounds halibut fillet with the skin, cut in 4 pieces
2	pounds yellow onions (about 4 large), thinly sliced	2	teaspoons unbleached all-purpose flour
2	teaspoons wildflower honey	1	tablespoon light olive or canola oil
2	whole cloves	1	lime, cut in 8 wedges, for garnish
	Salt and freshly ground pepper		

1. Heat the butter in a deep, medium skillet over medium-high heat. Add the onions, stirring until they are coated. Cook until they wilt, stirring occasionally, 6 minutes. Mix in the honey and cloves. Cover the pan tightly and cook 10 minutes longer.

2. Uncover and continue cooking, stirring frequently, until the onions are soft and honey-colored, 15 minutes. Remove the cloves and season to taste with salt and pepper. There will be about 2 cups of cooked onions.

3. Preheat the oven to 500°F. Rub each piece of fish with ½ teaspoon of flour. Season the fish with salt and pepper. In a medium ovenproof skillet, heat the oil over medium-high heat. Add the fish and cook skin side down for 2 minutes. Turn and cook until the fish is golden brown, 6 minutes.

4. Transfer the skillet to the oven and roast the fish 4 minutes, or until it feels firm when pressed in the center with your fingertip. To serve, set each piece of the roasted halibut skin side down in the center of a dinner plate. Top with one-quarter of the caramelized onions. Arrange 2 lime wedges on top.

Makes 4 servings

Per serving: 382 calories, 13 g fat, 5 g saturated fat, 39 g protein, 28 g carbohydrates, 5 g fiber

Make the onions up to 3 days ahead and this dish assembles very easily. Simply reheat the onions, wrapped in foil, at 350°F for 20 minutes, then increase the temperature to roast the fish.

FOOD FACT

Halibut provides a good amount of omega-3s, but stick to fish caught in the Pacific as Atlantic halibut is endangered.

SHRIMP WITH
CHERRY TOMATOES AND FETA

FOOD FACT

Shrimp contain a moderate amount of omega-3 fatty acids.

Plump cherry tomatoes, sautéed just until their skin cracks, are the stars of this Greek-accented dish. The large cherry ones, also called cocktail tomatoes, that come in a net bag are best. Their flavor is worth the premium you pay. If you buy shelled shrimp, this dish is ready to cook in 5 minutes.

2	teaspoons extra-virgin olive oil	¼	cup dry white wine, or fat-free, reduced-sodium chicken broth
¾	pound medium shrimp, shelled		
1	clove garlic, minced	3	tablespoons chopped flat-leaf parsley
1	(12-ounce) bag cherry tomatoes on the vine	2	tablespoons crumbled reduced-fat feta cheese
1	tablespoon chopped fresh oregano, or 1 teaspoon dried	½	teaspoon salt
			Freshly ground black pepper

1. Heat the oil in a medium skillet over medium-high heat. Add the shrimp and stir with a wooden spoon until they just lose their raw color, 1 to 2 minutes.

2. Add the garlic, tomatoes, oregano, and wine or broth. Cook, using a spoon to roll the tomatoes around, until most of the liquid has boiled off, 1 to 2 minutes. Add the parsley and cheese, and cook 1 minute longer, stirring occasionally. Season with salt and pepper, and serve immediately.

Makes 4 servings

Per serving: 154 calories, 5 g fat, 1 g saturated fat, 19 g protein, 5 g carbohydrates, 1 g fiber

SALMON HASH

Here the deeply browned potatoes and onions of classic hash are combined with salmon instead of corned beef. Tomatillos contribute the sharp edge traditionally provided by the pickled meat. For the salmon, I use leftover Roasted Salmon (page 148), but other baked or sautéed fish is good, too.

Enjoy this enlightened hash alone or with a poached egg on top, if you wish.

1	large Yukon Gold or other yellow-fleshed potato, quartered	3	cups leftover baked, broiled, or grilled salmon, or 12 ounces Roasted Salmon fillet (page 148), in 1" flakes
1	tablespoon extra-virgin olive oil		
1	medium red onion, chopped	2	tablespoons ketchup
2	medium tomatillos, chopped	1	tablespoon low-fat sour cream
1	clove garlic, finely chopped		Salt and freshly ground black pepper

1. Boil the potato until it is soft but gives some resistance when pierced with a knife, 15 minutes. When cool enough to handle, peel and dice.

2. Heat the oil in a medium nonstick skillet over medium-high heat. Sauté the onion until it is translucent, 4 minutes. Stir in the tomatillos and garlic, and cook 1 minute longer. Add the diced potato, spreading it in 1 layer, and cook until lightly browned on the bottom, 5 minutes. Turn and brown on the second side. Add the salmon to the pan and mix until it is heated through.

3. In a small bowl, combine the ketchup and sour cream. Off the heat, stir it into the hash. Season to taste with salt and pepper. Divide among 4 plates and serve immediately.

Makes 4 servings

Per serving: 344 calories, 19 g fat, 4 g saturated fat, 27 g protein, 16 g carbohydrates, 2 g fiber

SALMON FRIED RICE

Using refrigerated or frozen rice is the secret for getting fluffy fried rice. While I prefer an aromatic white jasmine, using rice leftover from Chinese take-out is handy. Do not add soy sauce to the rice; Asians would not dream of using it to darken the white color they prize.

1	tablespoon peanut oil	1	medium tomato, seeded and chopped
1	small red onion, halved and sliced vertically in thin crescents	1	long green chile pepper, thinly sliced, optional
1	clove garlic, finely chopped	1	teaspoon salt
2	cups cooked jasmine or basmati rice, chilled or frozen	⅛	teaspoon ground white or black pepper
6	ounces cooked fresh salmon, flaked	2	tablespoons shredded Thai or Italian basil, for garnish
3	scallions, green and white parts, chopped	1	tablespoon chopped cilantro, for garnish

Rice that has been refrigerated or frozen does not stick together when you fry it.

Pressing the rice against the hot wok helps it pick up a slightly smoky flavor.

1. Place a wok over high heat. Drizzle in the oil and stir-fry the onion and garlic until the garlic starts to color, 30 seconds.

2. Add the rice, and stir-fry for 3 minutes, alternately pressing the rice firmly against the side of the wok and tossing it. When the grains start to look fluffy, add the salmon, scallions, tomato, chile pepper (if using), salt, and ground pepper. Stir-fry until all the ingredients are evenly combined with the rice, 1 minute. Scoop the fried rice into a serving bowl, garnish it with the basil and cilantro, and serve immediately.

Makes 4 servings

Per serving: 244 calories, 9 g fat, 2 g saturated fat, 12 g protein, 27 g carbohydrates, 2 g fiber

SALMON SOONG

Cantonese restaurants serve Squab Soong, a stir-fry of minced poultry, crisp vegetables, and toasted nuts you eat wrapped in a chilled lettuce leaf. Even if squab were easily available, I would still prefer it made with salmon. I also use jicama in place of the customary water chestnuts because it has better crunch and flavor, unless you are able to get them fresh at an Asian market.

TOP WOKKING TAKES TWO

Restaurant-perfect stir-fries require super-high heat to create *wok hay*, the smoky taste of the wok found in good Chinese cooking. At home, it also takes 2 pairs of hands to produce perfectly seared food, with 1 person keeping the ingredients moving constantly while the other makes split-second additions to the wok.

3	dried shiitake mushrooms	1	small head iceberg lettuce, halved
3	tablespoons pine nuts	1	tablespoon peanut oil
1	teaspoon cornstarch	¾	pound salmon fillet, skinned and cut
½	teaspoon sugar		in ¾" cubes
⅛	teaspoon ground white or black pepper	1	rib celery, finely chopped
1	teaspoon salt	½	red bell pepper, seeded and cut in ½" dice
1	tablespoon dry sherry	½	cup ½" diced jicama
1	tablespoon hoisin sauce	⅓	cup chopped scallion, green and white
¼	cup fat-free, low-sodium chicken broth		parts
¼	teaspoon roasted sesame oil	1	clove garlic, finely chopped

1. In a small bowl, soak the mushrooms in warm water to cover for 20 to 30 minutes until soft. Drain, reserving the soaking liquid for another use. Remove and discard the mushroom stems. Finely chop the mushrooms and set aside.

2. Preheat the oven to 325°F.

3. Spread the pine nuts on a baking sheet and toast until they are golden, 8 minutes, stirring several times so the nuts color evenly. Set the nuts aside to cool.

4. Combine the cornstarch, sugar, pepper, and salt in a small bowl. Mix in the sherry, then the hoisin sauce. Add the chicken broth and sesame oil. Set the seasoning sauce aside, leaving the spoon in the bowl.

5. Gently lift 2 or 3 layers of lettuce from 1 of the halves, keeping them as cup-shaped as possible, then lift off another set of layers. Repeat, using the

other half of the lettuce. Set a lettuce cup on 1 of 4 plates, and refrigerate the remaining lettuce for another use.

6. Set a wok over the highest possible heat and drizzle with the peanut oil. Stir-fry the salmon 1 minute. Remove it to a plate. Stir-fry the celery, bell pepper, jicama, scallion, garlic, and chopped mushrooms for 30 seconds. Return the salmon to the wok. Stir the seasoning sauce and pour it into the wok. Cook until the sauce thickens, 1 minute, and mix in the nuts. Spoon the Soong over the lettuce and serve immediately.

Makes 4 servings

Per serving: 276 calories, 17 g fat, 3 g saturated fat, 20 g protein, 11 g carbohydrates, 3 g fiber

BROCCOLI-STUFFED BAKED POTATO WITH SALMON

When fresh sockeye salmon is available, its firm texture is ideal for this casual dish. It can be roasted, steamed, or grilled.

1	large baking potato	½	teaspoon dried oregano
⅛	teaspoon canola oil	⅛	teaspoon ground turmeric
2	small broccoli florets, cut very small		Salt and freshly ground black pepper
1	teaspoon butter or olive oil	2	(3-ounce) pieces cooked sockeye salmon

1. Place a rack in the center of the oven. Preheat the oven to 400°F.

2. Coat the potato with the oil (or use cooking spray). Pierce it in 3 or 4 places with the tip of a small, sharp knife, and bake for 1 hour, until the skin is crisp and the inside is very soft.

3. Shortly before the potato is done, steam the broccoli until it is soft, about 6 minutes. Drain well, and place the broccoli in a bowl. Using the side of a fork, chop the florets into bits.

4. When the potato is done, halve it lengthwise. Scoop the flesh out of both halves and add it to the broccoli. Add the butter, oregano, and turmeric and mash with a fork until the mixture is almost smooth. Season the filling to taste with salt and pepper.

5. Heap the filling into the shells, mounding it generously. Set a piece of salmon on top of each shell, and serve.

Makes 2 servings

Per serving: 284 calories, 12 g fat, 3 g saturated fat, 27 g protein, 20 g carbohydrates, 3 g fiber

TWO FOR ONE

If cooking for one, cool the second stuffed potato to room temperature and wrap it in foil. It will keep in the refrigerator for 1 to 2 days. To serve, preheat the oven to 350°F. Open the foil, coat the salmon with cooking spray, reseal, and bake 15 minutes or until heated through.

TUNA, BROCCOLI, AND WHITE BEAN SKILLET DINNER

Farm-stand broccoli and home-cooked beans will elevate this quick, simple meal to a treat, especially when you also use a pungent Tuscan olive oil or Olio Verde from Sicily. But even if you opt for frozen broccoli and canned beans when time is short, you'll still have a tasty dinner.

1	bunch broccoli, cut in 1" florets, or 4 cups frozen broccoli florets
2	teaspoons extra-virgin olive oil
1	small red onion, chopped
1	clove garlic, finely chopped
¼	teaspoon red-pepper flakes
1	(6-ounce) can light tuna packed in olive oil, drained

1	(14–19-ounce) can cannellini beans, drained and rinsed
¼	cup chopped oil-packed sun-dried tomatoes
	Salt and freshly ground black pepper

1. Steam the broccoli 4 minutes, or until crisp-tender. Plunge it immediately into a bowl of ice water or run cold water over it until it is chilled. Drain well and set aside.

2. In a deep, medium skillet, heat the oil over medium-high heat. Sauté the onion for 1 minute, then mix in the garlic and pepper flakes. Cook until the onion is soft, 3 minutes longer. Add the tuna, breaking it into 1" pieces. Add the broccoli, beans, and tomatoes to the skillet, and cook 4 minutes, until they are heated through. Season with salt and pepper, and serve. If there are leftovers, serve them at room temperature as a salad.

Makes 4 servings

Per serving: 199 calories, 7 g fat, 1 g saturated fat, 20 g protein, 21 g carbohydrates, 7 g fiber

SUN-DRIED AND SKINNY

If you need to avoid the fat in oil-packed sun-dried tomatoes (although it is usually health-promoting olive oil), substitute the dry ones. To soften them, blanch the tomatoes in boiling water for 3 minutes, and set aside to soak until soft but not mushy, 10 to 15 minutes. Squeeze out any excess water.

CHAPTER SEVEN

PASTA, SAUCES, AND GRAINS

Skipping a speech on why eating whole grains is good—they provide fiber, complex carbs, and so on—I would rather share delicious ways to enjoy them, including whole wheat pasta. Pairing these grains and dark pastas with the right ingredients avoids dull-tasting "brown" food. For example, long-grain brown rice perks up when cooked with a cinnamon stick and a clove, and it comes out fluffy, too, in Cinnamon Rice with Lentils. Wild rice, which has as much fiber as brown rice, goes perfectly with wild blueberries.

Pasta has borne the brunt of concerns about carbs, obesity, and insulin resistance. And admittedly, semolina pasta is highly refined. But there is room for everything, in moderation, particularly if you eat pasta as Italians do: in sensible portions combined with lots of vegetables. A modest amount of pasta shells tossed with broccoli and browned onions, or rigatoni topped with Roasted Vegetable Sauce combining chunky roasted tomatoes and red peppers with a touch of balsamic vinegar, is so satisfying. Even fettuccine with smoked salmon and cream is reasonable on occasion when prepared with a light touch. Spinach pasta has more fiber than plain semolina, thanks to the spinach powder that turns it green, and it goes splendidly with Spinach Pesto.

Farro or spelt pasta tastes so good that chefs use it, as well as imported Italian whole wheat pastas. Excellent with properly assertive toppings, they pair well with arugula and edamame and with Ginger Tomato Sauce. In addition to their earthy flavor, these dark, rustic pastas provide good quantities of fiber and complex carbohydrates.

Red sauces, are an ideal way to fit lycopene-rich cooked tomatoes into meals. Here you'll find three. Serve them with pasta and use them as cooking sauces for chicken, turkey sausages, halibut, and other seafood, or to accompany rice and beans.

WHOLE WHEAT LINGUINE
WITH ARUGULA AND EDAMAME

Arugula, a cruciferous vegetable rich in beta-carotene, gets its bite from sulfur compounds related to those in watercress.

COOK SMART

To save time, Italians boil vegetables in a large pot, then use the same water to cook the pasta. The veggies are easily lifted out if you use a pot that has a pasta insert or use a colander that sits securely on the pot.

Edamame—sweet green soybeans—are perfect partners with pungent dark greens and garlic. Combine them all with imported Italian whole wheat linguine or farro spaghetti from Manicaretti and you have a dish packed with flavor and fiber.

2	cups shelled edamame	8	cups coarsely chopped arugula
8	ounces whole wheat linguine or farro		Salt and freshly ground pepper
1	tablespoon extra-virgin olive oil, divided	½	cup freshly grated Parmigiano-
2	cloves garlic, minced		Reggiano cheese

1. Cook the edamame in boiling salted water until they are crisp-tender, 3 minutes. Remove them to a bowl with a slotted spoon.

2. Add the pasta to the same water, and cook according to package directions. Drain it in a colander, drizzle with ½ teaspoon of the oil, and set it aside.

3. In a large, nonstick skillet, heat the remaining oil over medium-high heat. Add the garlic and cook 15 seconds. Mix in the arugula, coating it with the oil, and cook until wilted, 2 minutes. Mix in the edamame and remove the pan from the heat. Add the drained pasta, stirring until it is warmed through, and season to taste with salt and pepper.

4. Divide the pasta and vegetables among 4 shallow pasta bowls or dinner plates, and top with equal amounts of the cheese. Serve hot or at room temperature.

Makes 4 servings

Per serving: 475 calories, 16 g fat, 4 g saturated fat, 30 g protein, 59 g carbohydrates, 13 g fiber

SPINACH FUSILLI
WITH SPINACH PESTO

A pasta and sauce that are green on green: Dark Spinach Pesto made with walnuts nestles into the twists of spinach fusilli, making it easy to mop up every creamy bit.

Raw spinach contains more folate than cooked spinach because this water-soluble B vitamin is lost through cooking.

2	*teaspoons extra-virgin olive oil*	¾	*cup Spinach Pesto (opposite page)*
4	*cloves garlic, sliced lengthwise*		*Salt and freshly ground black pepper*
8	*ounces spinach fusilli pasta*		

1. Heat the oil in a small skillet over medium-high heat and sauté the garlic until it is golden on both sides, 3 minutes. Drain the garlic on a paper towel and set it aside.

2. Cook the pasta according to package directions. Drain it, reserving 1 cup of the cooking water.

3. Divide the pesto among 4 warm pasta bowls or deep plates. Add the pasta, and 2 tablespoons of the reserved pasta water to each bowl. Toss to combine, adding more of the water if needed to coat the pasta with the sauce. Season to taste with salt and pepper, sprinkle with the browned garlic, and serve.

Makes 4 servings

Per serving: 441 calories, 21 g fat, 3 g saturated fat, 17 g protein, 46 g carbohydrates, 3 g fiber

SPINACH PESTO

Italians use fresh spinach to make pesto, particularly in winter when local, garden-fresh basil is out of season. Adding a touch of tofu produces a creamy sauce containing far less oil than traditional recipes. Enjoy it on pasta, in soups, and on steamed zucchini or green beans.

½	cup walnuts	1	tablespoon soft silken tofu
2	cups coarsely chopped flat-leaf spinach leaves	¼	cup freshly grated Parmigiano-Reggiano cheese
8	large basil leaves, torn in pieces	2	tablespoons extra-virgin olive oil
1	medium clove garlic, coarsely chopped		Salt and freshly ground black pepper

In a food processor, whirl the nuts until finely chopped, 30 seconds. Add the spinach, basil, and garlic. Whirl until they are finely chopped, 15 seconds. Add the tofu and cheese. Pulse 3 or 4 times, just to blend. With the motor running, drizzle in the oil. Season the pesto to taste with salt and pepper.

Makes 4 servings

Per serving: 192 calories, 18 g fat, 3 g saturated fat, 5 g protein, 3 g carbohydrates, 3 g fiber

FETTUCCINE WITH GOAT CHEESE AND WALNUTS

Goat's milk is lower in cholesterol than cow's milk, and it contains virtually no casein, a trigger for dairy allergies.

Creamy goat cheese makes this pasta seem more sinful than it is. Blending the cheese with a bit of the pasta cooking water, an Italian trick, turns it into a smooth sauce.

¾	cup shelled walnuts	2	teaspoons chopped flat-leaf parsley
2	ounces fresh goat cheese	2	tablespoons freshly grated
	Salt and freshly ground black pepper		Parmigiano-Reggiano cheese
16	ounces fettuccine pasta		

1. Preheat the oven to 350°F.

2. Toast the walnuts on a baking sheet for 10 minutes, stirring them 2 or 3 times. Set the nuts aside to cool.

3. Finely chop the nuts by hand or in a mini food processor. Place them in a mixing bowl, stir in the goat cheese, and season the mixture to taste with salt and pepper.

4. Cook the pasta according to package directions. Drain, reserving ½ cup of the cooking water, and place the pasta in a warmed serving bowl.

5. Thin the goat cheese mixture with the reserved pasta water, starting with ¼ cup. It should have the consistency of heavy cream. Pour the sauce over the pasta and sprinkle on the parsley and Parmigiano-Reggiano cheese. Toss to combine and serve immediately.

Makes 4 servings

Per serving: 630 calories, 24 g fat, 5 g saturated fat, 24 g protein, 83 g carbohydrates, 9 g fiber

SHELLS WITH BROCCOLI AND ONION

This dish combines the robust flavors of garlic, well-browned onions, and pecorino cheese. Splurge by using 3 tablespoons of a grassy-tasting Tuscan olive oil, and it will be even better. Chiocciole pasta is similar to shells, but any short, whole grain pasta will work in this dish.

8	cups bite-size broccoli florets	1	large onion, chopped
6	ounces whole wheat chiocciole		Salt and freshly ground black pepper
2	tablespoons extra-virgin olive oil	¼	cup freshly grated pecorino cheese
3	cloves garlic, thinly sliced lengthwise		

1. Cook the broccoli in boiling water for 2 minutes. Remove it to a colander with a slotted spoon, and place it under cold running water to stop the cooking. Drain well.

2. Toss the shells into the boiling water and cook them according to package directions. Drain in a colander but leave some water clinging to the pasta. Turn the shells into a large, warm serving bowl.

3. While the pasta cooks, heat the oil in a medium skillet over medium-high heat. Add the garlic, cooking until it starts to color, 3 minutes, then remove it with a slotted spoon and set it aside. Add the onion to the pan and sauté until well-browned, with some blackened bits. Add the broccoli to the skillet and sauté just until it is heated through.

4. Spoon the broccoli and onion over the pasta, scraping out the pan. Add the reserved garlic, and toss to combine. Season the pasta to taste with salt and pepper, sprinkle with the cheese, toss, and serve immediately.

Makes 4 servings

Per serving: 299 calories, 10 g fat, 2 g saturated fat, 13 g protein, 46 g carbohydrates, 11 g fiber

Whole wheat pasta provides 4 grams of fiber per serving, twice as much as semolina pasta.

GREEN AND GOLD

Extra-virgin olive oils ranging in color from warm gold to deep green may taste mild and fruity or harsh and peppery. Excellent-quality oils come from Umbria, Apulia, Sicily, and other parts of Italy besides Tuscany—as well as from Spain, Greece, France, and Tunisia. California, too, produces top-quality choices. Keep on hand 2 or 3 that please you. Use less-expensive ones for cooking and costlier ones with more complex flavor on salads, and to drizzle on vegetables or in soups.

SPELT PENNE WITH ROCK SHRIMP AND GINGER TOMATO SAUCE

A sturdy pasta like penne complements the robust flavor in Ginger Tomato Sauce (page 175). The sweet flavor of rock shrimp makes a good addition and keeps this a speedy dish, since they come already shelled. Keep in mind that whole grain pasta takes longer to cook than semolina pasta.

8	ounces spelt penne or ziti pasta	2	cups Ginger Tomato Sauce
2	teaspoons extra-virgin olive oil		(page 175)
¾	cup finely chopped onion	2	tablespoons chopped flat-leaf parsley,
¾	pound rock shrimp		for garnish

1. In a large pot of boiling water, cook the pasta according to package directions. Drain it in a colander and shake it, but leave some water clinging to the pasta.

2. Meanwhile, heat the oil in a medium nonstick skillet over medium-high heat. Sauté the onion until it softens, 4 minutes, then mix in the shrimp. As soon as the shrimp lose their raw color and turn red, add the sauce. When the sauce boils, reduce the heat and simmer until the shrimp are cooked through, about 4 minutes.

3. Divide the pasta among 4 wide shallow bowls. Top with the sauce, garnish with the parsley, and serve immediately.

Makes 4 servings

Per serving: 371 calories, 5 g fat, 1 g saturated fat, 28 g protein, 54 g carbohydrates, 4 g fiber

Spelt is an ancient form of wheat. Processed as a whole grain, it is similar to farro but tastes somewhat more like whole wheat in American brands like Vita-Spelt. People allergic to wheat can often comfortably eat spelt or farro.

FETTUCCINE WITH SMOKED SALMON AND BABY GREEN PEAS

Enjoy everything in moderation, including this lavish pasta. Just 2 tablespoons of cream and a scant teaspoon of butter per serving make it indulgent without wrecking an otherwise reasonable diet. Use a premium quality cream that is not ultrapasteurized and tastes of fresh fields and sunshine.

¾	pound fresh fettuccine	½	cup heavy cream
1	tablespoon unsalted butter	4	ounces good-quality smoked salmon,
1	large shallot, thinly sliced		cut in thin strips
1	cup frozen baby green peas, defrosted		Freshly ground black pepper

1. Cook the pasta in boiling salted water until tender, 3 to 4 minutes. Drain it and divide it among 4 warm pasta bowls or shallow soup plates.

2. While the pasta cooks, melt the butter in a large skillet over medium-high heat. Sauté the shallot until it is translucent, 2 minutes, then add the peas and cream. As soon as the cream boils, pour the sauce over the pasta. Top each serving with one-quarter of the smoked salmon, season generously with pepper, and serve immediately.

Makes 4 servings

Per serving: 436 calories, 17 g fat, 9 g saturated fat, 17 g protein, 54 g carbohydrates, 5 g fiber

Place the frozen peas in a colander and run hot tap water over them for 1 to 2 minutes to defrost them quickly.

Tender, tiny green peas provide 6 grams of fiber per cup.

ROASTED VEGETABLE SAUCE

So flavorful you will want to eat it on its own, serve this chunky sauce over penne or rigatoni. I also spread ½ cup in the center of a plate and top it with a piece of grilled chicken, halibut, or boneless pork chop.

Red bell peppers contain over 10 times more beta-carotene than green.

2	pounds plum tomatoes, halved lengthwise	2	cloves roasted garlic (see page 49)
		½	teaspoon balsamic vinegar
2	red bell peppers, seeded and quartered	½–1	teaspoon salt
1	red onion, halved lengthwise		Freshly ground black pepper
2	tablespoons extra-virgin olive oil, divided		

1. Set racks in the upper and the lower thirds of the oven. Preheat the oven to 425°F. Cover 2 baking sheets with foil and coat the foil with cooking spray or brush it with olive oil.

2. In a large bowl, toss the tomatoes, bell peppers, and onion with 1 table-spoon of the oil until evenly coated. Arrange the tomatoes, cut side down, on 1 baking sheet and place it on the bottom rack of the oven. Arrange the peppers and onion on the second sheet and place it on the top rack.

3. Bake the tomatoes until their skin is blistered and the tomatoes are soft but still hold their shape, 25 minutes. Turn up the edges of the foil so it holds in the juices and, using tongs, lift off the skin. When the onion is translucent but not soft, 25 to 30 minutes, remove it from the oven, and set aside. Bake the peppers until soft, 30 minutes. Transfer them to a small bowl, and cover with plastic wrap. Let the peppers steam for 10 minutes.

4. Lift the skin from the peppers and remove the outer layer from the onion. Chop all the vegetables coarsely, reserving any liquid from the peppers remaining in the bowl.

5. Heat the remaining 1 tablespoon of oil in a deep medium skillet. Add the garlic, tomatoes with their liquid, peppers plus their liquid, and the onion. Add the vinegar and sauté the vegetables 5 minutes, using the back of a wooden spoon to break them into small chunks. Continue cooking until almost all the liquid has evaporated, 5 minutes longer. Season the sauce to taste with salt and pepper. This sauce keeps for 5 days, tightly covered in the refrigerator.

Makes 4 servings

Per serving: 139 calories, 8 g fat, 1 g saturated fat, 3 g protein, 17 g carbohydrates, 4 g fiber

CUMIN TOMATO SAUCE

At Rice, a casual Asian-fusion restaurant in New York City, this sauce is served with deep-fried spinach rice balls. I prefer using it with Spinach and Rice Torta (page 192), my healthier way to this great combination. This sauce is also delicious with a white, meaty fish like cod or halibut and for making spicy stewed chicken.

To chop canned tomatoes, work a knife up and down in the can and push it toward the sides, cutting the tomatoes into chunks.

Tomatoes contain lycopene, an antioxidant. Foods rich in lycopene, vitamin E, and beta-carotene help defend against skin cancer by increasing the body's natural sun protection factor.

1	tablespoon extra-virgin olive oil	1½	tablespoons tomato paste
1	clove garlic, halved lengthwise	1	tablespoon ground cumin
1	Spanish onion, chopped	¼	teaspoon ground turmeric
1	tablespoon raisins		Salt and freshly ground black pepper
1	(28-ounce) can whole tomatoes with the liquid, coarsely chopped		

1. Heat the oil in a medium Dutch oven over medium-high heat and sauté the garlic until it begins to color, turning the slices, 1 minute total. Remove the garlic and discard. Add the onion and sauté until it is soft, 4 minutes.

2. Add the raisins, tomatoes with their liquid, tomato paste, cumin, and turmeric. Bring to a boil, reduce the heat, and simmer until the tomatoes are soft, 30 minutes.

3. Puree the sauce in a food processor until it is pulpy. Return the pureed sauce to the pot, and cook until it is reduced to 3 cups, about 20 minutes. Season to taste with salt and pepper.

Makes 6 servings

Per serving: 76 calories, 3 g fat, 0 g saturated fat, 2 g protein, 12 g carbohydrates, 3 g fiber

GINGER TOMATO SAUCE

This tomato sauce is full of surprises. Ginger and jalapeño pepper hit your mouth with heat, carrots give it a sweet base, and vermouth adds herbal notes. Grating the onion lets it disappear while also adding more pungency. Serve this sauce on ziti, curly cavatappi, or spinach fusilli and with seafood.

1	tablespoon + 1 teaspoon canola oil	1	medium carrot, finely shredded
1	tablespoon freshly grated ginger	⅓	cup sweet vermouth
2	cloves garlic, finely chopped	1	(28-ounce) can chopped tomatoes
1	small jalapeño pepper, seeded and finely chopped	1	teaspoon sugar
½	cup grated or finely chopped onion		Salt and freshly ground black pepper

1. Heat the oil in a deep, large saucepan over medium heat. Sauté the ginger, garlic, and jalapeño until they cling together, 4 minutes.

2. Mix in the onion and increase the heat to medium-high. Cook, stirring occasionally, until the onion is soft, 5 minutes, taking care not to let it color. Mix in the carrot and cook, stirring often, until the mixture in the pan is nearly dry and clings together, 8 minutes.

3. Pour in the vermouth and cook until it has boiled off and the vegetables are almost dry, 6 minutes. Add the tomatoes and sugar. Simmer the sauce, stirring occasionally, until it is thick enough to plop from a spoon, 15 minutes. Season to taste with salt and pepper.

Makes 6 servings

Per serving: 95 calories, 4 g fat, 0 g saturated fat, 2 g protein, 12 g carbohydrates, 2 g fiber

WILD RICE PILAF
WITH BLUEBERRIES

A pilaf when served hot, this fruited rice is a whole grain salad when served at room temperature. Its dual personality make this dish an excellent choice for potlucks and buffet parties.

This versatile dish comes together in less than 20 minutes if you cook the rice, soak the blueberries ahead, and have the vegetables coarsely chopped.

Turn it into a vegetarian main course by mixing in cubes of marinated or smoked tofu.

FOOD FACT

Wild rice is a good source of folate and zinc.

⅓	cup dried blueberries	½	teaspoon chopped fresh rosemary,
½	cup apple cider		or 1 teaspoon dried
1	rib celery, cut in 1" slices	¼	teaspoon ground ginger
1	medium leek, white part only, chopped	1	cup fat-free, reduced-sodium chicken
½	medium red onion, coarsely chopped		broth
1	shallot, quartered		Salt and freshly ground black pepper
1	tablespoon extra-virgin olive oil	¼	cup toasted sliced almonds, optional,
2	cups cooked wild rice		for garnish

1. In a small bowl, plump the blueberries by soaking them in the cider for 20 minutes. Drain, saving the cider for another use, and set the berries aside.

2. Place the celery, leek, onion, and shallot in a food processor and whirl until they are finely chopped.

3. Heat the oil in a medium skillet over medium-high heat. Sauté the chopped vegetables until they are lightly cooked, 6 minutes. Add the wild rice, blueberries, rosemary, and ginger. Pour in the broth plus 1 cup water. Simmer vigorously, stirring occasionally, until the liquid evaporates and the rice is very tender, 10 minutes. Season to taste with salt and pepper.

4. Garnish the rice with the almonds and serve at room temperature.

Makes 4 servings

Per serving: 235 calories, 4 g fat, 1 g saturated fat, 6 g protein, 46 g carbohydrates, 4 g fiber

CINNAMON RICE WITH LENTILS

Pyramida, a little Egyptian restaurant around the corner from me, offers this nicely spiced rice and lentil pilaf. Make it the cornerstone of a meatless meal, or serve it with sautéed chicken breast.

¾	cup long-grain brown rice	2	tablespoons extra-virgin olive oil
1	(4") cinnamon stick	1	large red onion, thinly sliced
1	whole clove		Salt and freshly ground black pepper
½	cup green lentils		

1. Place the rice, cinnamon stick, and clove in a medium saucepan. Pour in 2 cups cold water and bring to a boil over medium-high heat. Cover and simmer gently until the rice is tender, 50 minutes. Off the heat, let sit, covered, 10 minutes. Remove the cinnamon stick and clove.

2. In a second pot, cook the lentils, covered, in 2 cups water, until they are tender, 40 minutes. Drain any remaining liquid.

3. Heat the oil in a medium skillet over medium-high heat and sauté the onion until it is soft and lightly colored, 8 minutes.

4. Fluff the rice with a fork and place it in a mixing bowl. Add the lentils and onions and season to taste with salt and pepper, mixing with a fork to combine.

Makes 4 servings

Per serving: 288 calories, 8 g fat, 1 g saturated fat, 10 g protein, 44 g carbohydrates, 9 g fiber

Cinnamon sticks with both sides rolled in are actually cassia, a bark that is richer than true cinnamon in fragrant and health-protective essential oils.

INDIAN SPINACH RICE

For special occasions, I prepare this dish, which has spices sizzled in oil to release their flavor. Curry leaves add an exotic aroma and flavor. If they are not available, use chopped basil. Serve with grilled salmon, Pan-Roasted Halibut with Caramelized Onions (page 153), or Turkey-Walnut Meat Loaf (page 134).

1	cup white basmati rice	1½	cups frozen chopped spinach
1	tablespoon canola oil	2	(¼" × 1") slices fresh ginger
1	teaspoon black mustard seeds	1	teaspoon salt
3 or 4	whole dried chile peppers	¼	cup cilantro leaves, optional, for garnish
12	curry leaves, optional		

1. In a colander, rinse the rice under cold running water, stirring it with your fingers until the water runs clear, about 2 minutes. Place the rice in a bowl, cover it to a depth of 1" with cold water, and let it soak for 20 minutes. Drain well.

2. Heat the oil in a deep, medium saucepan over medium-high heat. Add the mustard seeds, chile peppers, and curry leaves, if using. When the mustard seeds start to pop, partially cover the pot. When the popping slows down, after about 1 minute, add the rice and spinach.

3. Carefully pour in 1½ cups cold water, standing back as it will splatter. Add the ginger and salt. Bring the liquid to a boil, stir, and reduce the heat. Simmer uncovered for 5 minutes, until the rice grains are long and opaque. Cover and cook 10 minutes longer. Remove from the heat and let sit, covered, for 5 minutes. With a fork, fluff the rice, removing the chile peppers and the ginger slices. Serve the rice in a bowl, garnished with coarsely chopped cilantro, if desired.

Makes 6 servings

Per serving: 165 calories, 3 g fat, 0 g saturated fat, 5 g protein, 31 g carbohydrates, 3 g fiber

If you soak basmati rice for 20 minutes, the grains will swell to nearly 1" long as they cook.

FOOD FACT
Mustard seeds contain curcumin, an antioxidant with anti-inflammatory properties.

CHAPTER EIGHT
EGGS, BEANS, AND SOY

If I had to pick a favorite chapter, except for desserts, this would be it. Its meatless and mostly meatless dishes will light up your senses with their zest. If you eat vegetarian only occasionally, these substantial dishes with mouth-filling flavors will help you happily eat meatless more often.

The first dish, a Tunisian ojja, shows how eggs and potatoes scrambled with a touch of tomato paste come out creamy and soft as shirred eggs. Huevo Ranchero, a healthier version of the Tex-Mex favorite, includes a generous portion of refried black beans and baked corn chips. Green Eggs and Ham provides two full servings of fresh greens in a quick breakfast kids of all ages will actually ask for.

Two recipes show how much flavor just two strips of preservative-free bacon add to legume dishes. Reduced-fat turkey bacon infuses a generous pot of Braised Black Beans with Red Wine with smoky taste, while crumbled crisp bacon, an option suggested for Black Soybean and Butternut Squash Stew, does the same for this autumnal, otherwise meatless main dish. This stew is a perfect introduction to black soybeans, too. Sturdy and nutty tasting, they are everything tofu-haters will enjoy.

Whether you love soy or are leery of it, here are numerous dishes that use it in various forms to show its many possibilities. Dirty Rice uses tempeh, one of the most flavorful, protein-rich, underappreciated forms of soy. One stir-fry features edamame and crunchy broccoli in black bean sauce, the Chinese condiment made from dried black soybeans. The other, a trio of red pepper, green asparagus, and golden-crisped tofu, uses curry as Chinese cooks do, balancing its heat with the natural sweetness of the peppers. Braised Tofu with Kohlrabi and Pears, with a sauce featuring mustard and aromatic coriander, is perfect for your next dinner party. It has layers of flavor as refined as those in dishes at a three-star restaurant.

OJJA TUNISIAN SCRAMBLED EGGS

When Tunisians scramble eggs, they add diced potatoes, shrimp, sliced sausage, or other ingredients that make an ojja a full meal. Tomato paste makes these colorful eggs creamy. Harissa, the North African pepper paste, helps make Tunisian food the hottest in North Africa—here it's replaced by red-pepper flakes, paprika, and crushed caraway seed that have the same effect. Use whole eggs for an even softer ojja, if you wish.

1	tablespoon extra-virgin olive oil	½	teaspoon salt
2	tablespoons tomato paste	1	cup peeled, cubed russet potato
1	clove garlic, finely chopped		(½ medium)
½	teaspoon crushed caraway seed	2	whole large eggs + 3 large whites, or
½	teaspoon sweet or hot paprika		4 whole large eggs
⅛–¼	teaspoon red-pepper flakes		

1. Heat the oil in a small skillet over medium-high heat. Mix in the tomato paste, garlic, caraway seed, paprika, pepper flakes (to taste), and salt. Pour in ½ cup water. Stand back, as it will splatter.

2. Mix in the potato, reduce the heat to medium-low, and cover the pan tightly. Cook for 10 minutes.

3. Beat the eggs and whites together very well, and pour them into the pan. Using a wooden paddle or a heatproof rubber spatula, stir the eggs constantly until they are creamy and moist, 4 minutes. They should coagulate rather than be scrambled. Serve immediately.

Makes 2 servings

Per serving: 267 calories, 17 g fat, 4 g saturated fat, 14 g protein, 14 g carbohydrates, 2 g fiber

GREEN EGGS AND HAM

Popeye would approve of the way I make Dr. Seuss's favorite dish, using spinach and other fresh greens. Serve it with Scottish Oatmeal Scones (page 218) and Ginger-Tomato Marmalade (page 305) for a good meal any time of day. If making brunch for 4, simply double the recipe.

2	*large eggs + 2 large egg whites*	⅓	*cup chopped flat-leaf parsley*
½	*teaspoon salt*	3	*scallions, green part only, chopped*
	Freshly ground black pepper	½	*cup chopped low-fat ham*
1	*cup chopped fresh spinach, or frozen chopped spinach, defrosted and squeezed dry*		

1. Combine the eggs and whites in a mixing bowl. Add the salt and 2 or 3 grinds of black pepper. Whisk until well combined.

2. Coat a medium nonstick skillet with cooking spray and heat it over medium-high heat. Add the spinach, pulling the frozen spinach apart, if using. Mix in the parsley, scallions, and ham. Cook the greens, stirring with a wooden spoon, until they are wilted, 2 minutes. Pour in the beaten eggs and stir constantly until they are combined with the other ingredients and scrambled, about 2 minutes. Divide the cooked eggs between 2 plates and serve immediately.

Makes 2 servings

Per serving: 188 calories, 8 g fat, 3 g saturated fat, 21 g protein, 6 g carbohydrates, 2 g fiber

HUEVO RANCHERO

I put together the ingredients for this popular Mexican dish in a different way, starting with just 1 egg on a generous bed of refried black beans. Instead of a fried tortilla under the beans, I scatter a handful of tortilla chips around them, then add a light, spicy tomato sauce. Strips of roasted poblano chiles and a sprinkling of cheese add the finishing touches.

1	(28-ounce) can plum tomatoes, drained		Refried Black Beans, recipe doubled (page 186)
2–5	serrano chile peppers, stemmed and coarsely chopped, seeding optional	4	large eggs
½	small yellow or white onion, chopped	2	cups yellow corn tortilla chips, baked or regular
1	large clove garlic, chopped	1	roasted poblano chile for rajas
1	tablespoon + 1 teaspoon canola oil	2	tablespoons queso fresco, queso añejo, or feta cheese, crumbled
	Salt		

1. For the sauce, place the tomatoes, serrano chiles, onion, and garlic in a blender. Whirl until the tomatoes are pulpy. Heat 1 tablespoon of the oil in a medium skillet over medium-high heat. When it is very hot, pour in the pureed sauce, which should sizzle. Cook, stirring to prevent sticking and reduce splattering, until the sauce is orange-red and has the consistency of pizza sauce, 5 minutes. Season to taste with salt. This sauce can be made a day ahead and reheated.

2. Make the refried beans, or reheat them if previously prepared.

3. To fry the eggs, coat a large nonstick skillet with cooking spray and heat the remaining 1 teaspoon oil. One at a time, add the eggs, leaving enough space between them so that they don't run together. Cook until they are done the way you like fried eggs.

4. Meanwhile, divide the beans equally among 4 plates. With the back of a large spoon, make a slight indentation in the beans. With a spatula, place an egg on each bed of beans. Scatter the tortilla chips around the beans, dividing them evenly. Spoon the sauce generously over the egg and beans and arrange 2 or 3 rajas over each. Sprinkle on some of the cheese and serve immediately.

Makes 4 servings

Per serving: 505 calories, 17 g fat, 4 g saturated fat, 23 g protein, 69 g carbohydrates, 16 g fiber

REFRIED BLACK BEANS

Black beans make refried beans with more flavor and, I think, a more interesting texture than pinto beans. Canned beans actually work better than home-cooked because they are softer. I season them to serve as a good companion to grilled salmon, vegetables, and grains. When making them for Huevo Ranchero (page 184), omit the cumin and use 1 teaspoon dried oregano.

1	teaspoon canola or extra-virgin olive oil	½	teaspoon ground cumin
1	(15-ounce) can black beans, drained, or 2 cups soft-cooked	2	teaspoons chopped fresh oregano, or ½ teaspoon dried
			Salt and freshly ground black pepper

Heat the oil in a medium nonstick skillet over medium-high heat. Using a fork, mix in the beans, coating them with the oil. Add the cumin and oregano and mash for about 1 minute, until the beans are creamy but some are still whole or partially mashed, or until they have the texture you like. Season the beans to taste with salt and pepper.

Makes 2 servings

Per serving: 177 calories, 4 g fat, 0 g saturated fat, 10 g protein, 24 g carbohydrates, 10 g fiber

SPANISH CHICKPEAS WITH SPINACH AND EGGS

Spinach sautéed with garlic, chickpeas, and breadcrumbs is a distinctly Mediterranean combination. In Spain, I have enjoyed them topped with hard-cooked eggs and served in an earthenware *cazuela* accompanied by grilled crusty bread. It makes a good weekend lunch or light evening meal accompanied by a light red wine.

2	teaspoons extra-virgin olive oil	¼	teaspoon ground cumin
10	ounces baby spinach	½	teaspoon salt, or to taste
2	cloves garlic, 1 finely chopped and 1 halved lengthwise		Freshly ground black pepper
½	cup dry breadcrumbs	2	teaspoons sherry vinegar
1	(14–19-ounce) can chickpeas, drained	2	hard-cooked eggs, sliced
½	teaspoon sweet paprika	2	(1"-thick) slices Italian peasant bread

1. Heat the oil in a medium skillet over medium-high heat. Sauté the spinach until it wilts, 2 minutes. Mix in the chopped garlic and cook until the spinach is soft. Add the breadcrumbs, chickpeas, paprika, cumin, salt, and a few grinds of pepper, cooking until the beans are heated through, 3 to 4 minutes. Stir in the sherry vinegar. Spoon the cooked spinach into a serving dish and top it with the sliced eggs.

2. Coat both sides of the bread with cooking spray and grill on both sides. Rub 1 side of the grilled bread with the remaining halved garlic. Serve warm with the eggs.

Makes 2 servings

Per serving: 493 calories, 14 g fat, 3 g saturated fat, 22 g protein, 71 g carbohydrates, 12 g fiber

MEXICAN RED BEANS AND RICE

Ordinary though it looks, this dish has surprising flavor. Whether you need dinner from scratch in 20 minutes or need a meal to reheat, this recipe is reliable. Serve it as a meatless main dish or as an accompaniment to grilled chicken breast or fajitas.

To make the rice from scratch, cook ⅔ cup raw in 2 cups water.

2	tablespoon canola oil	1	(15-ounce) can diced tomatoes, with their liquid
1	medium red onion, chopped		
1	medium green bell pepper, seeded and chopped	1	(15-ounce) can red beans, rinsed
		2	cups cooked long-grain brown rice
1	large clove garlic, finely chopped		Salt and freshly ground black pepper
1	teaspoon dried oregano		Chopped cilantro, optional, for garnish
½	chipotle chile in adobo or ½ teaspoon chipotle powder		

1. Heat the oil in a medium skillet over medium-high heat. Sauté the onion and green pepper until the onion is translucent, 4 minutes. Mix in the garlic and cook 1 minute longer. Add the oregano and chipotle.

2. Add the tomatoes with their liquid, reduce the heat, and simmer until the tomatoes are soft and some of their liquid has evaporated, about 10 minutes.

3. Mix in the beans and cooked rice. When they are heated through, season to taste with salt and pepper. Garnish with cilantro, if using, and serve.

Makes 4 servings

Per serving: 334 calories, 8 g fat, 1 g saturated fat, 11 g protein, 55 g carbohydrates, 13 g fiber

BLACK BEAN BLINI
WITH FRESH GARDEN SALSA

These velvety blini make a light meal and are perfect for entertaining because they hold for hours. Serve them with the Fresh Garden Salsa or topped with smoked salmon.

Read the package when buying liquid egg whites. Not all brands can be whipped.

2	tablespoons canola oil, divided		Salt and freshly ground black pepper
1	(15-ounce) can black beans, drained, or 2 cups soft-cooked	3	large egg whites, or the liquid equivalent
1	tablespoon chopped oregano, or 1 teaspoon dried	⅔	cup fresh yellow corn kernels, or defrosted frozen
			Fresh Garden Salsa (page 44)
1	teaspoon ground cumin	½	lime, cut lengthwise into 4 wedges,
¼	teaspoon ground chipotle chile pepper		for garnish

1. Heat 1 tablespoon of the oil in a large nonstick skillet over medium-high heat. Add the beans, oregano, cumin, and chipotle. Add 2 tablespoons water and mash the beans until they are creamy, but with some bits remaining, about 2 minutes. Season the beans to taste with salt and pepper and set them aside to cool. Rinse and dry the pan.

2. Beat the egg whites until soft peaks form. Fold in the black bean mixture until it is evenly combined with the whites, making a soft, fluffy batter.

3. Heat 2 teaspoons of the oil in the pan over medium-high heat. For each blini, drop a scant ¼ cup of the bean mixture into the pan. Cook until well browned on the bottom, 2 minutes. Turn and brown well on the second side, 2 minutes. Set the cooked blini in 1 layer on a warm platter. Add the remaining oil to the pan as needed.

4. To serve, combine the corn with the salsa. Arrange 3 blini on each plate with the salsa and garnish with a lime wedge set on top.

Makes 4 servings (12 blini)

Per serving: 198 calories, 9 g fat, 2 g saturated fat, 11 g protein, 28 g carbohydrates, 9 g fiber

SWEET POTATO AND BROCCOLI SHEPHERD'S PIE

Keeping only the mashed potatoes of traditional Shepherd's Pie, this meatless version replaces the usual minced lamb with generous layers of broccoli and cheese, making it as comforting as the British classic but much lighter. It freezes well and reheats beautifully.

To reheat, bring the Shepherd's Pie to room temperature, cover it with foil, and bake at 350°F for 20 minutes.

FOOD FACT

Three kinds of cheese, plus buttermilk, make this dish calcium-rich.

2	pounds Beauregard, Garnet, or Jewel yams
1	teaspoon freshly grated ginger
½	teaspoon five-spice powder
2	teaspoons salt, divided
	Freshly ground black pepper
1	large egg white
3	cups broccoli florets + 1 cup broccoli stems, thinly sliced crosswise
1	tablespoon fresh lemon juice
1½	cups reduced-fat ricotta cheese
¼	cup crumbled fat-free feta cheese
¼	cup buttermilk
½	teaspoon dried oregano
2	tablespoons dry breadcrumbs
¼	cup freshly grated Parmigiano-Reggiano cheese

1. Preheat the oven to 400°F.

2. Bake the yams 1 hour, until they are soft. When cool enough to handle, peel the sweet potatoes and place their flesh in a mixing bowl. Add the ginger, five-spice powder, and ½ teaspoon of the salt. Mash with a fork until the potatoes are creamy. Season with pepper, and mix in the egg white.

3. Steam the broccoli florets and stems until tender, 8 minutes. Place them in a bowl and season with the lemon juice and ½ teaspoon of the salt.

4. Place the ricotta, feta, buttermilk, and the remaining 1 teaspoon salt in a food processor. Whirl until the mixture is smooth, 2 minutes. Add the oregano, and pulse to distribute it evenly. Season the mixture with pepper.

5. Coat a deep 1½-quart heatproof casserole with cooking spray. Spread half the potato mixture over the bottom of the baking dish. Spoon half the cheese mixture over the sweet potatoes. Arrange the broccoli on top of the cheese. Cover the broccoli with the remaining cheese mixture. Cover the cheese with the remaining sweet potatoes. Sprinkle with the breadcrumbs. Cover the top of the casserole with the grated Parmesan.

6. Bake the pie uncovered for 30 minutes, or until it is bubbling around the edges and hot in the center. Remove from the oven and let sit 20 minutes before serving.

Makes 6 servings

Per serving: 200 calories, 7 g fat, 4 g saturated fat, 12 g protein, 22 g carbohydrates, 3 g fiber

SPINACH AND RICE TORTA

Simplifying the deep-fried spinach and rice balls served at Rice, a casual New York eatery, I have also slimmed them down. Instead of making the balls, I press the spinach and rice mixture into a pan and bake it. Cut into wedges and served with Cumin Tomato Sauce (page 174), as they do at Rice, this dish is mega-hot, but you can turn down the heat if you like while still enjoying all its other bold flavors.

¾	cup brown basmati rice
1	tablespoon canola oil
1	small red onion, finely chopped
3	cloves garlic, finely chopped
2	tablespoons pine nuts
1	(10-ounce) package frozen chopped spinach, defrosted and squeezed dry

3	tablespoons freshly grated Parmigiano-Reggiano cheese
¼–½	teaspoon cayenne pepper
1	teaspoon salt
1	large egg, beaten
¼	cup dry breadcrumbs
	Cumin Tomato Sauce (page 174)

1. Place the rice in a deep saucepan. Add 3 cups cold water, cover the pot tightly, and boil until the rice is soft, 45 to 50 minutes. Off the heat, let it stand, covered, for 10 minutes.

2. Preheat the oven to 350°F.

3. Heat the oil in a medium, nonstick skillet over medium-high heat. Sauté the onion until it is translucent, 3 minutes. Mix in the garlic and nuts and cook, stirring often, until the nuts color, 2 minutes. Turn the contents of the pan into a mixing bowl and add the spinach, pulling it apart with your fingers.

4. Add 2½ cups of the hot rice to the spinach, reserving the remaining ½ cup for another use. Add the cheese, cayenne, and salt. Mix with a fork to combine. Mix in the egg, stirring vigorously until the mixture becomes sticky.

5. Coat an 8" round springform pan with cooking spray. Coat the bottom and sides of the pan with the breadcrumbs. Tilt the pan over a plate, and knock out any excess, reserving the extra crumbs. Turn the rice mixture into the pan, pressing it into an even layer with your fingertips, then sprinkle the reserved crumbs over the top. Using your finger, wipe away any crumbs clinging to the sides of the pan above the torta, letting them fall onto it.

6. Bake 40 minutes, until the torta is firm to the touch in the middle and a knife inserted into the center comes out clean. Cool the torta in the pan for 20 minutes. Before removing the sides of the pan, run a thin knife around the edge of the pan. Slide a thin spatula under the torta to loosen it from the bottom, cut it in wedges, and serve with Cumin Tomato Sauce spooned generously over each portion.

Makes 6 servings

Per serving: 258 calories, 9 g fat, 2 g saturated fat, 9 g protein, 34 g carbohydrates, 6 g fiber

DIRTY RICE

FOOD FACT

The paprika and other spices add a generous amount of antioxidants.

In Creole cooking, finely chopped duck gizzards and liver create the "dirty" effect that gives this dish its name. This meatless version makes a rousing *laisser les bon temps rouler* dinner. Some of its jazz comes from Cajun spices, the rest from tempeh's hearty flavor. Usually I recommend eating brown rice, but white rice is preferable for this dish. Serve it with steamed collard greens.

1	cup long-grain white rice	1	tablespoon olive oil
1	green bell pepper, seeded and chopped		Blackening Spice (opposite page)
1	rib celery, coarsely chopped	1	tablespoon cider vinegar
1	medium onion, coarsely chopped		Salt
1	(8-ounce) package soy tempeh, cubed	¼	cup chopped flat-leaf parsley

1. Cook the rice according to package directions. Set aside.

2. Place the bell pepper, celery, and onion in a food processor and pulse 5 or 6 times to chop the vegetables. Add the tempeh and pulse 5 or 6 times, until the mixture includes medium and finely chopped pieces.

3. Coat a deep medium skillet with cooking spray. Set the pan over medium-high heat and add the oil. When the oil is hot, stir in the chopped tempeh mixture using a wooden spoon, coating the mixture with oil. Sauté until the onion and tempeh brown, 9 minutes, scraping up the dark brown to black bits stuck to the bottom of the pan. Mix in the Blackening Spice and vinegar, scraping vigorously for 2 minutes to gather up as much of the dark coating on the bottom of the pan as possible. Remove the pan from the heat and mix in the warm rice, fluffing it with a fork. Season with salt, garnish with the parsley, and serve.

Makes 8 servings

Per serving: 159 calories, 4 g fat, 1 g saturated fat, 8 g protein, 23 g carbohydrates, 3 g fiber

BLACKENING SPICE

Most recipes for spice blends leave you with extra that goes unused. This one makes just the right amount for Dirty Rice, but you can easily multiply it to make a larger quantity if you wish. It is also good for seasoning fish, chicken, or pork chops.

2	teaspoons sweet paprika	½	teaspoon ground white pepper
½	teaspoon freshly ground black pepper	½	teaspoon garlic powder
½	teaspoon cayenne pepper	¼	teaspoon dried oregano
½	teaspoon onion powder	¼	teaspoon dried thyme

Combine all the spices in a small bowl.

Makes 5 teaspoons

Per serving (1 teaspoon): 6 calories, 0 g fat, 0 g saturated fat, 0 g protein, 1 g carbohydrates, 0 g fiber

BLACK SOYBEAN
AND BUTTERNUT SQUASH STEW

Some of my favorite dishes result from improvising with ingredients at hand. This chunky stew with Southwestern flair started with the remaining half of a large butternut squash, a few slices of bacon, and a couple kinds of peppers.

FOOD FACT

Retaining the soybeans' cooking liquid gives this dish a nutrient boost.

1	tablespoon canola oil	
1	large red onion, diced	
1	small green bell pepper, seeded and diced	
1	clove garlic, finely chopped	
1	teaspoon ground cumin	
½	teaspoon ground sweet paprika	
2	tablespoons tomato paste	
1	small butternut squash (1¼ pounds), peeled, seeded, and cut in 1½" chunks	

Black Soybeans (page 198) with their cooking liquid, or 2 (15-ounce) cans black soybeans, drained, + 1 (15.5-ounce) can vegetable broth

Salt and freshly ground black pepper

2   slices preservative-free bacon, cooked and crumbled, optional

Chopped jalapeño, for garnish

Chopped cilantro, for garnish

1. Heat the oil in a large Dutch oven over medium-high heat. Sauté the onion and pepper until the onion is translucent, 4 minutes. Mix in the garlic, cumin, and paprika, cooking until they are fragrant, 30 seconds. Stir in the tomato paste.

2. Add the squash and beans with their cooking liquid or the canned beans and vegetable broth. When the liquid boils, reduce the heat and simmer, partially covered, until the squash is tender, 30 minutes. Season to taste with salt and pepper.

3. Ladle the stew into deep bowls. Sprinkle with the bacon, if using, and garnish with the chopped jalapeño and cilantro.

Makes 6 servings

Per serving: 171 calories, 4 g fat, 0 g saturated fat, 11 g protein, 24 g carbohydrates, 9 g fiber

BLACK SOYBEANS

Black soybeans have a nutty, almost sweet flavor that is far nicer than the flat taste of yellow soybeans. They remain slightly firm, even when they are completely cooked, and turn from ebony black to a burnished mahogany brown.

1	*cup dried black soybeans*	1	*onion, quartered*
1	*bay leaf*	1	*teaspoon ground cumin*

1. Soak the beans in cold water for 8 hours or overnight.

2. Drain the beans and place them in a deep saucepan. Pour in 4 cups cold water and add the bay leaf, onion, and cumin. Cook, covered, over medium-high heat until the water starts to boil. Reduce the heat and simmer until the beans are slightly al dente if using them in a stew or chili, about 1 hour. Cook until tender, about 1½ hours, if using in a salad. Remove bay leaf before serving. Cooked black soybeans keep for 3 days tightly covered in the refrigerator.

Makes 6 servings

Per serving: 122 calories, 1 g fat, 0 g saturated fat, 7 g protein, 23 g carbohydrates, 5 g fiber

BRAISED BLACK BEANS WITH RED WINE

Red wine gives these tender beans French flavor reminiscent of coq au vin. Turkey bacon adds a smoky note. Starting with dried beans is essential for soaking up all these flavors.

1½	cups dried black turtle beans	⅓	cup dry red wine
1	tablespoon extra-virgin olive oil	1	clove garlic, cut in 4 pieces
1	small red onion, finely chopped	4	sprigs flat-leaf parsley
1	small carrot, finely chopped	1	bay leaf
½	rib celery, finely chopped	1	teaspoon dried thyme
2	strips uncured, reduced-fat turkey bacon, chopped	1	whole clove
			Salt and freshly ground black pepper

1. Soak the beans in cold water overnight. Drain and set aside.

2. Preheat the oven to 300°F.

3. In a small Dutch oven, heat the oil over medium-high heat. Sauté the onion, carrot, and celery until the onion is lightly browned, 6 minutes. Mix in the bacon and cook, stirring occasionally, for 2 minutes longer.

4. Pour in the wine. Add the drained beans and 1½ cups cold water. Add the garlic, parsley, bay leaf, thyme, and clove. Cook uncovered, until the liquid starts to bubble, then cover the pot and transfer it to the oven.

5. Bake 45 to 60 minutes, until the beans are tender. Drain and discard any remaining liquid. Remove the parsley, bay leaf, and clove. Season to taste with salt and pepper. Serve the beans hot or warm.

Makes 4 servings

Per serving: 304 calories, 6 g fat, 1 g saturated fat, 17 g protein, 47 g carbohydrates, 15 g fiber

FOOD FACT

Red wine adds resveratrol to these beans.

To use an earthenware bean pot, sauté the vegetables and bacon in a skillet, then transfer them to the clay pot. Add boiling water instead of cold.

Hard cider is drier in flavor than apple juice and only mildly alcoholic. What you don't pour into the pot is delicious served chilled along with this dish.

This dish keeps 2 to 3 days and reheats well. Warm gently over the stovetop.

FOOD FACT
One medium pear contains 4 grams of fiber.

BRAISED TOFU WITH KOHLRABI AND PEARS

Do not skip this recipe because of the kohlrabi. When I ran a catering service, this was my most popular main dish because of its blend of mellow, sharp, and sweet flavors. Serve it over rice, accompanied by a green salad and baby carrots braised in orange juice.

2	tablespoons canola oil	1	(12–16-ounce) package firm regular tofu, drained, pressed (page 22), cut into ¾" cubes, and pan-crisped (page 22)
1	cup finely chopped onion		
2	tablespoons finely minced shallot		
2	heaping tablespoons unbleached all-purpose flour	1	medium kohlrabi, peeled, cut in ½" cubes (1½ cups)
1	cup hard cider	1	Bosc pear, peeled, cored, and cut in ¾" pieces
½	cup Dijon mustard		
1	tablespoon ground coriander	8	ounces mushrooms, stemmed and quartered (1½ cups)
¼	teaspoon ground turmeric		
			Salt and freshly ground pepper

1. In a large, deep saucepan, heat the oil over medium-high heat. Add the onion and shallots and, stirring occasionally, cook until soft, about 5 minutes. Stir in the flour, and cook 3 minutes, stirring constantly so the flour does not color.

2. Using a wooden spoon, stir in ¼ cup of the cider. Scrape the bottom and side of the pan with the wooden spoon to dissolve all the flour. As soon as the mixture thickens, add the remaining cider, stirring until you have a thick sauce. Mix in the mustard, coriander, and turmeric. Add the tofu and kohlrabi, and simmer gently for 15 minutes.

3. Add the pear and mushrooms and simmer until the pear is tender, 10 to 15 minutes. Season to taste with salt and pepper.

Makes 6 servings

Per serving: 191 calories, 10 g fat, 1 g saturated fat, 9 g protein, 21 g carbohydrates, 4 g fiber

BROCCOLI, BLACK MUSHROOMS, AND EDAMAME WITH BLACK BEAN SAUCE

Edamame provide enough protein to make this stir-fry a solid main dish. Black bean sauce is made with fermented soybeans, adding a second form of soy. Serve this with Double Miso Soup (page 89), and your meal will have a soy trio.

4	medium dried shiitake mushrooms	¼	cup fat-free, reduced-sodium chicken
1	cup frozen shelled edamame		or vegetable broth
4	cups broccoli florets	1	tablespoons peanut oil
1	tablespoon black bean sauce	2	scallions, green and white part, chopped
1	teaspoon sugar	1	large clove garlic, chopped
⅛–¼	teaspoon red-pepper flakes	2	teaspoons freshly grated ginger
¾	teaspoon salt	½	teaspoon roasted sesame oil

1. Soak the mushrooms in hot tap water until soft, 30 minutes. Remove and discard the stems. Squeeze the moisture from the caps and cut them into thin strips.

2. Steam the edamame for 5 minutes. Add the broccoli, and steam until it is bright green, 2 minutes. Set the cooked vegetables aside.

3. In a measuring cup, combine the black bean sauce, sugar, red-pepper flakes, salt, and broth. Set aside, leaving a spoon in the cup.

4. Heat the oil in a wok over the highest possible heat. Stir-fry the scallions, garlic, and ginger until fragrant, 30 seconds. Add the mushrooms, broccoli, and edamame. Stir the seasoning sauce and add it into the wok. Stir-fry for 2 minutes to concentrate the sauce. Off the heat, add the sesame oil, toss to combine, and serve immediately.

Makes 4 servings

Per serving: 148 calories, 7 g fat, 1 g saturated fat, 9 g protein, 15 g carbohydrates, 5 g fiber

I use Kame Black Bean Sauce, which contains no MSG. Check the label of other brands.

STIR AND POUR

When you stir-fry, combine the ingredients for the seasoning sauce in a measuring cup. Leave in a spoon to quickly restir it and pour it into the wok.

ASPARAGUS, RED PEPPER, AND CURRIED TOFU

The mild curry powder I like best is sold in Chinese and Southeast Asian food markets. It has a lovely combination of gentle heat and sweet spices like fennel, coriander, and cinnamon. It is particularly suited to this stir-fry where chewy pan-crisped tofu drinks up the golden sauce. Served over rice noodles, this dish is reminiscent of Shanghai Noodles. It can also be served over brown rice.

1	tablespoon cornstarch	2	teaspoons grated or finely chopped ginger
2	teaspoons curry powder		
1	teaspoon sugar	1	large clove garlic, finely chopped
1	tablespoon dry sherry	1	medium red onion, diced
1	tablespoon reduced-sodium soy sauce	8	asparagus, cut in 1" pieces
		1	red bell pepper, seeded and diced
¾	cup fat-free, reduced-sodium chicken broth	3	tofu steaks, cut in 1" cubes and pan-crisped (page 22), or 1 pound firm tofu, pressed and cubed (page 22)
1	tablespoon peanut oil		

1. In a measuring cup, combine the cornstarch, curry powder, and sugar. Mix in the sherry, soy sauce, and broth, leaving the spoon in the cup. Set aside.

2. Heat the oil in a wok over the highest possible heat. Add the ginger and garlic and stir-fry until fragrant, 30 seconds. Add the onion, asparagus, and pepper, and stir-fry until they are brightly colored, 1 minute. Add the tofu.

3. Stir the seasoning sauce and pour it into the wok. Stir-fry until the sauce boils and thickens, 2 to 3 minutes.

Makes 4 servings

Per serving: 151 calories, 8 g fat, 1 g saturated fat, 10 g protein, 12 g carbohydrates, 2 g fiber

CHAPTER NINE
SANDWICHES
AND BAKED GOODS

Eating whole grains is important because of the fiber, vitamins, and minerals they provide. Bread-based meals and snacks—sandwiches, pizza and focaccia, scones, muffins, and tea bread—are perfect opportunities to add them to your day. Besides oats, they also include other Best Foods, plus other vegetables, soy, nuts, and fruit.

Using whole grain breads for making sandwiches is a significant first step. Today you can buy so many kinds, and such good ones, from sliced oat bran or multigrain loaves to crusty whole wheat Italian bread and artisanal creations studded with walnuts. You can make any sandwich on a whole grain bread that enhances it.

Now, take two giant steps. First, make a Raw Vegetable Wrap with Feta. This "handwich" containing a whole leafy salad in a delicious sprouted-wheat tortilla lets you neatly eat fresh leafy vegetables out of hand anywhere. Next, discover how well soy and sandwiches go together, too. Tempeh, used instead of bacon, makes a good and guilt-free TLT. Then, for an open-face, warm sandwich that will pleasantly surprise you, try Grape and Red Onion Focaccia.

If you like making pizza, here is a whole wheat dough that bakes up crisp yet tender and tastes good as well. Old-Fashioned Onion Board, a yeasted flatbread, also includes whole wheat flour. It offers bread bakers a change of pace.

For faster, simpler baking, Scottish Oatmeal Scones also contain the right proportion of whole grain and white flour to have good taste and a light texture. The rest of the baked goods here use only white flour, but they include generous amounts of blueberries, sweet potato, walnuts, and other foods that make them good and good for you.

RAW VEGETABLE WRAP WITH FETA

This whole grain wrap lets you eat a leafy green salad at your computer—and do it neatly, too. My favorite wrapper for this "handwich" is Alvarado Street Bakery's sprouted wheat tortilla (page 63).

FOOD FACT

A mere ¼ cup of zingy, bright green broccoli sprouts adds cancer-fighting power equal to 6½ cups of chopped raw broccoli to sandwiches and salads.

1	(10") sprouted wheat or whole wheat tortilla	4	thin seedless cucumber slices
2	romaine lettuce leaves, cut crosswise in ½" strips	1	plum tomato, thinly sliced
6	watercress sprigs	¼	cup crumbled feta cheese
1	scallion, green part only, cut in 6" lengths	1	tablespoon tahini
¼	cup broccoli sprouts		Pinch of powdered red pepper
		2	tablespoons fresh lemon juice
			Salt and freshly ground black pepper

1. Lay the tortilla on the counter. Arrange the lettuce strips down the center third of the tortilla. Tear the tough bottom part off the watercress, and arrange the sprigs on top of the lettuce. Lay the scallions on top of the watercress. Arrange the sprouts over this. Arrange the cucumber and tomato slices in 1 layer over the greens. Sprinkle the cheese over the tomatoes.

2. For the dressing, in a small bowl, whisk the tahini and red pepper with the lemon juice until creamy. Add cool water just until the dressing is thin enough to drizzle, about 1 tablespoon. Season to taste with salt and pepper. Drizzle the dressing over the filling. Fold in the 2 sides of the tortilla, making a fat roll. Serve immediately. Or, wrap in plastic wrap or foil and refrigerate. This wrap keeps up to 24 hours, tightly wrapped, in the refrigerator.

Makes 1 serving

Per serving: 312 calories, 17 g fat, 7 g saturated fat, 13 g protein, 36 g carbohydrates, 6 g fiber

TEMPEH, LETTUCE, AND TOMATO SANDWICH ON RYE

Try it, you'll like this sandwich made with the soy tempeh called Smoky Tempeh Strips, from Lightlife, in place of bacon. This meat alternative does not pretend to be bacon, but it does taste great, especially on toasted rye bread with all the trimmings.

1	teaspoon canola oil	2	thin tomato slices
3	tempeh bacon strips	1	romaine lettuce leaf
2	slices old-fashioned rye bread	1	tablespoon reduced-fat mayonnaise

1. Heat the oil in a medium skillet over medium-high heat. Brown the tempeh strips, 1½ minutes. Turn and brown the tempeh on the second side, 1½ minutes.

2. While the tempeh browns, toast the bread. Arrange the tempeh on 1 slice, and top with the tomato slices, then the lettuce, folding and flattening the leaf. Spread the mayonnaise on the other slice of bread and close the sandwich. Serve immediately.

Makes 1 serving

Per serving: 338 calories, 14 g fat, 2 g saturated fat, 14 g protein, 39 g carbohydrates, 5 g fiber

HONEY SOYNUT
BUTTER SANDWICH

This sandwich is akin to the traditional PBJ, though it's made with peanut butter that I blend with honey and crunchy soynuts. For your sandwich, either use grape jelly or try orange marmalade, my personal favorite.

2	slices whole grain bread	1½	tablespoons grape jelly or orange
2	tablespoons Honey Soynut Butter, or		marmalade, or to taste
	to taste		

For each sandwich, spread the amount of Honey Soynut Butter you like on 1 slice of whole grain bread. Top it with jelly or marmalade and the remaining slice of bread. Cut the sandwich diagonally into 4 pieces and serve.

Makes 1 sandwich

Per sandwich: 430 calories, 15 g fat, 3 g saturated fat, 12 g protein, 65 g carbohydrates, 5 g fiber

HONEY SOYNUT BUTTER

This powerhouse spread is so yummy you can eat it off the spoon. Make sure to use the soynuts that look like split peanuts, not the whole, round kind.

½	cup peanut butter, smooth or crunchy	2	tablespoons roasted soynuts, salted or
¼	cup wildflower or blueberry honey		plain, chopped

In a bowl, mix the peanut butter, honey, and soynuts together. This spread keeps at least 2 weeks in a tightly covered jar.

Makes ⅔ cup

Per serving (2 tablespoons): 202 calories, 13 g fat, 3 g saturated fat, 7 g protein, 19 g carbohydrates, 2 g fiber

GRAPE AND RED ONION FOCACCIA

Using a Boboli or other baked shell lets you enjoy this aromatic, savory, and sweet focaccia without having to bake a dough from scratch. If you are counting carbs, halve the crust horizontally, and save 1 half to use another time.

1	(10-ounce) prebaked Italian pizza bread shell or focaccia	1	teaspoon chopped thyme, or ¼ teaspoon dried
2	teaspoons extra-virgin olive oil	2	tablespoons freshly grated Parmigiano-Reggiano cheese
1	large red onion, sliced in ¼" crescents		
1	cup red seedless grapes, halved		

1. Preheat the oven to 450°F. Place the pizza shell or focaccia on a perforated pizza heating pan or a baking sheet and set aside.

2. Heat the oil in a medium nonstick skillet over medium-high heat. Sauté the onion for 3 minutes, just until it begins to soften. Mix in the grapes and thyme, coating them with the oil. Arrange the grape mixture on the pizza shell, leaving a 1" border all around. Sprinkle the cheese over the topping.

3. Bake for 6 to 8 minutes, or until the crust is hot and crisp and the onions are wilted but still al dente.

Makes 4 servings

Per serving: 297 calories, 9 g fat, 2 g saturated fat, 7 g protein, 49 g carbohydrates, 1 g fiber

GRILLED PIZZA

The smoky flavor this free-form pizza offers sets it apart from the usual oven baked pies. Watch carefully so the topping does not dry out.

Whole Wheat Pizza Dough (opposite page), ⅔ recipe	2 generous cups 1" broccoli florets, steamed
¾ cup prepared light tomato sauce	1 roasted red pepper, cut in ¼" strips
1 cup shredded, smoked tofu	4 tablespoons freshly grated
1 cup shredded smoked mozzarella cheese	Parmigiano-Reggiano cheese

1. Prepare a grill for medium heat.

2. Making one pizza at a time, grill the dough until lightly marked, about 2 minutes. Turn. Spread 3 tablespoons sauce over the crisped dough, leaving a ½" border. Sprinkle on one-quarter of the smoked tofu and mozzarella cheese. Top with one-quarter of the broccoli and red pepper strips. Sprinkle with 1 tablespoon of the Parmesan cheese. Grill, with top closed, until the cheese is melted, about 4 minutes. Serve immediately.

Makes 4 pizzas

Per pizza: 520 calories, 17 g fat, 7 g saturated fat, 32 g protein, 62 g carbohydrates, 7 g fiber

CHILL OUT

Smoked mozzarella and smoked tofu, sold at natural food stores, enhance this flavor. They are easier to shred if you first place them in the freezer for 15 minutes.

WHOLE WHEAT PIZZA DOUGH

Using pastry flour, not bread flour, produces a pizza crust that is both crisp and tender.

½	teaspoon sugar	1	cup whole wheat pastry flour
1	(¼-ounce) package active dry yeast	2	teaspoons salt
2½	cups unbleached all-purpose flour	1	tablespoon extra-virgin olive oil

1. Dissolve the sugar in 1 cup warm water (110°F). Sprinkle on the yeast and set aside until foamy, 10 minutes.

2. Combine 2 cups of the all-purpose flour, the whole wheat flour, and salt in a large bowl. Pour in the yeast mixture and the oil. Mix with a fork to form a shaggy dough. Sprinkle some of the remaining flour on a work surface and turn the dough out onto it. Knead, adding just a little flour as needed, until the dough is smooth and elastic, about 8 minutes.

3. Lightly coat a bowl with cooking spray. Form the dough into a disk, and turn it in the bowl to lightly coat it with the oil. Cover with a dish towel and set in a warm place until the dough has doubled in bulk, 45 to 60 minutes.

4. Punch down the dough and turn it onto a lightly floured work surface. Cut it into 6 pieces. Wrap the pieces in plastic wrap and set aside. Roll out 1 piece of the dough into a circle, 8" in diameter and ¼" thick. Place it on a foil-covered baking sheet coated with cooking spray and spray the top of the dough. Cover it with a dish towel and roll out the remaining dough, 1 piece at a time. Let the covered dough rise 15 minutes before adding a topping.

Makes 6 pizza crusts

Per crust: 274 calories, 3 g fat, 0 g saturated fat, 9 g protein, 53 g carbohydrates, 4 g fiber

OLD-FASHIONED ONION BOARD

My grandparents called this thick and thin bread a pletzl. It remains one of my favorites. Keeping the dough thin is key to making crisp squares. Spanish onions taste milder than large yellow onions. Which you use is a matter of personal taste. When the onions char on the edges, they are even more flavorful.

Leave the dough a bit thicker, about ¼" when rolled out before the second rise, and your free-form boards will turn out more breadlike.

DOUGH

1	teaspoon sugar
2¼	teaspoons dry yeast
1¾	cups + ⅓ cup unbleached all-purpose flour
1¼	cups whole wheat flour
1½	teaspoons salt
2	tablespoons extra-virgin olive oil, divided
3	tablespoons yellow cornmeal

TOPPING

1	large onion, halved and thinly sliced
2	tablespoons extra-virgin olive oil
	Coarse sea salt or kosher salt
1½	teaspoons poppy seeds, or dried thyme

1. Dissolve the sugar in 1 cup warm water (110°F). Sprinkle in the yeast and let it sit until foamy, 10 minutes.

2. In a large mixing bowl, combine the 1¾ cups all-purpose flour with the whole wheat flour and salt. Pour in the yeast mixture and 1 tablespoon of the oil. Mix with a fork to form a sticky dough. Sprinkle 1 tablespoon of the remaining all-purpose flour on a work surface and turn the dough out onto it. Knead, adding the remaining flour 1 tablespoon at a time, until the dough is smooth and elastic, 6 minutes. It will feel tacky but will not stick to your hands or the work surface.

3. Lightly coat a clean bowl with 1 teaspoon of the remaining oil. Form the dough into a disk and turn it in the bowl to lightly coat it with the oil. Cover the bowl with a dish towel and set it in a warm place until the dough doubles in bulk, 30 to 45 minutes.

4. Place a rack in the upper third of the oven. Preheat the oven to 475°F.

5. To form and bake the onion boards, punch down the dough, turn it onto a lightly floured surface, and cut it into 6 pieces. Shape each piece into a 6" square, patting it with your hands. Cover and set aside for 15 minutes.

6. One at a time, roll out 2 of the squares of dough into a ¼"-thick, free-form 9" square. Sprinkle 1 tablespoon of the cornmeal on a dark metal baking sheet. Transfer the 2 squares to the baking sheet. Cover them with a dish towel and set them in a warm place for 15 minutes. Repeat, using 1 tablespoon of the remaining cornmeal for each baking sheet.

7. With your fingertips, pound the squares all over, leaving a ½" border. Brush them all over, using the remaining 2 teaspoons oil.

8. For the topping, place the onion in a mixing bowl and toss with the oil. Arrange the onion over the center of each square. Sprinkle with salt and poppy seeds or thyme.

9. Bake the Onion Boards in batches 12 minutes, or until golden brown around the edges and deep brown on the bottom. Serve warm or at room temperature.

Makes 6 pieces

Per piece: 358 calories, 11 g fat, 2 g saturated fat, 10 g protein, 57 g carbohydrates, 6 g fiber

BLUEBERRY-POLENTA MUFFIN TOPS

If you prefer the crusty top of a muffin, these golden muffin tops are heaven. They are the perfect size as well—enough to enjoy, not so big that you feel guilty. Minimally sweet, they have full corn flavor and crunch, thanks to the polenta. They also make fine tea cakes.

1	large egg	½	cup quick-cooking polenta
⅓	cup sugar	1	teaspoon baking powder
⅓	cup orange juice	⅛	teaspoon salt
½	teaspoon grated orange zest	1¼	cups fresh or frozen blueberries,
¼	cup canola oil		or ¾ cup dried
½	cup unbleached all-purpose flour		

1. Place a rack in the center of the oven. Preheat the oven to 350°F. Coat an 8-cavity muffin-top pan with cooking spray.

2. In a mixing bowl, using an electric mixer on medium-high speed, beat the egg with the sugar until thick and pale, 2 minutes. Mix in the juice, zest, and oil. Stir in the flour, polenta, baking powder, and salt. Mix in the blueberries. Spoon the batter into the prepared pan, filling the cavities to the top.

3. Bake 15 minutes, until a toothpick inserted into the center of a muffin top comes out clean and the tops are rounded and browned around the edges. Cool the muffin tops in the pan for 2 minutes. Unmold and cool on a wire rack. Serve warm or at room temperature. Tops keep for up to 3 days wrapped in foil.

Makes 8 muffin tops

Per muffin top: 187 calories, 8 g fat, 1 g saturated fat, 3 g protein, 27 g carbohydrates, 2 g fiber

OAT MUFFINS
WITH PEAR AND PECANS

Diced pear is one of two surprises in these tender, moist muffins. The other is browned butter, which gives them a rich, nutty taste.

MUFFINS

2	tablespoons unsalted butter
1	cup quick oats
¾	cup chopped pecans
1	cup unbleached all-purpose flour
1½	teaspoons baking powder
½	teaspoon baking soda
¼	teaspoon salt
¾	cup buttermilk

⅓	cup brown sugar, packed
1	large egg
4	canned Bartlett pear halves in juice, drained and chopped

TOPPING

1	tablespoon old-fashioned rolled oats
1	tablespoon pumpkin seeds
1	tablespoon sunflower seeds
1	tablespoon brown sugar

1. Preheat the oven to 400°F. Grease an 8-cup muffin tin and set it aside. Heat the butter in a small pan over medium heat until it is nut brown, 2 minutes, and set it aside to cool.

2. Toast the oats and pecans in a dry skillet over medium-high heat, stirring until the oats are fragrant, 2 minutes. Cool and transfer to a mixing bowl.

3. Add the flour, baking powder, baking soda, and salt to the oats. Combine the buttermilk, sugar, and egg in a large mixing cup. Pour them into the dry ingredients. Add the butter. Stir with a wooden spoon to combine. Mix in the pears. Spoon the batter into the prepared pan. Combine the topping ingredients and sprinkle over the muffins.

4. Bake 22 minutes, or until the muffins are golden and a toothpick inserted into the center comes out clean. Cool in the pan 5 minutes. Unmold them and let cool completely on a wire rack.

Makes 8 muffins

Per muffin: 258 calories, 12 g fat, 3 g saturated fat, 6 g protein, 32 g carbohydrates, 2 g fiber

One of these muffins in the morning, with a cup of yogurt, can be breakfast.

FOOD FACT

Canned pears contain as much fiber as fresh.

SWEET POTATO MUFFINS

Spicy and moist, these muffins are almost creamy in the center. Serve them warm from the oven as a snack accompanied by Sweet Potato Butter (page 41), or as a portable breakfast.

1	cup unbleached all-purpose flour	1	large egg
1	teaspoon baking powder	⅓	cup low-fat yogurt
¼	teaspoon baking soda	1	teaspoon vanilla extract
1	teaspoon ground cinnamon	¾	cup shredded carrot
½	teaspoon ground ginger	½	cup mashed roasted Beauregard,
½	teaspoon salt		Garnet, or Jewel yams
¼	cup light olive oil or canola oil	2	tablespoons sesame seeds
⅓	cup brown sugar	1	tablespoon pumpkin seeds

1. Preheat the oven to 375°F. Place paper liners in the cups of a 6-cup muffin pan.

2. In a mixing bowl, whisk together the flour, baking powder, baking soda, cinnamon, ginger, and salt. In another bowl, combine the oil, sugar, and egg. Mix in the yogurt and vanilla. Stir in the carrot and sweet potato. Add the wet ingredients to the bowl of dry ingredients, and mix just until blended. Spoon the batter into the muffin cups, filling them to the top. Sprinkle 1 teaspoon sesame seeds and a few pumpkin seeds over the top of each muffin.

3. Bake 22 to 27 minutes, until the muffins are lightly colored and a toothpick inserted in the center comes out clean. Cool 5 minutes in the pan, then unmold, and cool completely on a wire rack.

Makes 6 muffins

Per muffin: 264 calories, 12 g fat, 2 g saturated fat, 5 g protein, 35 g carbohydrates, 2 g fiber

To speed preparation and cleanup time, I combine the sugar, egg, and other wet ingredients with the oil in a 4-cup measuring cup, then mix in the carrot and sweet potato.

PICTURE PERFECT

For muffins like these in the photograph, cut baking parchment into 6" squares. Center a piece of parchment over a cavity in the baking pan, pressing it down in the center, then flattening the creases to make the paper fit. Fill with batter and bake as usual.

FOOD FACT

The fiber in the carrot and seeds can slow down the body's absorption of the sugar, helping to keep blood sugar levels from spiking.

SCOTTISH OATMEAL SCONES

Whole buttermilk contains 4 grams of fat per cup; low-fat buttermilk, 1.5 grams. Use either, or fat-free.

These rustic scones are good spread with homemade Blueberry Butter (page 304) or Walnut Honey (page 291). Use whole wheat pastry flour, which is made from soft wheat. It has a milder taste than the whole wheat flour made from winter wheat.

1	cup quick-cooking oats (not instant)	2	teaspoons baking powder
½	cup whole wheat pastry flour	¼	teaspoon baking soda
½	cup unbleached all-purpose flour	¼	cup cold unsalted butter, diced
2	tablespoons sugar	1	large egg, at room temperature
¾	teaspoon salt	¼	cup buttermilk

1. Place a rack in the center of the oven. Preheat the oven to 375°F. Make an 8" circle of flour in the center of a baking sheet and set it aside.

2. In a mixing bowl, combine the oats, whole wheat and white flours, sugar, salt, baking powder, and baking soda. Cut in the butter, using a sturdy fork or 2 knives, until the mixture resembles coarse cornmeal.

3. Whisk the egg and buttermilk together. Pour the liquid into the oat mixture. Stir with a fork to combine them, finally using your hands to gather the dough into a crumbly ball. Transfer the dough to the prepared baking sheet, patting it with your hands to shape it into an 8" disk about ½" thick. With a sharp knife, score the scones into 8 wedges.

4. Bake 20 minutes, or until the scones are lightly colored on top and golden around the edge. Cool slightly on the baking sheet. Cut into wedges and serve warm. They will keep 1 day wrapped in foil. Reheat in a 350°F oven until warm, 5 minutes.

Makes 8 scones

Per scone: 164 calories, 7 g fat, 4 g saturated fat, 4 g protein, 21 g carbohydrates, 2 g fiber

CHOCOLATE ZUCCHINI TEA CAKE

Adding chocolate takes this quick bread to a whole new level. While working to cut down fat and still make a conventionally good quick bread, I discovered a specific technique that helps make this work (see note).

¼	cup light olive oil		⅛	teaspoon ground cloves
1	large, cold egg		½	teaspoon baking soda
¾	cup sugar		¼	teaspoon baking powder
1	teaspoon vanilla extract		¼	teaspoon salt
1¼	cups unbleached all-purpose flour		¼	cup regular or low-fat plain yogurt
2	tablespoons Dutch-process cocoa powder		1	cup shredded zucchini
			1	cup broken or chopped walnuts
½	teaspoon ground cinnamon		1	cup bittersweet chocolate chips

1. Preheat the oven to 350 degrees. Set a rack in the center of the oven. Lightly coat an 8" × 4" × 2½" loaf pan with oil or cooking spray.

2. In a mixing bowl, whisk the oil and egg together until they resemble homemade mayonnaise, 15 strokes. Beat in the sugar and vanilla.

3. Add the flour, cocoa, cinnamon, cloves, baking soda, baking powder, and salt, mixing with a rubber spatula to combine the wet and dry ingredients into a thick batter. Mix in the yogurt, then the zucchini, then the walnuts plus half the chocolate chips. Turn the batter into the prepared pan and sprinkle the remaining chocolate chips over the top.

4. Set the pan on a light-colored baking sheet and bake 50 minutes or until a bamboo skewer inserted into the center comes out clean. Cool the bread in the pan for 20 minutes, then unmold and cool completely on a wire rack before refrigerating, wrapped in foil, until it is chilled through, 6 hours. This bread keeps up to 5 days.

Makes 1 loaf, eight 1" slices

Per slice: 448 calories, 24 g fat, 6 g saturated fat, 8 g protein, 56 g carbohydrates, 3 g fiber

An 8" pan is essential for a moist bread. So is refrigerating the finished bread wrapped in foil, as it crumbles unless it is sliced cold; allow it to warm to room temperature before serving.

AN EGG-CITING DISCOVERY

If you whisk the oil vigorously with a very cold egg, the mayonnaise-like texture helps to produce a moister quick bread.

CHAPTER TEN
VEGETABLES AND SIDE DISHES

When side dishes are interesting, you can eat a couple of servings of vegetables before you realize it. A half-cup serving of cooked broccoli or spinach (the USDA's official serving size for all cooked vegetables), appealingly prepared, virtually disappears. So with steamed Broccoli Balsamico or Sweet and Sour Red Cabbage, even stopping at a double serving is difficult. Preparing them does not mean spending a lot of time in the kitchen, either.

Cooking transforms the flavor of many vegetables. It can also make them look brighter and more attractive, and it makes the vital nutrients they contain more available to our bodies. This is one reason I always cook broccoli, even if I just steam it for 1 minute or give it a 30-second plunge into boiling water. Besides breaking down the vegetable's cell walls, even brief cooking makes the broccoli taste milder and sweeter. (Steaming is preferable, as it causes the least loss of vitamin C and other water-soluble nutrients, but sometimes boiling is more efficient, as when you are making pasta and already have a pot of water going.)

With certain vegetables, the cooking method can affect their taste noticeably. For example, boiled and roasted yams are as different as chalk and cheese. Boiled yams are bland and mushy, while roasting turns their flesh butter-soft and creamy and brings out their natural sweetness by caramelizing the sugars.

With onions, the longer and more gently they are cooked, the greater their transformation from crisp and pungent to tender, even creamy, and sugar-sweet. The cooking method matters, too. On the grill, charring enhances an onion's pungency, while the extreme heat caramelizes their surface a bit. Roasting onions brings out more sweetness, but it does not caramelize them as much as the long, slow cooking.

Savory herbs, spices, sweetness, and heat—used in different combinations—provide other ways to give vegetables variety. Serve thyme-perfumed Sweet Potato Steak Fries one night, spiced Moroccan Sweet Potato Puree the next, then fruit-sweetened Scalloped Sweet Potato with Apple the third, and I guarantee you will enjoy eating sweet potatoes as a side dish 3 days in a row. All the recipes here use the moist, deep orange-fleshed sweet potato varieties called yams, such as Beauregard, Garnet, and Jewel.

GARLIC-ROASTED TOMATOES

Generously flavored with garlic and herbs, these baked tomatoes serve as a side dish or an antipasto. They are delicious even made with hard, unripe tomatoes. Serve with Turkey-Walnut Meat Loaf (page 134) or Pan-Roasted Halibut with Caramelized Onions (page 153).

4½	teaspoons extra-virgin olive oil, divided	2	cloves garlic, finely chopped
1	teaspoon fine sea salt or kosher salt, divided	⅓	cup dry breadcrumbs
		¼	cup chopped flat-leaf parsley
6	large plum tomatoes, halved lengthwise		Freshly ground black pepper

1. Preheat the oven to 400°F. Brush an 8" square baking dish with ½ teaspoon of the oil or coat it with cooking spray.

2. Salt the cut sides of the tomatoes with half the salt. Set them on a plate.

3. Heat 1 tablespoon of the remaining oil in a medium nonstick skillet over medium-high heat. Arrange the tomatoes in 1 layer, cut side down, in the pan and cook until lightly browned, 3 minutes. You may have to do this in 2 batches. Fit the tomatoes cut side up in the prepared baking dish, making 1 snug layer. If the skillet is burnt, wipe it out.

4. Return the skillet to medium-high heat and add the remaining oil. Sauté the garlic until it starts to color, 2 minutes. Off the heat, mix in the breadcrumbs, parsley, the remaining salt, and 3 or 4 grinds of pepper. Sprinkle the seasoned breadcrumbs over the tomatoes.

5. Bake the tomatoes uncovered for 10 minutes, until the breadcrumb topping is browned. Cool 20 minutes and serve warm or at room temperature.

Makes 6 servings

Per serving: 69 calories, 4 g fat, 1 g saturated fat, 1 g protein, 8 g carbohydrates, 1 g fiber

To substitute frozen spinach, defrost it and squeeze out most of the moisture without wringing it dry. Continue as in step 2, adding the spinach all at once.

FEEL THE HEAT

The heat level in jalapeños is notoriously unpredictable. To find out whether you have a 3-alarm sizzler or a 1-alarm wimp, taste a thin sliver when cutting the pepper open. If you want more heat, slice a second jalapeño into fine strips and use it to garnish the cooked spinach.

FOOD FACT

Letting the chile water sit gives the sulfur compounds in the garlic time to develop and become more pungent.

JALAPEÑO SPINACH

Everyone will want the recipe for this dish with 2-alarm flavor. The cooked spinach should be tender but still have body.

1	jalapeño, seeded and chopped	2	teaspoons extra-virgin olive oil
1	clove garlic, chopped	16	ounces fresh curly or flat-leaf spinach,
½	teaspoon salt		stemmed

1. In a blender, whirl the jalapeño, garlic, and salt with ½ cup cold water until the mixture resembles pale green water, 1 minute. Set aside for 10 minutes.

2. Heat the oil in a medium nonstick skillet over medium-high heat. Add the spinach in 2 or 3 batches, stirring after each addition to coat the leaves with the oil. When all the spinach is wilted, 2 minutes, pour in the chile water. Cook until the spinach is dark green and half the liquid has evaporated, 3 minutes. Transfer the spinach to a serving bowl and serve hot or at room temperature.

Makes 4 servings

Per serving: 42 calories, 3 g fat, 0 g saturated fat, 2 g protein, 4 g carbohydrates, 2 g fiber

STIR-FRIED SPINACH
WITH CHARRED GARLIC

Barbara Tropp featured this combination of spinach leaves and the starlike clusters where the stems come together at her restaurant, the China Moon Café, in San Francisco, California. It requires using firm-leafed curly spinach. Charring the garlic adds a smoky flavor to the dish.

1	pound curly spinach, in clusters	¼	teaspoon sugar
1	tablespoon peanut oil	¼	teaspoon salt
3	cloves garlic, halved lengthwise		

FOOD FACT

Including the spinach stems increases the fiber in this dish.

1. Using scissors, cut the leaves from each spinach cluster into 2" ribbons. For the stars, cut off all but 1" of the stem above the root cluster. Using a small knife, pare away any tough root tip and cut large clusters vertically in half or quarters. Thoroughly wash the spinach and stem clusters in several changes of cold water and drain well.

2. Set a bowl of ice water in the sink. Drop the spinach and clusters into a pot of boiling water for 1 minute. Drain in a colander, then plunge the spinach into the ice water. When completely cool, squeeze the moisture out of the leaves and shake off the water clinging to the clusters. The cooked spinach can be refrigerated up to 24 hours at this point.

3. Heat a wok over high heat. Drizzle the oil into the wok, add the garlic, and stir-fry 30 seconds until it is dark brown, or lightly char it by pressing the garlic against the side of the wok. Add the spinach and clusters and stir-fry just to coat them with the oil, 30 seconds. Add the sugar and salt and toss to distribute them. Turn the stir-fried spinach into a serving bowl and serve hot or at room temperature.

Makes 4 servings

Per serving: 50 calories, 4 g fat, 1 g saturated fat, 2 g protein, 4 g carbohydrates, 2 g fiber

BROCCOLI BALSAMICO

For this dish, skip using a steamer basket or insert so you can steam broccoli, then glaze it with a flavorful sauce, all in the same pot. This method lets the florets absorb the sauce, which concentrates as the liquid boils off.

2	tablespoons balsamic vinegar	½	teaspoon salt
1	tablespoon brown sugar	3 or 4	grinds black pepper
1	small clove garlic, finely chopped	2	teaspoons extra-virgin olive oil
½	teaspoon freshly grated ginger	5	cups broccoli florets

1. In a small bowl, whisk the vinegar, sugar, garlic, ginger, salt, and pepper together. Add the oil and set aside.

2. Place the broccoli in a deep saucepan. Pour in ½ cup water, cover, and set over medium-high heat. Cook until the tips of the florets are tender but the stems are firm when pierced with a knife, about 5 minutes. Off the heat, add the balsamic mixture, pouring it down the side of the pot so it mixes with the cooking water.

3. Return the pot to the heat and cook, stirring, until the liquid has almost completely evaporated, about 30 seconds. Serve immediately.

Makes 4 servings

Per serving: 66 calories, 3 g fat, 0 g saturated fat, 3 g protein, 10 g carbohydrates, 3 g fiber

BROCCOLI SMASHED POTATOES

Even youngsters will love this dish, an unexpected way to enjoy a whole cup of broccoli.

1	pound Yukon Gold or other yellow-fleshed potatoes, peeled	½	cup low-fat (1%) milk
4	cups medium broccoli florets		Salt and freshly ground black pepper
1	leek, white part only, thinly sliced	4	teaspoons unsalted butter
		½	teaspoon ground mace

FOOD FACT

Yellow-fleshed potatoes get their color from carotenoids.

1. Place the potatoes in a deep saucepan and cover with cold water to a depth of 2". Cook uncovered over high heat until the potatoes can be easily pierced with a knife, about 20 minutes.

2. While the potatoes cook, steam the broccoli and leek until the broccoli is very soft, about 15 minutes. Drain in a colander.

3. Drain the potatoes and place them in a deep bowl. Using a sturdy fork, mash the potatoes into roughly 1" chunks. Add the broccoli and leek, mashing until only small lumps of the broccoli remain. Add the milk, 2 tablespoons at a time, mashing until the texture is pleasing to you. Season to taste with salt and pepper.

4. In a small saucepan, melt the butter over medium heat until it is golden brown, 1 to 2 minutes, taking care it does not burn. Stir in the mace.

5. To serve, spoon the smashed potatoes into a serving bowl. With the back of the spoon, smooth the top, leaving several shallow indentations. Drizzle the butter, letting it pool in the hollows. Serve immediately.

Makes 4 servings

Per serving: 169 calories, 5 g fat, 2 g saturated fat, 7 g protein, 32 g carbohydrates, 5 g fiber

TOMATO BROCCOLI

Inspired by a dish created in the 1970s by Burt Greene, an inventive caterer, this tangy combination of steamed broccoli and creamy tomato sauce can be served as either a side dish or a warm salad. It goes with chicken, salmon, shrimp, and other seafood.

	Florets from 1 bunch broccoli	1	cup canned diced tomatoes, with their liquid
2	teaspoons extra-virgin olive oil		
1	small onion, chopped	2	tablespoons reduced-fat mayonnaise
1	clove garlic, chopped		Salt and freshly ground black pepper

1. Steam the broccoli until tender-crisp, 5 minutes. Drain in a colander and rinse under cold water to stop the cooking. Drain well again and place the broccoli in a serving bowl.

2. Heat the oil in a 7" skillet over medium-high heat. Sauté the onion for 2 minutes, then mix in the garlic and cook, stirring 1 minute longer. Add the tomatoes with their liquid and cook until most of the liquid has evaporated, 5 minutes longer. Set the sauce aside to cool slightly.

3. Transfer the tomato mixture to a food processor or blender and whirl until the sauce is a pulpy puree. Add the mayonnaise and whirl to blend. Season the sauce to taste with salt and pepper. Spoon it over the broccoli and serve immediately.

Makes 4 servings

Per serving: 92 calories, 5 g fat, 1 g saturated fat, 3 g protein, 11 g carbohydrates, 4 g fiber

For potlucks, carry the broccoli and the tomato dressing in separate containers. Reheat the dressing just before serving.

FOOD FACT

Olive oil and mayonnaise provide fat, which helps your body to absorb the lycopene in this dish.

BROCCOLI PUREE

The slight texture in this puree adds interest for me. If you prefer it smooth, simply whirl the broccoli longer when you puree it. Soy creamer adds richness without cholesterol.

8	cups small broccoli florets			Fresh nutmeg
1	clove roasted garlic (page 49)	1		teaspoon fresh lemon juice
2–3	tablespoons soy coffee creamer or			Salt and freshly ground black pepper
	heavy cream			

1. Steam the broccoli until very tender, 15 minutes, and transfer it to a food processor.

2. Coarsely chop the broccoli by pulsing 6 times. Add the garlic, creamer, 6 gratings of nutmeg, and lemon juice. Whirl to puree, stopping when the broccoli still has a bit of texture. Season to taste with salt and pepper and serve immediately.

Makes 4 servings

Per serving: 54 calories, 2 g fat, 1 g saturated fat, 4 g protein, 8 g carbohydrates, 4 g fiber

Soy coffee creamer adds just ½ gram of fat per serving and contains no cholesterol or saturated fat. You won't taste the difference, even if you are used to heavy cream.

CORN AND BROCCOLI PUDDING

Slimmed down from a recipe calling for instant stuffing mix and a stick of butter, this dish is a sure crowd-pleaser. While using frozen corn and dried basil is fine, it's better when it has the crunch of fresh broccoli. To save time, though, check the salad bar where you shop. It may include steamed florets you can use.

This casserole becomes a main dish when you mix in 1 cup cottage cheese or squeezed, crumbled firm tofu.

3	cups fresh or frozen broccoli florets	6	large basil leaves, cut crosswise into fine strips, or 1 teaspoon dried
1	tablespoon unsalted butter		
1	small onion, finely chopped	1	teaspoon sugar
3	scallions, white and green parts, chopped	1	teaspoon salt
			Freshly ground white or black pepper
2	large eggs	⅛	teaspoon turmeric, optional
1	(14¾-ounce) can creamed corn	2	slices firm white bread, crusts removed, cut in ½" cubes
2	cups frozen yellow corn kernels, defrosted		

1. Place a rack in the center of the oven. Preheat the oven to 350°F. Coat a 1½-quart baking dish with cooking spray, or brush it lightly with oil, and set aside.

2. Steam the broccoli until tender, 4 minutes. Drain well.

3. Melt the butter in a medium skillet over medium-high heat. When it stops foaming, stir in the onion and scallions, sautéing until the onion is soft, 4 minutes.

4. In a large mixing bowl, beat the eggs. Mix in the sautéed onion and scallions, scraping the pan to include any unabsorbed butter. Add the creamed corn, corn kernels, basil, sugar, salt, pepper to taste, and turmeric, if using. Add the broccoli and mix to combine well. Pour the corn and broccoli mixture into the prepared baking dish.

5. Sprinkle the cubed bread in an even layer over the top of the pudding. Coat the bread liberally with cooking spray.

6. Bake 40 minutes, or until the center of the pudding feels springy to the touch and a knife inserted all the way to the bottom of the pan comes out clean. Let the pudding sit 15 minutes before serving or serve it lukewarm.

Makes 6 servings as a side dish, 4 as a main course

Per side dish serving: 191 calories, 8 g fat, 2 g saturated fat, 7 g protein, 33 g carbohydrates, 5 g fiber

SWEET POTATO STEAK FRIES

Coarse-grained kosher or sea salt is the perfect garnish for these potatoes. *Fleur de Sel*, the elegant French salt, is even better.

FOOD FACT

Leaving the potatoes unpeeled increases the fiber in this dish.

While Beauregards are fairly even in shape, Garnet and Jewel yams are often twisted or bulge in the middle. Whichever kind you use, pick out fairly regularly shaped potatoes so you can make long, straight fries. If you like your fries with the skins on, consider using organic potatoes for this dish.

2   large (1 pound each) Beauregard, Garnet, or Jewel yams, unpeeled
1   tablespoon extra-virgin olive oil
1   teaspoon kosher or sea salt, divided

2   teaspoons chopped fresh thyme
¼   teaspoon chopped fresh rosemary
     Freshly ground black pepper

1. Preheat the oven to 450°F.

2. Halve the yams crosswise. Stand each half on the cut end and halve it vertically, then cut each piece lengthwise into 4 to 6 half-inch slabs.

3. Pour half the oil onto a baking sheet and sprinkle with ½ teaspoon of the salt. Add the sliced potatoes and drizzle the remaining oil over them. Add the thyme, rosemary, and 4 or 5 grinds of pepper. Using your hands, toss the potatoes to coat them with the oil and seasonings.

4. Bake for 15 minutes. Using tongs, turn each slice. Bake 10 minutes longer, or until the potatoes are browned and easily pierced with a fork. Sprinkle with the remaining ½ teaspoon salt, and serve immediately.

Makes 6 servings

Per serving: 200 calories, 3 g fat, 0 g saturated fat, 2 g protein, 42 g carbohydrates, 6 g fiber

MOROCCAN SWEET POTATO PUREE

Moroccan food is spicy but not necessarily hot. These creamy sweet potatoes are quick and easy, making them a good weeknight dish. To dress them up for special occasions, garnish with finely chopped mint and parsley.

2	pounds Beauregard, Garnet, or Jewel yams	⅛	teaspoon ground coriander
¼	teaspoon ground cinnamon	1	tablespoon extra-virgin olive oil
½	teaspoon ground ginger		Salt and freshly ground black pepper

1. Preheat the oven to 400°F.

2. Bake the sweet potatoes until a small knife inserted at the widest part easily pierces them, 25 to 50 minutes, depending on their size and shape. Place the potatoes in a medium bowl and when cool enough to handle, peel them with your fingers.

3. Add the cinnamon, ginger, coriander, and oil to the potatoes. Mash them with a fork until they are creamy and well combined. Season to taste with salt and pepper and serve hot, lukewarm, or at room temperature.

Makes 4 servings

Per serving: 303 calories, 4 g fat, 1 g saturated fat, 4 g protein, 64 g carbohydrates, 10 g fiber

When you want to save time, use smaller sweet potatoes, which bake significantly faster than large ones. For easy peeling, coat them very lightly with oil (see page 29).

SCALLOPED SWEET POTATO WITH APPLE

Cutting the potatoes on the diagonal gives the slices an attractive, oval shape. Make them no more than ¼" thick.

FOOD FACT

Dried apricots provide a generous amount of vitamin A and fiber.

THE YUMMIEST APRICOTS

The best-tasting dried apricots are Blenheims, sold at Trader Joe's. They taste like an apricot does in your imagination.

Rather than baking yams with marshmallows, this recipe uses honey and apricots to give them a pleasing balance of sweet and tart. It makes an almost fat-free dish to serve with Sesame-Oat Chicken Fingers (page 123), Pork Tenderloin in Chipotle Mole (page 142), and other poultry and pork dishes.

2	pounds Beauregard, Garnet, or Jewel yams, peeled and thinly sliced on the diagonal	¼	cup blueberry or wildflower honey
		2	tablespoons frozen orange juice concentrate
1	Granny Smith apple, peeled, cored, and thinly sliced	½	cup apple cider
		½	teaspoon salt
12	dried California apricot halves, chopped		Freshly ground black pepper

1. Preheat the oven to 375°F. Coat an 8" square baking dish with cooking spray or brush it lightly with oil, and set aside.

2. Cover the bottom of the baking dish with a layer of potato, arranging the slices in 4 overlapping rows, like roof tiles. Cover the potatoes with the apple. Add a second layer of potatoes. Sprinkle the apricots over the potatoes.

3. Whisk the honey, orange juice concentrate, cider, salt, and 4 or 5 grinds of pepper together until the honey dissolves. Pour the mixture over the potatoes.

4. Cover the dish with foil and bake 40 minutes. Uncover and bake 15 minutes longer, or until the potatoes are tender when pierced with a knife. They will still hold their shape. Let stand 15 minutes before serving.

Makes 8 servings

Per serving: 196 calories, 0 g fat, 0 g saturated fat, 2 g protein, 48 g carbohydrates, 6 g fiber

GINGER-CANDIED YAMS

FOOD FACT

Orange juice concentrate contains considerably more vitamin C than juice.

Brown sugar combined with orange juice and lots of ginger creates a spicy glaze on these chunky potatoes. Unlike most other recipes, these candied yams are almost fat-free. They are perfect with roast turkey, of course, but also with pork and as part of a winter vegetable plate, along with BBQ Collard Greens with Edamame (page 240).

1½	pounds Beauregard, Garnet, or Jewel yams, peeled and cut in 1" pieces	1	tablespoon frozen orange juice concentrate
½	cup brown sugar, packed	¾	teaspoon salt
½	teaspoon ground ginger		Freshly ground black pepper

1. Preheat the oven to 400°F. Coat a 1½-quart baking dish with cooking spray or brush it lightly with oil.

2. Place the sweet potatoes in the prepared baking dish. In a small bowl, combine the sugar, ginger, orange juice concentrate, salt, and 3 or 4 grinds of black pepper. Sprinkle the sugar mixture over the yams.

3. Bake uncovered for 20 minutes. Stir the potatoes and continue baking until the yams are soft but hold their shape, 25 minutes longer. Let them sit 20 minutes to allow the flavors to meld before serving. Or bake them ahead, cool, and refrigerate, tightly covered, for up to 2 days. To reheat, cover the pan with foil and place in a 350°F oven for 20 minutes.

Makes 4 servings

Per serving: 182 calories, 0 g fat, 0 g saturated fat, 3 g protein, 43 g carbohydrates, 5 g fiber

SWEET POTATO KUGEL

Kugel, a kind of moist pudding, traditionally is loaded with cholesterol and can be quite sweet. Instead, I prefer this enlightened kugel made using chicken broth in place of dairy products. It requires just enough matzoh meal to hold it together, plus a touch of oil.

1	pound Beauregard, Garnet, or Jewel yams, peeled	1	cup fat-free, reduced-sodium chicken broth
2	large eggs	1	teaspoon salt
¼	cup finely chopped onion	¼	teaspoon freshly ground black pepper
1	tablespoon canola oil	⅔	cup matzoh meal

1. Preheat the oven to 350°F. Coat a 1½-quart rectangular baking dish with cooking spray.

2. Using a medium-fine grater, shred the sweet potatoes. There should be 4 cups. Place the shredded yams in a mixing bowl.

3. Add the eggs, onion, oil, broth, salt, and pepper. Mix with a fork to combine. Add the matzoh meal and combine well. Spread the mixture evenly in the prepared baking dish.

4. Bake the kugel uncovered for 45 minutes, or until the top is golden and a knife inserted into the center comes out clean. Let it sit for 20 minutes before serving. Or let it cool to room temperature, cover with foil, and refrigerate for up to 2 days. Reheat the kugel, covered, at 350°F for 25 minutes.

Makes 6 servings

Per serving: 194 calories, 7 g fat, 1 g saturated fat, 5 g protein, 29 g carbohydrates, 3 g fiber

SOYCOTASH

In late summer, when fresh edamame, local corn, and sweet red peppers are all in season locally, this vegetable medley is so good I can make a meal of it. The rest of the year, made with frozen edamame and corn, it is still delicious. Serve with Turkey-Walnut Meat Loaf (page 134) or pork chops.

½	vegetable bouillon cube
1	small red onion, chopped
½	medium red bell pepper, chopped
1	cup fresh or frozen shelled edamame

2	cups fresh or frozen yellow corn kernels
1	teaspoon unsalted butter
	Salt and freshly ground black pepper

1. In a medium saucepan, dissolve the bouillon cube in ¼ cup water. Bring the broth to a boil. Add the onion and bell pepper and cook, stirring often, until the onion is translucent, 2 minutes.

2. In another saucepan, cook the edamame in boiling salted water. If using fresh vegetables, boil the edamame for 6 minutes, add the corn, and cook 2 minutes longer. For frozen vegetables, boil the edamame for 5 minutes, add the corn, and cook 2 minutes longer. Either way, the vegetables should be tender-crisp.

3. Drain and add the cooked edamame and corn to the onion and red pepper. Mix in the butter until it melts. Season to taste with salt and pepper. Serve hot or at room temperature. Soycotash keeps for 2 days, tightly covered in the refrigerator. Reheat it in a tightly covered saucepan, adding a minimal amount of water if needed.

Makes 4 servings

Per serving: 150 calories, 6 g fat, 1 g saturated fat, 10 g protein, 18 g carbohydrates, 4 g fiber

BBQ COLLARD GREENS WITH EDAMAME

Using smoke-flavored barbecue sauce gives these greens all the savor of Texas BBQ. Serve them with long-grain brown rice to help sop it up.

1	(10-ounce) package frozen chopped collard greens	3	tablespoons smoke-flavored barbecue sauce
1	cup frozen shelled edamame	2	strips crumbled uncured bacon, optional, for garnish
1	small yellow onion, finely chopped		
½	small green bell pepper, finely chopped		

1. Place the collards in a medium saucepan. Add ⅓ cup water, cover, and cook for 6 minutes.

2. Add the edamame, onion, and pepper. Cover and cook 8 minutes longer. Stir in the barbecue sauce and serve, garnished with the bacon, if desired.

Makes 4 servings

Per serving: 171 calories, 6 g fat, 1 g saturated fat, 11 g protein, 20 g carbohydrates, 6 g fiber

For a meatless meal, mix in 1½ cups cooked brown rice and serve with black beans.

FOOD FACT

One cup of cooked collards provides 4 grams of protein.

MISO MASHED POTATOES

Miso plus olive oil makes light, creamy mashed potatoes, especially when the potatoes are of the yellow-fleshed variety. It is important to work quickly, while the cooked potatoes are still hot and moist.

1¼	pounds Yukon Gold or other yellow-fleshed potatoes	4	teaspoons extra-virgin olive oil
2	tablespoons shiro or mellow white miso	2	cloves roasted garlic (page 49)
			Salt and freshly ground black pepper

1. In a medium saucepan, boil the potatoes until they are soft when pierced with a knife, about 20 minutes. Drain and place the potatoes in a mixing bowl. As soon as they are cool enough to handle, peel the potatoes.

2. Roughly mash the flesh with a fork, working in the miso, oil, and garlic until the potatoes are smooth—or leave some lumps, if you prefer. Season to taste with salt and pepper and serve immediately.

Makes 4 servings

Per serving: 157 calories, 5 g fat, 1 g saturated fat, 5 g protein, 28 g carbohydrates, 3 g fiber

FOOD FACT

Miso, criticized for being high in sodium, contains 210 milligrams per teaspoon, versus kosher salt, which has 1,880 milligrams per teaspoon.

SWEET AND SOUR RED CABBAGE

Many recipes call for sugar, but I prefer using apple cider, raisins, and dried blueberries for sweetness in this dish. A cinnamon stick adds a touch of spice.

2	tablespoons olive oil	¼	cup dried blueberries
1	small head red cabbage (1½ pounds),	½	cup apple cider
	quartered and shredded lengthwise	¼	cup apple cider vinegar
1	medium red onion, sliced	1	bay leaf
1	teaspoon salt	1	cinnamon stick
½	cup golden raisins		Freshly ground black pepper

1. Heat the oil in a large skillet over medium-high heat. Add half the cabbage and the onion, stirring to coat the vegetables with the oil. Cook, stirring often, until they wilt, 2 minutes. Mix in the remaining cabbage, sprinkle with the salt, and cook, stirring occasionally, until all the cabbage is wilted, 2 minutes. Add the raisins and blueberries.

2. Pour in the cider and vinegar. Add the bay leaf and cinnamon stick. Cook uncovered, stirring often, until the cabbage is crisp-tender, 6 minutes, or if you prefer it softer, 10 minutes. Remove the bay leaf and cinnamon stick. Adjust the salt and season to taste with pepper. Serve hot. The cabbage keeps for 3 days, tightly covered in the refrigerator. Reheat it in a covered baking dish in a 350°F oven for 20 minutes.

Makes 4 servings

Per serving: 230 calories, 8 g fat, 1 g saturated fat, 4 g protein, 43 g carbohydrates, 5 g fiber

PAN-GRILLED RED ONION

Sautéing onions in a dry pan gives them a grilled flavor. It's a good way to enjoy them if you don't like—or can't tolerate—raw onions. Keep them on hand to add to salads, sandwiches, and soups. I also serve them as a side dish with fish, poultry, beans, and rice.

1   large red onion, cut in ⅛" slices
        or crescents

Set a large, well-seasoned cast-iron skillet or nonstick pan over medium-high heat. Heat the dry pan for 1 minute, then spread the onions to cover the pan in 1 layer. Cook until most of the onions are well-browned on the bottoms, 2 to 3 minutes. If using crescents, about one-quarter of the tips will be darkened as well. Stir to turn the onions and cook 1 minute longer. Continue to cook, stirring constantly, until the onions are golden, 2 minutes longer. The onions are done when they are limp but still slightly crunchy. They keep for up to 3 days, tightly covered in the refrigerator.

Makes 1 cup

Per serving (⅓ cup): 21 calories, 0 g fat, 0 g saturated fat, 1 g protein, 5 g carbohydrates, 1 g fiber

SICILIAN UGLY ONIONS

Capers preserved in sea salt let you taste the bud's tangy flavor. My favorite ones, big as raisins, come from the Sicilian islands of Salina and Pantelleria.

Roasted until their skin chars to dark bronze and beads of blackened juices form, these onions are certainly ugly when they come from the oven. Inside, however, their flesh is moist and sweet. In Sicily, this is an everyday dish served as a salad or a condiment with grilled fish. It is good with roast chicken, too.

4	*Spanish onions, preferably of equal size, 3 pounds total*	1	*tablespoon chopped fresh oregano or thyme leaves*
2	*tablespoons capers, preferably salted*	2	*tablespoons extra-virgin olive oil*
1	*tablespoon chopped fresh basil*		*Salt and freshly ground black pepper*

1. Preheat the oven to 475°F. Line a light-colored 8" square metal baking pan with a piece of foil large enough to hang over all 4 sides.

2. Remove any loose, papery skin from the onions, leaving the tight-fitting layers. Roast the onions in the pan until collapsing, about 1 hour and 15 minutes. (The tops may be charred and black.) Set aside to cool.

3. In a small bowl, soak salted capers in cold water for 20 minutes. Rinse under cold water and drain. (Just rinse pickled capers.) Dry and set aside.

4. Place each onion on a cutting board and slice off the root end. Pull the onions open, tearing through up to 4 tough outer layers. Use kitchen shears if necessary. Pull out the insides and discard the tough, burnt outer layers. Coarsely chop the remaining flesh.

5. Place the onion in a mixing bowl. Mix in the capers, basil, oregano, and oil. Season to taste with salt and pepper. Let sit for 30 minutes at room temperature so the flavors meld. Keep for up to 4 days, tightly covered in the refrigerator.

Makes 6 servings

Per serving: 82 calories, 3 g fat, 0 g saturated fat, 2 g protein, 13 g carbohydrates, 3 g fiber

BEET AND WALNUT RELISH

In Georgia (the Caucasian republic), walnuts are often a main ingredient. Serve this pungent relish with Pan-Roasted Halibut with Caramelized Onions (page 153) or Black Soybean and Butternut Squash Stew (page 196).

Some supermarkets sell cooked beets. Use them, if you like.

3	medium beets		Salt and freshly ground black pepper
¼	cup walnuts	1	tablespoon fresh lemon juice
2	tablespoons coarsely chopped cilantro leaves	1	tablespoon red wine vinegar
1	clove garlic, coarsely chopped		Chopped flat-leaf parsley, for garnish

1. Place the beets in a large saucepan. Cover them to a depth of 2" with cold water. Boil until a thin knife pierces them easily, about 45 minutes. Drain and cool the beets for 20 minutes. Peel them with your fingers or use the edge of a small knife to help lift off the skin in strips. The beets can be prepared up to this point a day ahead and refrigerated, individually wrapped in plastic wrap.

2. Coarsely chop the beets. Place them in a food processor and whirl 30 seconds to chop them finely. Add the walnuts, cilantro, garlic, ½ teaspoon of salt, and 3 or 4 grinds of black pepper. Pulse 5 or 6 times. Add the lemon juice and vinegar. Pulse 3 times to blend. Adjust the seasoning if desired. Garnish with parsley and serve. This relish keeps for 2 days, tightly covered in the refrigerator.

Makes 2 cups

Per serving (½ cup): 40 calories, 3 g fat, 0 g saturated fat, 1 g protein, 4 g carbohydrates, 1 g fiber

BLUEBERRY AND
RED ONION COMPOTE

Related to the savory onion marmalade you see on many restaurant menus, this condiment dresses up grilled or roasted chicken breast, roast turkey, or plain pork chops. Having it on hand is especially nice when your meat or poultry is store-bought and already cooked.

2	teaspoons unsalted sweet butter	2	tablespoons light brown sugar
2	teaspoons canola oil	1	tablespoon balsamic vinegar
2	large red onions, halved vertically and		Pinch of salt
	cut crosswise in ¼" slices	½	cup blueberries, fresh or frozen

1. Melt the butter with the oil in a heavy, deep saucepan over medium heat. Stir in the onions and cook, stirring often, until they are wilted, about 5 minutes.

2. Mix in the sugar and vinegar. Cook, stirring until the sugar dissolves, about 1 minute, then add 1 cup water and the salt. Cook until most of the water has evaporated and the onions are simmering in a thick, bubbly syrup, about 25 minutes. Add the blueberries and cook until the compote thickens to the consistency of jam, about 20 minutes. Cool to room temperature before serving. This compote keeps up to 2 weeks, tightly covered in the refrigerator.

Makes 2 cups

Per serving (⅓ cup): 56 calories, 3 g fat, 1 g saturated fat, 1 g protein, 7 g carbohydrates, 1 g fiber

WALNUT CHUTNEY

Chutney normally does not contain nuts, but after I thought of this savory combination I found several walnut chutney recipes in older British cookbooks. It goes beautifully with roasted and grilled poultry and cottage cheese.

1	Golden Delicious apple, peeled, cored, and finely chopped	1	teaspoon ground cinnamon
1	cup chopped onion	1	teaspoon freshly grated ginger
⅔	cup chopped walnuts	½	teaspoon freshly grated orange zest
2	Turkish dried figs, chopped	¼	teaspoon ground allspice
⅓	cup pitted dates, chopped	¼	teaspoon red-pepper flakes
¼	cup golden raisins	½	cup apple juice
½	cup dark brown sugar, firmly packed	½	cup apple cider vinegar

Place the apple, onion, nuts, figs, dates, raisins, sugar, cinnamon, ginger, zest, allspice, and pepper flakes in a deep, medium saucepan. Pour in the apple juice and vinegar. Cover and bring to a boil. Stir to combine the ingredients and boil gently, uncovered, until the chutney plops from the spoon, 30 minutes. Spoon into 2 freshly washed and dried 1-cup glass jars, cover tightly, and cool to room temperature. Store in the refrigerator.

Makes 2 cups

Per serving (¼ cup): 193 calories, 7 g fat, 1 g saturated fat, 2 g protein, 34 g carbohydrates, 3 g fiber

Double the recipe, if you like, increasing the liquids to ¾ cup each and allowing a longer time to cook.

FOOD FACT
Dried fruit plus nuts and apple makes a fiber-full combination.

CHAPTER ELEVEN
DESSERTS

Does dessert go with healthy eating? If it is good for you, can it still be irresistible? Absolutely. Blueberries, chocolate, walnuts, oats, spinach, and sweet potatoes, all Best Foods, make memorable desserts. I also use butter and sugar, though less than most recipes usually call for. I even have a dessert made with . . . how shocking . . . whipped cream!

Where familiar ingredients show up, I sometimes use them unexpectedly. Since heat affects anthocyanins, my blueberry pie filling is uncooked and glazed with melted blueberry fruit spread, which also sweetens it. There are oats in the Cherry Berry Crisp's crust, as you would expect, and in the Apple-Spice Biscotti, as you might not. They taste like nuts, which they in fact replace in the crisp cookies. Almonds, not usually found in Oatmeal-Raisin Cookies, make mine distinctively special. Walnuts, which appear in expected places, a cobbler and brownies, star in Walnut Crisps, little wafers that rate three stars for flavor, simplicity, and satisfying crunch.

Taking advantage of the good news about chocolate's antioxidant powers, I provide many ways to indulge, always using either 70% bittersweet or dark chocolate made by Dove that is processed so its antioxidants are most available. From stunning Hot Chocolate Soufflés with Strawberry Salsa and The Ultimate Bittersweet Brownie, to intense Chocolate-Nut Chewies and the instant fix of Chocolate Bruschetta, these desserts satisfy your chocolate craving with good conscience. A number of them also include beneficial fruit and nuts.

Indulging my own fondness for dishes with soy that are supremely good, soymilk enhances the opulent flavors of Chocolate-Cherry Bread Pudding and its accompanying Dark Cherry-Chocolate Sauce. Similarly, tofu makes Key Lime Tartlets luscious but light.

We eat fruits as vegetables all the time, most commonly cucumbers and avocados as well as tomatoes. Here, vegetables serve as dessert, in a middle European Spinach Strudel and a Sweet Potato Pudding that tastes like pure New England.

In sum, here are desserts to please your sweet tooth and the rest of you, too.

KEY LIME TARTLETS

The filling for these creamy tartlets keeps, tightly covered, in the refrigerator for up to 4 days.

Bottled key lime juice turns the creamy filling in these phyllo tartlets a lovely golden shade. Use a microplane grater to shred the lime zest for them and everyone will think this is the latest creation from the best pastry shop in town. Say they are made with soy, and they won't believe you.

½   package soft regular tofu (about
       1¾ cups)

¼   cup light cream cheese

⅔   cup confectioners' sugar

3   tablespoons fresh or bottled key lime
       juice

2½   teaspoons grated lime zest, divided
       Pinch of salt

4   phyllo sheets, whole wheat or regular

2   tablespoons unsalted butter, melted

1. Break the tofu into pieces and squeeze out about half the moisture (see page 22). It should resemble cottage cheese. Place the tofu in a food processor, add the cream cheese and sugar, and whirl to a smooth puree. Add the lime juice, 1½ teaspoons of the zest, and salt and whirl to blend.

2. Preheat the oven to 375°F. Lay out 1 sheet of the phyllo with the long side facing you. Brush it with melted butter. Top with another sheet of phyllo and brush again with butter. Repeat, ending with the fourth phyllo sheet brushed with butter. Cut the layered dough into 6 rectangles. Fit the dough into the cups of a 6-cup muffin tin. Bake 12 minutes, or until golden brown with dark tips. Cool 2 minutes in the tin, lift out the phyllo cups, and cool completely on a wire rack. If not filling immediately, arrange the cups on a plate, cover with foil, and set aside for up to 24 hours.

3. To assemble, place the phyllo cups on individual dessert plates. Spoon ⅓ cup of the key lime filling into each cup, sprinkle the remaining 1 teaspoon grated lime zest over the cream, and serve.

Makes 6 servings

Per serving: 201 calories, 9 g fat, 4 g saturated fat, 7 g protein, 26 g carbohydrates, 0 g fiber

BLUEBERRY-LEMON TRIFLE

The layers of crushed gingersnaps, creamy yogurt, fruit, and jam in these individual parfaits remind me of British trifle, though this refreshing dessert is light and far easier to make. My lemon curd is lower in fat and calories, but use a commercially made curd if you prefer.

20	reduced-fat gingersnap cookies	¼	cup soy cream cheese or fat-free dairy cream cheese
1½	cups (two 6-ounce containers) lemon soy yogurt or low-fat dairy yogurt	½	cup blueberry fruit spread
½	cup Lemon Curd (opposite page)	¼	cup fresh blueberries, optional, for garnish

1. Place the gingersnaps in a resealable plastic bag and crush them into coarse crumbs with a rolling pin. There will be about 1½ cups of crumbs.

2. In a food processor or blender, combine the yogurt, lemon curd, and cream cheese. Process or blend until smooth.

3. Set out 4 6-ounce or ½-cup ramekins, custard cups, or small bowls (clear glass would be nice). Spoon 2 tablespoons of the crumbs into each ramekin and cover them with ¼ cup of the yogurt mixture, spreading it with the back of the spoon. Top with another 2 tablespoons of cookie crumbs. Dollop 2 tablespoons of the blueberry spread into the center of the crumbs and cover with the remaining yogurt mixture. Sprinkle on the remaining crumbs. Arrange 5 or 6 fresh blueberries in a ring on top of each trifle, if desired, and serve. Or cover with plastic wrap and refrigerate for up to 24 hours, letting the trifles sit at room temperature for 20 minutes before serving.

Makes 4 servings

Per serving: 330 calories, 7 g fat, 2 g saturated fat, 6 g protein, 62 g carbohydrates, 1 g fiber

LEMON CURD

This recipe contains far less sugar and fat than commercial ones, and less than most other recipes, yet is pleasingly rich.

5	large egg yolks	½	cup sugar
½	cup fresh lemon juice	3	tablespoons cold, unsalted butter, cut in small pieces
	Pinch of salt		

1. In the top of a double boiler, whisk together the egg yolks, lemon juice, salt, and sugar. Set over simmering water, making sure the water does not touch the bottom of the upper pot. Cook, stirring constantly with a wooden spoon, until the curd thickens enough to leave a straight track when you draw your finger down the back of the coated spoon, about 15 minutes.

2. Off the heat, while stirring vigorously, add the butter and stir until it has melted into the curd. Transfer the hot curd to a small bowl and cover it with plastic wrap, pressing the plastic onto the surface of the curd. Let it sit at room temperature until lukewarm, then refrigerate until chilled, at least 6 hours. The curd will thicken as it cools.

Makes 1 cup

Per serving (2 tablespoons): 127 calories, 7 g fat, 4 g saturated fat, 2 g protein, 14 g carbohydrates, 0 g fiber

BAKED PEARS WITH CRANBERRIES AND CIDER SAUCE

Its dried-fruit filling sparkling with a honey glaze makes this dish look like an autumn still life. A light brushing with butter helps the pears glow.

4	*medium Bartlett pears*
½	*lemon*
1	*tablespoon unsalted butter, melted*
2	*tablespoons dried cranberries, coarsely chopped*
2	*tablespoons raisins, coarsely chopped*
1	*tablespoon minced crystallized ginger*
⅓	*cup chopped walnuts*
¼	*cup + 1 tablespoon blueberry honey or other mild variety*
2	*cups apple cider*

1. Preheat the oven to 350°F.

2. Peel the pears. Cut off the top one-third of the way down from the stem and rub the cut ends with the lemon half. Set the tops aside and, using a melon baller, scoop out the pear, making a 1½" cavity. Rub the bottoms with the lemon, then brush them lightly inside and out with the butter. Set the pears in a baking dish just large enough to hold them upright.

3. Combine the cranberries, raisins, ginger, and nuts in a small bowl. Mix in the ¼ cup of honey and spoon the mixture evenly into the pears. Brush the tops lightly with butter and set them on top of the filling. Reserve the remaining butter. Pour the cider into the baking dish.

4. Bake uncovered for 20 minutes, or until the pears are easily pierced with a knife. Lift the pears onto a serving plate.

5. For the sauce, pour the liquid from the baking dish into a small saucepan and boil it over high heat until reduced by half. Add the remaining honey and the reserved butter and boil down to ½ cup.

Makes 4 servings

Per serving: 362 calories, 10 g fat, 2 g saturated fat, 3 g protein, 71 g carbohydrates, 5 g fiber

CHERRY BERRY CRISP

When you serve this crisp, everyone gets a piece of golden crust and a generous helping of fruit bubbling with juices. Since berries need little preparation, you can assemble this dessert and get it into the oven in a mere 10 minutes.

FOOD FACT

The fruit in this crisp pro-vides more than 3 grams of fiber per serving.

FILLING

2	cups frozen sweet cherries
1	pint fresh blueberries or 2 cups frozen
½	pint raspberries
½	cup granulated sugar

TOPPING

⅔	cup unbleached all-purpose flour
⅓	cup whole wheat pastry flour
¾	cup firmly packed light brown sugar
4	tablespoons cold, unsalted butter, cut in small pieces

1. Place a rack in the center of the oven. Preheat the oven to 400°F. Coat a 9" square baking pan with cooking spray.

2. Combine the cherries, blueberries, raspberries, and granulated sugar in the prepared pan. Set aside.

3. In a mixing bowl, using a fork, combine the white and whole wheat flours with the brown sugar. With the fork, then your fingertips, work the butter into the dry ingredients until it looks sandy. Sprinkle the mixture over the fruit in the baking dish, leaving a ½" border of fruit exposed around the edge of the pan. With your finger, pat the topping to form a compact crust.

4. Bake the crisp for 10 minutes. Reduce the heat to 375°F and bake 30 minutes longer, or until the juices from the fruit bubble up around the edges of the dough and the crust is browned, 35 to 40 minutes. Cool to lukewarm on a wire rack and serve.

Makes 6 servings

Per serving: 276 calories, 9 g fat, 5 g saturated fat, 3 g protein, 50 g carbohydrates, 5 g fiber

OAT CRANACHAN
WITH RASPBERRIES

You are surprised, no doubt, to see this whipped cream dessert. It is so delicious and simple that I do serve it occasionally. For me, its oats and fresh berries compensate for the cream, and I believe that a healthy diet can accommodate such indulgence once in a while. The Scots mix uncooked oats with the cream, while my version using cooked oatmeal is more like a mousse.

1	cup heavy cream, chilled		Scotch Oats (page 290), at room
2	tablespoons sugar		temperature
1	tablespoon Scotch whiskey	1	cup fresh raspberries
½	cup toasted walnuts		

1. Whip the cream with an electric mixer on medium-high speed until it thickens. Add the sugar, 1 tablespoon at a time, continuing to beat until the cream is stiff but not dry looking. Using a rubber spatula, mix in the whiskey, then the walnuts and Scotch Oats. This can be done up to 24 hours ahead, and the mixture refrigerated, tightly covered.

2. To serve, place a few raspberries in the bottom of 4 footed dessert dishes or small clear glass bowls. Top with the oatmeal cream mixture. Sprinkle a few more berries on top and serve chilled.

Makes 4 servings

Per serving: 182 calories, 9 g fat, 1 g saturated fat, 4 g protein, 22 g carbohydrates, 5 g fiber

SWEET POTATO PUDDING

This baked pudding looks and tastes like Indian pudding. Serve it warm, topped with a small scoop of frozen yogurt, which makes the perfect sauce as it melts.

2	cups mashed roasted yams (about 1¼ pounds Beauregard, Garnet, or Jewel yams)	⅛	teaspoon allspice
		⅛	teaspoon ground nutmeg
		1	teaspoon vanilla extract
¼	cup maple syrup	2	large egg whites
2	large eggs, separated	1	cup vanilla frozen yogurt or dairy-free frozen dessert
1	teaspoon freshly grated orange zest		
1½	teaspoons ground cinnamon		

1. Set a rack in the center of the oven. Preheat the oven to 350°F. Coat a 6-cup rectangular baking dish with cooking spray.

2. In a food processor, blend the sweet potatoes, maple syrup, egg yolks, orange zest, cinnamon, allspice, nutmeg, and vanilla to a smooth puree. Turn the puree into a mixing bowl.

3. In another bowl, beat the 4 egg whites to soft peaks. Using a rubber spatula, fold one-third of the whites into the yam puree to lighten it. Then scoop this mixture into the remaining whites and fold gently to combine. Turn the mixture into the prepared baking dish.

4. Set a pan large enough to hold the baking dish onto the oven rack. Place the filled baking dish in it and carefully pour boiling water into the larger pan until it comes halfway up the sides of the baking dish.

5. Bake 50 minutes, or until a toothpick inserted into the center of the pudding comes out clean. Serve warm, topped with frozen yogurt.

Makes 4 servings

Per serving: 258 calories, 3 g fat, 1 g saturated fat, 9 g protein, 48 g carbohydrates, 4 g fiber

SPINACH STRUDEL

Test-kitchen staffs taste a lot of dishes, and this was one of the favorites at Rodale. Its combination of spinach, lemon zest, and walnuts drew raves.

1	bunch spinach, or 1 (10-ounce) bag, stemmed and rinsed	½	cup chopped walnuts
½	Granny Smith apple, peeled, cored, and finely chopped	¼	cup + 1 tablespoon sugar
		1	teaspoon grated lemon zest
⅓	cup dried currants	4	sheets whole wheat phyllo
		2	tablespoons unsalted butter, melted

I find whole wheat phyllo dough much easier to handle than the usual kind. I like one made by The Phyllo Factory, which is sold in natural food markets. It stays crisper around fillings and also tastes the same as other phyllo.

1. Preheat the oven to 375°F. Line a baking sheet with foil, coat it lightly with oil or cooking spray, and set it aside.

2. Sauté the spinach in a skillet until tender but not soft, 4 minutes. Transfer it to a colander and cool under cold running water. Squeeze out most of the moisture (there will be 1½ cups cooked) spinach. Finely chop, then fluff the spinach. In a mixing bowl, combine the spinach, apple, currants, nuts, ¼ cup of the sugar, and the zest. Set the filling aside.

3. Lay out 1 sheet of the phyllo with the long side facing you and brush lightly with butter. Sprinkle with 1 teaspoon of sugar. Top with another sheet, brush lightly with butter, and sprinkle with another teaspoon of sugar. Repeat, ending with the fourth sheet brushed lightly with butter. Arrange the filling 2" above the bottom of the dough in a long log, leaving 1" at either end. Fold the bottom edge up to cover the filling. Fold in the sides and roll up. Press the seam with your fingers to seal it. Transfer to the baking sheet, seam side down. Brush with the remaining butter.

4. Bake 45 minutes, or until golden brown. Cool it on the baking sheet. Use a serrated knife to cut the strudel, serving it at room temperature.

Makes 6 servings

Per serving: 222 calories, 11 g fat, 3 g saturated fat, 4 g protein, 30 g carbohydrates, 3 g fiber

BLUEBERRY AND STRAWBERRY PIE

This simple dessert of sliced strawberries arranged over fresh blueberries in a prebaked pie shell always comes out picture perfect. The berries mixed with melted fruit spread, which sweetens and glazes them, are ready in mere minutes. Because the fruit is uncooked, it provides maximum health benefits.

1	cup wild blueberry fruit spread	1	9" prebaked pie shell
¼	teaspoon ground cinnamon	¼	cup strawberry fruit spread
1½	pints fresh blueberries	6–8	large strawberries, hulled and cut
1½	teaspoons grated lemon zest		vertically into ¼" slices

1. In a medium saucepan, melt the blueberry spread with the cinnamon over medium heat. Off the heat, mix in the blueberries and lemon zest until the berries are coated. Spoon the berries into the crust.

2. Melt the strawberry spread in a small pot over medium heat. Mix the strawberries into the melted spread to coat them. Using a fork, arrange the glazed strawberries in a ring on top of the blueberry filling, placing them with the wide end against the edge of the crust and the point inward. Form an 8-pointed star in the center, with 4 slices pointing outward and add 4 smaller ones arranged on top of them. Serve within 1 hour of filling.

Makes 6 servings

Per serving: 310 calories, 7 g fat, 3 g saturated fat, 2 g protein, 61 g carbohydrates, 2 g fiber

BLUEBERRY PEACH CROSTATA

Use only blueberry jam.
Fruit spread does not seal
the crust.

FOOD FACT

Peaches are a good source
of vitamins A and C, potassium, and fiber, in addition
to carotenoids.

I am skeptical about frozen food, but frozen peaches taste better than most of the fresh ones available. (Unfortunately, this is true even during the summer.) To see for yourself, make this golden-crusted Italian tart. Leftovers, if there are any, are great for breakfast.

CRUST

1⅓	cups unbleached all-purpose flour
1	teaspoon grated lemon zest
¼	teaspoon salt
1	large egg
6	tablespoons unsalted butter, at room temperature
⅓	cup granulated sugar

FILLING

¼	cup fresh orange juice
3	tablespoons brown sugar
¼	teaspoon ground cinnamon
16	ounces frozen sliced peaches
¼	cup peach or apricot preserves, or fruit spread
1	cup fresh or frozen blueberries
¼	cup blueberry jam

1. Set a rack in the center of the oven. Preheat the oven to 350°F.

2. For the crust, place the flour, lemon zest, and salt in a mixing bowl, making a well in the center. Place the egg, butter, and granulated sugar in the well. Using a fork, lightly mix the egg, then gradually work the flour into the egg and butter until the mixture is crumbly. Rub the dough between your fingers for 2 minutes to blend the ingredients well. Press the dough into a ball and flatten it into a 5" × 1" disk on a sheet of waxed paper. Invert a bowl over the dough and let it rest for 30 minutes.

3. Roll out the dough between 2 sheets of waxed paper into an 11" disk. Removing 1 sheet of paper, fit the dough into a 9" loose-bottomed tart pan, fixing any tears with your fingers and bringing it three-quarters of the way up the sides. Line the crust with foil and weight it with dry beans.

4. Bake for 15 minutes. Remove the foil and bake 5 minutes longer, until it is just golden. Cool completely on a wire rack. Fill immediately or cover with foil and set the crust aside for up to 8 hours.

5. For the filling, combine the juice, brown sugar, and cinnamon in a medium skillet over medium-high heat, stirring until the sugar dissolves, 30 seconds. Add the peaches, cover, and cook 4 minutes. Uncover and cook until the fruit is translucent but still firm, 5 minutes longer. Reduce the heat. Pushing the fruit to 1 side, mix the preserves with the liquid, cooking until it melts, 1 minute. Add the blueberries and mix to glaze the fruit. Set aside to cool slightly, 10 minutes.

6. Coat the bottom of the crust with the blueberry jam. Spoon the warm fruit into the crust. Serve warm or at room temperature, within 2 hours.

Makes 6 servings

Per serving: 402 calories, 13 g fat, 7 g saturated fat, 5 g protein, 69 g carbohydrates, 3 g fiber

CHOCOLATE-CHERRY BREAD PUDDING

This sigh-inducing pudding is just the way I like dessert—intense but not too sweet. Served with warm Dark Cherry-Chocolate Sauce (page 266), it seems too decadent to include soy. I owe thanks to Chef Eddie Caereff at The Newsroom Café in West Hollywood, California, for the idea of using bananas and maple syrup for sweetening these individual puddings baked in a muffin tin.

1	1½-pound loaf challah or other egg bread	3	large eggs
¾	cup dried sour cherries	2	cups chocolate soymilk
2	small ripe bananas	½	cup maple syrup
2	tablespoons Dutch-process cocoa powder	1	teaspoon vanilla extract
			Dark Cherry-Chocolate Sauce (page 266)

1. Cut the bread into 1½"-thick slices. Trim off the crusts and cut the bread into 1½" cubes. There should be 8 cups. Place the bread in a large mixing bowl and add the cherries. Save any remaining bread and crusts for another use.

2. In another bowl, mash the bananas and cocoa together with a fork until smooth. Whisk in the eggs, soymilk, maple syrup, and vanilla until well combined. Pour the mixture over the bread and cherries and gently fold the 2 mixtures together with a rubber spatula to make sure the bread is evenly moistened. Set aside to soak for 30 minutes.

3. Preheat the oven to 350°F. Coat an 8-cup muffin tin with cooking spray.

4. Spoon the pudding into the prepared tin, filling the cups to just below the rim.

The riper the bananas, the sweeter the pudding and the more pronounced their flavor. I prefer bananas that are yellow all over and just beginning to show brown in the skin. They are still firm, so mashing them takes up to 4 minutes.

The crusts and leftover bread can be used to make a second, denser pudding. All the other ingredients are the same, but I bake this one in an 8" round cake pan. Eat it out of hand for breakfast and as a snack.

FOOD FACT

Arthritis sufferers say drinking sour cherry juice alleviates their pain, possibly because of anti-inflammatory anthocyanins. Researchers are currently investigating this claim.

5. Bake for 40 minutes, or until a toothpick inserted in the center comes out clean. Cool to lukewarm in the pan, then run a thin knife around the edge of each pudding to loosen it before unmolding.

6. To serve, spoon 2 tablespoons of the sauce in a ring on a dessert plate and place a warm pudding in the center. Or set the cooled puddings on a plate, cover with foil, and refrigerate up to 2 days. Let the puddings come to room temperature before serving with the warm sauce.

Makes 8 servings

Per serving: 429 calories, 8 g fat, 2 g saturated fat, 13 g protein, 76 g carbohydrates, 4 g fiber

DARK CHERRY-CHOCOLATE SAUCE

Cherry jam studded with plump Bing cherries adds intriguing flavor to this thick sauce and provides just enough sweetening to balance its dark chocolate edge. Depending on what the sauce accompanies, you can use orange marmalade or sour cherry jam instead. Use a chocolate with less than 70% chocolate if you prefer. Soymilk keeps down the fat so you can serve this sauce generously.

4	ounces bittersweet chocolate (70%), or dark chocolate, chopped	¼	cup black cherry fruit–sweetened spread
½	cup unsweetened plain soymilk	2	tablespoons light brown sugar
		¼	teaspoon vanilla extract

1. Place the chocolate in a small bowl.

2. Combine the soymilk, fruit spread, and sugar in a small, heavy saucepan and set it over medium-high heat. Cook, stirring with a wooden spoon, until the spread and sugar melt and bubbles begin to form around the edges of the pan, 4 minutes. Pour the hot milk mixture over the chocolate, add the vanilla, and stir until the chocolate melts and the sauce is thick and creamy. Serve warm. This sauce keeps, tightly covered in the refrigerator, for up to 3 days. To rewarm, set the container in a large bowl of boiling water to come halfway up the sides. Let it sit 4 minutes, then stir with a wooden spoon or a rubber spatula until the sauce is warm. Serve immediately.

Makes 1 cup

Per serving (2 tablespoons): 112 calories, 6 g fat, 3 g saturated fat, 2 g protein, 16 g carbohydrates, 1 g fiber

CHOCOLATE ANGEL FOOD CAKE

Cocoa powder gives this cake deep chocolate flavor and more body than the usual white angel cake. Serve with Dark Cherry-Chocolate Sauce (opposite page) or fresh berries.

1½	cups sugar, divided	1½	teaspoons cream of tartar
¾	cup unbleached all-purpose flour	¼	teaspoon salt
6	tablespoons Dutch-process cocoa	1½	teaspoons vanilla extract
10	large egg whites, or the equivalent, at room temperature		

1. Set a rack in the center of the oven. Preheat the oven to 350°F.

2. Sift half the sugar with the flour and cocoa.

3. In a large mixing bowl, beat the egg whites until frothy, using an electric mixer on medium speed. Add the cream of tartar and salt. Increase the speed to medium-high, beating until soft peaks form. Add the remaining sugar, 2 tablespoons at a time, mixing until incorporated before the next addition. When stiff peaks form, fold in the vanilla with a rubber spatula. Add the flour mixture in thirds, folding it in gently, adding the next third before the mixture is completely blended. Blend completely before turning the batter into an ungreased 10" tube pan. Run a knife through the batter to eliminate any air pockets.

4. Bake 45 minutes, or until a bamboo skewer inserted in the center comes out clean and the cake springs back when lightly pressed. Cool by hanging the inverted pan over the long neck of a wine bottle. When completely cool, run a metal spatula around the sides and turn the cake onto a plate. Wrap airtight in plastic for up to 3 days, until ready to serve.

Makes 12 servings

Per serving: 146 calories, 0 g fat, 0 g saturated fat, 4 g protein, 33 g carbohydrates, 1 g fiber

EGGS-TREME SUCCESS

To beat egg whites sky-high:

• Use older eggs.

• Separate eggs when cold, then bring them to room temperature.

• Make sure the bowl and beaters are immaculate. To do this, rinse them with white vinegar and salt, then hot water. Wipe them dry with a paper towel.

FOOD FACT

Natural cocoa may provide more antioxidants, but it produces a paler-looking cake than Dutch processed.

HOT CHOCOLATE SOUFFLÉS
WITH STRAWBERRY SALSA

I use only bittersweet (70%) chocolate for this recipe; you may get a softer, wetter soufflé using chocolate containing less chocolate liqueur.

FOOD FACT
Strawberries rank third among fresh berries for antioxidants.

Cakelike outside, like warm chocolate pudding inside, these little soufflés collapse quickly, so present them straight from the oven. (They are still heavenly, like flourless chocolate cake, if they fall.) Instead of a sauce, spoon Strawberry Salsa into each soufflé as you serve it.

1	tablespoon Dutch-process cocoa powder
3	tablespoons superfine sugar, divided
¾	cup warm Chocolate, Chocolate, Chocolate (page 270)
1	teaspoon vanilla extract
4	large egg whites

STRAWBERRY SALSA

4	large strawberries, hulled and finely chopped
1	teaspoon superfine sugar
1	teaspoon orange-flavored liquor, optional

1. Place a rack in the center of the oven. Preheat the oven to 400°F. Set a baking sheet on the rack.

2. Coat 4 1-cup soufflé dishes or heatproof custard cups with cooking spray. Combine the cocoa and 1 tablespoon of the sugar in a small bowl. Coat the inside of each soufflé dish with about 1 teaspoon of this mixture. Reserve the remaining cocoa mixture and set the prepared soufflé dishes aside.

3. Place the Chocolate, Chocolate, Chocolate in a mixing bowl. (If it has been refrigerated, warm it until molten in a medium saucepan over medium-low heat, or in the microwave, stirring occasionally.) Mix in the vanilla and set aside.

4. Beat the whites to soft peaks. Beat in the remaining sugar, 1 tablespoon at a time, mixing 15 seconds after each addition. When the whites form firm peaks but still look moist, use a rubber spatula to gently mix one-quarter of the whites into the chocolate. Scoop this mixture into the whites, and fold, leaving slight streaks to avoid collapsing the whites. Spoon the mixture into the prepared cups, filling them to within ½" of the top. Smooth

the tops with the back of a spoon. Holding a small knife vertically, use the tip to draw a circle ½" in from the side of the dish and 1" deep in each soufflé. Sprinkle the reserved cocoa mixture over the tops of the soufflés.

5. Bake for 15 minutes, until the soufflés are nicely puffed and the tops look dry.

6. Meanwhile, in a small bowl, combine the chopped berries, sugar, and liqueur, if using. Set aside for 10 minutes.

7. To serve the soufflés, use a large spoon to lift the tops and spoon one-quarter of the salsa into each one. Serve immediately.

Makes 4 servings

Per serving: 212 calories, 8 g fat, 4 g saturated fat, 7 g protein, 31 g carbohydrates, 3 g fiber

CHOCOLATE, CHOCOLATE, CHOCOLATE

This is chocoholic bliss. I first made this supernal blend of chocolate and cocoa as the base for hot and iced chocolate drinks, but found myself eating most of it off the spoon. Smooth as a truffle, it can be turned into seductive Hot Chocolate Soufflés (page 268) and is divine spread on toasted bread for Chocolate Bruschetta (page 274). Silk, soy coffee creamer, makes it more satiny than heavy cream and it contains no cholesterol.

SERENDIPITY

When I was 16, I thought the Frrrozen Hot Chocolate at Serendipity, a New York City institution, was the best thing I had ever eaten. Its secret is a base combining 20 or more kinds of the best-quality chocolate and cocoa. My version uses 4 kinds of premium bitter-sweet (70%) chocolate and 2 kinds of cocoa. Vary the brands according to your preference, but use only the finest.

FOOD FACT

Although chocolate is high in fat, it is a neutral kind of fat that does not elevate cholesterol levels the way saturated fat does.

2	tablespoons Dutch-process cocoa powder
2	tablespoons natural cocoa powder
¼	cup sugar
⅔	cup soy coffee creamer
2	ounces Scharffen Berger Bittersweet (70%) chocolate, chopped
2	ounces Dove Dark chocolate, in pieces
2	ounces Michel Cluizel Brut Amer (72%) chocolate, chopped
2	ounces Valrhona (72%) chocolate, chopped

1. Place the cocoa powders and sugar in the top of a double boiler. Add the creamer. Set the pot over simmering water, making sure no steam is escaping and heat, whisking, until the mixture is blended and smooth, 1 minute.

2. Add all the chocolate and stir until it is melted and the mixture is smooth and glossy, 5 minutes. Stored in a jar in the refrigerator, this base keeps for 2 weeks.

Makes 2 cups

Per serving (2 tablespoons): 87 calories, 5 g fat, 3 g saturated fat, 2 g protein, 12 g carbohydrates, 1 g fiber

THE ULTIMATE BITTERSWEET BROWNIE

I call these the ultimate brownie because they contain double the amount of chocolate used in the classic recipe, and all of it is deep, dark bittersweet. The result is a rich brownie with a shiny crust and fudge center.

8	ounces bittersweet (70%) or dark chocolate, coarsely chopped	1	cup sugar
			Pinch of salt
6	tablespoons unsalted butter	1	teaspoon vanilla extract
2	large eggs, at room temperature	⅓	cup unbleached all-purpose flour

1. Set a rack in the center of the oven. Preheat the oven to 350°F. Coat an 8" square light-colored metal baking pan with cooking spray and set aside.

2. Melt the chocolate and butter in a double boiler or the microwave. Cool the mixture to room temperature.

3. In a mixing bowl, beat the eggs with a hand mixer on medium until they are pale and doubled in volume, 2 minutes. Increase the speed to high. Gradually beat in the sugar, 2 tablespoons at a time, blending it in before the next addition. This should take 1 minute. Mix in the salt and vanilla. Continue beating until the batter has the consistency of soft whipped cream and leaves a trail that sits briefly on the surface when the beater is raised, 7 minutes. Decrease the speed to medium-low and mix in the cooled chocolate.

4. Sprinkle the flour over the batter. Using a rubber spatula, gently fold it in just until blended. Spread the batter evenly in the prepared pan.

5. Bake 35 minutes, or until the brownies are crusty on top and a toothpick inserted into the center comes out almost clean. Cool the brownies on a wire rack for 5 hours. Using a thin, sharp knife, cut the brownies into 16 squares.

Makes 16 brownies

Per brownie: 128 calories, 11 g fat, 6 g saturated fat, 2 g protein, 9 g carbohydrates, 1 g fiber

PATIENCE PAYS

Letting any dish made with chocolate rest overnight improves its flavor because the volatile compounds in the chocolate have time to meld and settle down.

CHOCOLATE-NUT BROWNIES

Loaded with cocoa, this all-American, cakelike brownie is light yet intense. Walnuts and chunks of chopped chocolate baked on top serve as an icing. A glass of milk won't find a better partner.

¾	cup natural cocoa, sifted	2	large eggs, lightly beaten
½	teaspoon baking soda	1	teaspoon vanilla extract
¼	teaspoon salt	1⅓	cups unbleached all-purpose flour
½	cup unsalted butter, melted	¾	cup walnuts
½	cup boiling water	2	ounces bittersweet (70%) or dark
1⅓	cups sugar		chocolate, chopped

1. Preheat the oven to 350°F. Coat a 9" square baking pan with cooking spray and set aside.

2. In a mixing bowl, whisk together the cocoa, baking soda, salt, butter, and the boiling water. Mix in the sugar, eggs, and vanilla. Fold in the flour until just combined with the wet ingredients. Spread the batter in the prepared pan and sprinkle the nuts and chocolate over the batter.

3. Bake for 30 minutes, or until a toothpick inserted in the center comes out clean. Cool completely on a wire rack. Cut into 16 squares. These brownies keep, wrapped in foil, for 3 days.

Makes 16 brownies

Per brownie: 215 calories, 12 g fat, 5 g saturated fat, 3 g protein, 29 g carbohydrates, 2 g fiber

CHOCOLATE BRUSCHETTA

FOOD FACT

Hazelnuts are high in monounsaturated fat, the same type that makes olive oil healthy.

After school, French children eat a *goûter*, buttered bread topped with chocolate. In French, *goûter* means "to spoil," and you will feel totally spoiled by this chocolate-lavished treat. I use *pane di casa* from a local Italian bakery, but any crusty bread with a light interior is good. Serve this with cappuccino, for breakfast as well as dessert.

4	(½"-thick) slices country-style white bread	4	teaspoons chopped roasted hazelnuts, or 4 large strawberries, hulled and thinly sliced
4	tablespoons Chocolate, Chocolate, Chocolate (page 270)		

1. Preheat the oven to 400°F.

2. Toast the bread directly on the oven rack for 5 minutes, turning it after 2 minutes. The slices should be crisp and golden to dark brown near the crust. Cool the toasted bread to lukewarm.

3. Spread 1 tablespoon of the chocolate on each slice of bread. Sprinkle with 1 teaspoon of the nuts or arrange the slices from 1 strawberry on the bread.

Makes 4 servings

Per serving: 132 calories, 5 g fat, 2 g saturated fat, 4 g protein, 21 g carbohydrates, 2 g fiber

CHOCOLATE-NUT CHEWIES

Glossy outside, fudgy inside, and studded with hazelnuts, these cookies are so good it is hard to believe nuts provide their only fat.

1	cup hazelnuts		Pinch of salt
3	cups confectioners' sugar	3	large egg whites, at room temperature
½	cup Dutch-process cocoa powder	1	cup coarsely chopped walnuts
2	tablespoons unbleached all-purpose flour		

1. Arrange racks in the upper and lower third of the oven. Preheat the oven to 350°F. Line 2 baking sheets with parchment paper and set aside.

2. Toast the hazelnuts until they are lightly colored and their skins have cracked, 10 minutes, stirring them 2 or 3 times so they toast evenly. Wrap the hot nuts in a dish towel and rub them together vigorously to remove any loose skin. Set the nuts aside to cool.

3. Combine the sugar, cocoa, flour, and salt in a mixing bowl. Beat in the egg whites one at a time using a hand mixer on medium speed. Scrape down the bowl. Increase the speed to high and beat 1 minute, until the batter resembles chocolate icing. Mix in the walnuts and toasted hazelnuts.

4. Drop the batter onto the prepared baking sheets, using 3 tablespoons for each cookie and leaving 3" between cookies.

5. Bake for 8 minutes. Switch the position of the pans in the oven and rotate them 180 degrees. Bake 7 minutes longer, until the cookies are shiny outside and slightly moist in the center. Cool the cookies on the baking sheets, then peel them off the parchment. These cookies keep up to 1 week in an airtight tin.

Makes 20 cookies

Per cookie: 156 calories, 8 g fat, 1 g saturated fat, 3 g protein, 21 g carbohydrates, 2 g fiber

Usually one avoids baking meringues on a damp day, but I first made these during a snowstorm and discovered that they are an exception, as they come out fine even on rainy days.

Giving credit where it is due, I found the original version of this recipe in the *New York Times.*

WALNUT CRISPS

These cookies with an elusive touch of cinnamon are perfect with fruit salad or a cup of espresso, and they make a delicious mid-afternoon nibble.

Air-cushioned baking sheets let these cookies brown nicely on the bottom without burning.

1	cup walnuts	¼	teaspoon ground cinnamon
1	large egg	⅛	teaspoon baking powder
½	cup dark brown sugar, packed		Pinch of salt
1½	tablespoons unbleached all-purpose flour		

1. Place racks in the upper and lower third of the oven. Preheat the oven to 350°F. Line 2 baking sheets with parchment paper.

2. In a food processor, finely chop the walnuts and set them aside.

3. In a mixing bowl, beat the egg, using a wooden spoon, until the yolk and white are blended. Stir in the sugar and beat vigorously until the mixture resembles grainy caramel, about 1 minute. Mix in the reserved nuts and stir in the flour, cinnamon, baking powder, and salt.

4. Using 2 spoons, drop the batter, 1 tablespoon at a time for large cookies or a heaping teaspoon for small ones, onto the prepared baking sheets, using 1 spoon to scrape the batter off the other. With the back of a spoon, flatten and smooth each cookie into rounds, leaving 2" between the large ones or 1½" between the smaller ones.

5. Bake the cookies 5 minutes. Switch the position of the pans in the oven and rotate them 180 degrees. Bake 5 to 8 minutes longer, or until the cookies are browned around the edges. The large cookies may still be slightly soft when they come out of the oven. They harden as they cool. Cool the cookies completely on the baking sheets, then lift them off the parchment.

Makes 24 large cookies

Per cookie: 55 calories, 3 g fat, 0 g saturated fat, 1 g protein, 6 g carbohydrates, 0 g fiber

Clockwise from right: Chocolate-Nut Chewies (page 275), Walnut Crisps (opposite page), Oatmeal-Raisin Cookies (page 279)

APPLE-SPICE BISCOTTI

Oats taste like toasted nuts in these cinnamon-accented biscotti.

FOOD FACT

Cup for cup, currants provide more fiber than raisins.

2	cups unbleached all-purpose flour	2	large eggs
2	teaspoons baking powder	½	teaspoon vanilla extract
¼	teaspoon ground cinnamon	½	cup old-fashioned rolled oats
⅛	teaspoon salt	⅔	cup finely chopped Golden Delicious apple
2	tablespoons unsalted butter, softened		
⅔	cup sugar	½	cup dried currants

1. Place a rack in the center of the oven. Preheat the oven to 350°F. Cover a baking sheet with parchment paper.

2. Combine the flour, baking powder, cinnamon, and salt in a bowl.

3. With an electric mixer, beat the butter and sugar together until they are fluffy, 1 minute. Add the eggs and beat until the mixture is pale yellow and has the thickness of stirred yogurt, 2 to 3 minutes. Add the vanilla, flour mixture, and oats, stirring until they are almost combined. Mix in the apple and currants.

4. Divide the stiff, sticky dough into 2 parts. Moistening your fingers lightly with cold water, smooth and shape each half into a 12" × 3" × ½" flattened log on the baking sheet.

5. Bake 25 minutes, or until the logs feel firm in the center and are lightly browned. Cool them on the pan for 10 minutes. On a cutting board, use a serrated knife to cut the logs into ½" slices. Stand the sliced biscotti on the baking sheet, nearly touching, in 2 or 3 rows. Bake for 20 to 25 minutes, or until the biscotti are dry. Cool them on the pan and store up to 1 week in an airtight container.

Makes 48 cookies

Per cookie: 45 calories, 1 g fat, 0 g saturated fat, 1 g protein, 8 g carbohydrates, 0 g fiber

OATMEAL-RAISIN COOKIES

Friends call this the posh oatmeal cookie. Rich as a Florentine, each golden cookie contains less than a half-teaspoon of butter. They also keep and ship well. To soften the butter quickly, divide it into a couple of pieces and knead it in your hand. When it is malleable, it is soft enough.

6	tablespoons unsalted butter, softened	1	cup all-purpose flour
1	cup sugar	1½	cups rolled oats
1	large egg, at room temperature	¾	teaspoon baking soda
1	tablespoon unsulfured molasses	½	teaspoon ground cinnamon
1	teaspoon vanilla extract	¾	cup raisins
1	teaspoon salt	¾	cup sliced almonds

1. Arrange racks in the upper and lower third of the oven. Preheat the oven to 350°F. Line 2 baking sheets with parchment paper and set aside.

2. In a mixing bowl, use an electric mixer on medium speed to cream the butter with the sugar until it is pale and fluffy, 2 minutes. Mix in the egg, molasses, vanilla, and salt. Using a rubber spatula, stir in the flour, oats, baking soda, and cinnamon until almost blended. Add the raisins and almonds, mixing gently until the ingredients are combined.

3. Drop the dough, 2 heaping tablespoons at a time (the size of a golf ball), onto the baking sheet, spacing them 3" apart. Flatten the cookies slightly.

4. Bake for 6 minutes. Switch the position of the pans in the oven and rotate them 180 degrees. Bake 5 minutes longer, or until the cookies are deep golden brown. Cool them for 1 minute on the pan, then transfer them to a wire rack and cool completely. The cookies become crisp as they cool. They keep for up to 2 weeks in an airtight container.

Makes 48 cookies

Per cookie: 67 calories, 2 g fat, 1 g saturated fat, 1 g protein, 10 g carbohydrates, 1 g fiber

WARM YOUR EGGS

Before cracking eggs, pastry chefs cover them in hot tap water and let them sit until slightly warm, about 20 minutes, so they will produce more volume in a recipe. Change the water once, if necessary.

FOOD FACT

Almonds contain more calcium and fiber than any other nut.

BLUEBERRY TURTLES

These chocolates melt on your fingers. Just lick them, then savor the juicy berries popping in your mouth through the hardened chocolate. This is a great recipe to make with kids, though it might get a bit messy.

4   ounces bittersweet chocolate
1   cup fresh blueberries, at room
        temperature

1. Cover a baking sheet with waxed paper.

2. Melt the chocolate in a mixing bowl in the microwave or over barely simmering hot water.

3. Mix the berries into the warm chocolate, stirring gently with a rubber spatula to coat them. With a fork, lift 6 to 8 of the berries and drop them in a cluster onto the waxed paper, nudging them into a nice shape. Scrape together any chocolate remaining in the bowl and drizzle it over the clusters.

4. Refrigerate until firm, about 45 minutes. Remove the clusters from the waxed paper and arrange them on a serving plate. Let them sit just until the chocolate loses its dull look, about 10 minutes. Serve immediately. Blueberry Turtles keep up to 24 hours, lightly covered with waxed paper in the refrigerator.

Makes 24 pieces

Per piece: 27 calories, 2 g fat, 1 g saturated fat, 0 g protein, 3 g carbohydrates, 1 g fiber

BLUEBERRY ICE

This deep, dark refresher is a speedy way to satisfy your sweet tooth while enjoying the phyto-feast in berries. Serve it as soon as it is whirled, as a luscious granita, or freeze it in a mold to eat as ice pops. Commercially frozen blueberries work better here than fresh ones you freeze at home. Use raspberry jam with or without seeds.

¾	cup frozen blueberries	1	tablespoon raspberry fruit spread or jam
½	cup frozen black cherries	¼	cup apple juice

Place the blueberries, cherries, fruit spread, and juice in a blender and whirl until they are blended into a fine slush. Pack the mixture into molds, insert sticks, and freeze. Or scoop it into dessert dishes and serve immediately.

Makes 4 servings

Per serving: 61 calories, 0 g fat, 0 g saturated fat, 1 g protein, 15 g carbohydrates, 1 g fiber

If making pops, the recipe can be multiplied up to 4 times. For more servings of granita, make it several times. If you simply make a larger batch, the slush at the bottom will melt before all the berries in a larger batch are pureed.

BROWN RICE CRISP TREATS

My recipe turns this well-loved, nutritionally dreadful confection into a delicious one made with whole grain, soy, and chocolate.

2	tablespoons unsalted butter	1	cup toasted brown rice cereal or whole
3	cups miniature marshmallows		grain flakes
	(½ of a 10-ounce bag)	½	cup salted roasted soynuts
2	cups crisp puffed brown rice cereal	2	ounces bittersweet chocolate, chopped

1. Coat an 8" square baking dish and a heat-resistant rubber spatula with cooking spray.

2. In a large saucepan over medium heat, melt the butter. Add the marshmallows and cook until they are melted but still look lumpy, about 3 minutes, stirring occasionally. Take the pot off the heat.

3. Using the coated spatula, stir in the cereals, nuts, and chocolate until they are combined with the marshmallow mixture. Work quickly so not all the chocolate melts.

4. Turn the sticky mixture into the prepared pan, smoothing and pressing it into an even layer. If it sticks to the spatula, use a little more cooking spray.

5. Refrigerate for 30 minutes, or until the treats are crisp. Using a sharp knife, cut into 16 squares. They will keep up to 2 weeks, stored in an airtight container with waxed paper between the layers.

Makes 16 squares

Per square: 94 calories, 4 g fat, 2 g saturated fat, 3 g protein, 14 g carbohydrates, 1 g fiber

Use Puffed Kashi, Uncle Sam's Flakes, or Grape-Nuts Flakes and an organic puffed rice cereal such as Erewhon. All of them are whole grain and have virtually no fat and little or no added sugar.

Use ½ cup raisins in place of the chocolate to increase fiber if you like.

WILD BLUEBERRY TRAIL MIX

Most trail mix strikes me as junk food pretending to be healthy. Here, you get lots of salty-sweet crunchies—including soynuts, almonds, and peanuts—sunflower seeds, dried blueberries, and crunchy cacao nibs for extra antioxidants, plus some sugar-coated chocolate candy such as M&M's.

½	cup Lemon-Blueberry Granola (page 294) or other granola	¼	cup salted peanuts
⅓	cup dried blueberries, preferably wild	¼	cup salted soynuts
¼	cup shelled almonds	2	tablespoons sunflower seeds
¼	cup sugar-coated chocolate candy, such as M&M's	2	tablespoons cacao nibs, optional

Combine all the ingredients in a bowl or plastic bag. Store in an airtight container.

Makes 1¼ cups

Per serving (¼ cup): 249 calories, 16 g fat, 3 g saturated fat, 10 g protein, 20 g carbohydrates, 5 g fiber

PRIMAL CHOCOLATE

Cacao nibs, crunchy bits of roasted cacao bean, are where chocolate-making begins. Their intense, faintly spicy, earthy flavor goes well with whole grains and nuts. They add a sophisticated touch to chocolate chip cookies and brownies. Also sprinkle them on Sweet Potato–Carrot Soup (page 80), as a garnish. You can find them—from Scharffen Berger, the American chocolate maker—at Whole Foods Markets and specialty food stores.

CHAPTER TWELVE

BREAKFASTS AND DRINKS

Breakfast *is* the most important meal of the day. It has been proved time and again that a healthy morning meal gives you more brain power, more even energy for the day, and fewer carbohydrate cravings later on. Good breakfast sets you up not just physically but emotionally, too. Feeling good, you head into the day better able to handle the rough spots.

A good breakfast does not have to be time-consuming, but it should include plenty of fiber to give you a jump-start toward the recommended 25 to 30 grams a day. Happily, many breakfast foods, including oatmeal, whole grain pancakes served with fiber-rich fresh and dried fruits, including berries and raisins, provide plenty of it.

Besides oatmeal, I like to have some protein at breakfast. This might be the lean poultry sausage, available now with no preservatives, or uncured bacon, particularly one with reduced fat (5 grams of fat per serving, 2 saturated). These are not everyday choices, but they make a nice occasional treat. Sometimes, I also enjoy having smoked salmon or nut butter on whole grain toast as part of my breakfast.

To keep oats interesting, here are 10 possibilities, including Muesli in a Glass, a terrific oat smoothie.

Fresh fruit goes with most breakfast dishes, so remember to include it on your cereal and, sliced, on top of toast. For pancakes, Apple Salsa will help. Blueberry Butter and Ginger-Tomato Marmalade are a couple of ways to serve fruit cooked. For drinks, there are many ways to enjoy blueberries and blueberry juice, especially the wild kind. The smoothies and fresh juices include some deliciously unexpected, nutrient-packed combinations that are good for an afternoon pickup, too.

Finally, considering it contains a little caffeine, have hot chocolate some mornings instead of coffee.

BEST EVERYDAY OATMEAL

Ready in 4 minutes, this is a lightly creamy oatmeal with substance. (The recipe can be doubled.) Instead of sugar, sweeten it with a generous topping of Maple-Walnut Crunch (opposite page).

⅓   cup low-fat (1%) milk or plain soymilk
⅛   teaspoon salt
½   cup quick oats (not instant)

Combine the milk and ⅔ cup cold water in a saucepan and bring the liquid to a boil. Add the salt. Gradually mix in the oats while stirring vigorously. Cook uncovered at a medium boil for 3 minutes. Off the heat, cover and set aside for 1 minute. Serve with Maple-Walnut Crunch (opposite page), raisins, dried blueberries, or brown sugar, as you prefer.

Makes 1 serving

Per serving: 204 calories, 5 g fat, 2 g saturated fat, 9 g protein, 30 g carbohydrates, 4 g fiber

MAPLE-WALNUT CRUNCH

Flax seeds bring a powerhouse of omega-3s and fiber to this versatile topper. Grinding them is essential for the body to utilize the fatty acids they contain. Sprinkle this topping over any cereal, hot or cold, or on warm toast spread with cream cheese.

1   cup walnuts

3   tablespoons flax seeds

¼   cup maple sugar

Maple sugar is costly but its flavor is worth the price, although you can use dark brown sugar in its place.

1. Preheat the oven to 350°F.

2. Spread the nuts in 1 layer on a baking sheet. Toast until they are fragrant and lightly colored, 10 minutes, stirring after 3 minutes and after 6 minutes so they toast evenly. Spread the nuts on a plate to cool.

3. Grind the flax seeds to a coarse meal in a clean coffee grinder or spice mill. Place them in a mixing bowl. Coarsely chop the walnuts or break them by hand into 4 or 5 pieces each, and add to the bowl with the flax. Mix in the maple sugar. Maple-Walnut Crunch keeps a week or more in the refrigerator in a tightly sealed jar.

Makes 1 cup

Per serving (1 tablespoon): 58 calories, 5 g fat, 0 g saturated fat, 1 g protein, 4 g carbohydrates, 1 g fiber

OLD-FASHIONED OATMEAL

This gutsy, chewy oatmeal should be made with the best quality thick-cut oats. It is good topped with cold milk or soymilk, and served with raisins or dried blueberries and chopped nuts. My own favorite toppings are dried currants and a sprinkling of *furikake*, a combination of sesame seeds and nori flakes, which the Japanese use on rice (see page 50).

⅛   *teaspoon salt*
½   *cup old-fashioned rolled oats*

In a saucepan, bring 1½ cups cold water to a boil. Gradually mix in the oats while stirring vigorously. Cook uncovered at a medium boil for 16 minutes. Off the heat, cover and set aside for 1 minute. Serve with a pat of butter and sprinkling of dark brown sugar, raisins or dried cranberries, and chopped walnuts—or any of the toppings suggested above.

Makes 1 serving

Per serving: 154 calories, 3 g fat, 0 g saturated fat, 6 g protein, 27 g carbohydrates, 4 g fiber

APPLE-CINNAMON PORRIDGE

Cooking Scotch or Irish steel-cut oats with apple cider, fresh apple, and cinnamon adds natural sweetness. These very American flavors are particularly good with the earthier one of steel-cut oats, as well as with old-fashioned oats.

½	cup steel-cut oats	½	Golden Delicious apple, peeled and
1	cup apple cider		shredded
1¼	cups low-fat (1%) milk or soymilk	¼	teaspoon ground cinnamon
	Pinch of salt		Buttermilk or vanilla yogurt, optional

1. In a heavy, dry skillet over medium heat, toast the oats until they are fragrant, 3 to 4 minutes, stirring constantly. Set aside.

2. Combine the cider and milk in a saucepan. Set the pot over medium-high heat until the liquid is boiling around the edges. Add the salt. While stirring, gradually mix in the toasted oats. Mix in the apple and cinnamon. Cook uncovered until the oats are cooked, about 30 minutes. Serve immediately, accompanied by cold buttermilk or vanilla yogurt, if desired.

Makes 2 servings

Per serving: 315 calories, 5 g fat, 2 g saturated fat, 11 g protein, 57 g carbohydrates, 6 g fiber

SCOTCH OATS
WITH WALNUT HONEY

This is oatmeal made the way they do it in the old country, cooked with water and salt. The Scots serve it with cold buttermilk on the side, dipping the hot cereal by the spoonful into the cold milk as they eat it. This canny method keeps the cereal hot and the milk cold, so you enjoy the contrast with every spoonful. Probably, though, you will prefer to top your oats with citrus-perfumed Walnut Honey and cold milk or soymilk.

¼	teaspoon salt		Walnut Honey (opposite page)
½	cup steel-cut oats	1	cup cold buttermilk, optional

1. Bring 2 cups cold water to a boil in a medium saucepan. Add the salt. While stirring, slowly sprinkle in the oats so the water continues to boil. Cook uncovered until the oats are tender, 30 minutes, reducing the heat if necessary to maintain a steady, gentle boil.

2. To serve, divide the hot oatmeal between 2 deep bowls. Spoon 2 table-spoons Walnut Honey over each serving. Pour the buttermilk into a smaller, shallow bowl, if using.

Makes 2 servings

Per serving: 310 calories, 8 g fat, 2 g saturated fat, 7 g protein, 54 g carbohydrates, 6 g fiber

WALNUT HONEY

Your inner Pooh will sigh over this nutty honey drizzled on hot oatmeal.

1 cup blueberry or wildflower honey	1 tablespoon grated lemon zest
1 cup walnuts	

Warm the honey in a small saucepan over medium heat until it liquefies, 4 minutes. Stir in the nuts and zest and pour into a container. Covered tightly, it will keep at room temperature for a few weeks.

Makes 1½ cups

Per serving (2 tablespoons): 140 calories, 5 g fat, 1 g saturated fat, 1 g protein, 25 g carbohydrates, 1 g fiber

WILD BLUEBERRY OATMEAL

It's not just the berries that are wild here. Baking buttered toasted oats with the berries makes a deep purple, chewy hot cereal like none you've had. A brilliant change for daily oatmeal eaters, this cereal has been declared irresistible even by dedicated oatmeal-haters. The preparation takes less time than making pancakes or French toast. The firmer texture of wild blueberries is just right. I particularly like this oatmeal served with a dollop of vanilla yogurt.

1	(10-ounce) bag frozen wild blueberries	2	tablespoons unsalted butter, cut in
½	cup blueberry fruit spread		pieces
1½	cups blueberry juice	4	teaspoons sugar
1	teaspoon ground cinnamon	1	teaspoon grated lemon zest
	Pinch of salt		Vanilla yogurt, optional
1½	cups old-fashioned rolled oats		

1. Place a rack in the center of the oven. Set a baking sheet on the rack. Preheat the oven to 350°F. Coat 4 2-cup soufflé dishes with cooking spray or coat them lightly with oil. Set them aside.

2. Combine the blueberries, fruit spread, juice, cinnamon, and salt in a medium saucepan. Cook over medium-high heat until the mixture comes to a boil. Stir to dissolve the fruit spread and set aside.

3. Toast the oats in a dry, medium cast-iron or other heavy skillet over medium-high heat, stirring constantly with a wooden spoon. When the oats are fragrant and start to color, 3 minutes, remove the pan from the heat. Push the oats to 1 side. Add the butter to the other side of the pan, stirring to help it melt. Mix the oats with the butter until they are coated. Spoon one-quarter of the oats into each of the prepared dishes.

4. Pour the berry mixture over the oats. Stir 2 or 3 times. Cover each dish with aluminum foil to seal it.

BLUEBERRY BOOST

Blueberry juice is another way to benefit from the antioxidants in blueberries. It can be unsweetened and solely blueberry, or it may contain a blend of blueberry and other fruit juices for added sweetness, so read the label to see what you are getting. For cooking, you may want to add more blueberry fruit spread when using juice that is straight blueberry.

5. Place the soufflé dishes on the baking sheet in the oven. Bake 40 to 45 minutes, until the oatmeal is cooked but still slightly chewy. Uncover the dishes.

6. Combine the sugar and lemon zest in a small bowl. Sprinkle the mixture over the hot oatmeal and let it sit 10 minutes to cool slightly before serving. Pass a bowl with the yogurt, if desired.

Makes 4 servings

Per serving: 323 calories, 8 g fat, 4 g saturated fat, 6 g protein, 60 g carbohydrates, 6 g fiber

LEMON-BLUEBERRY GRANOLA

When *Cooks Illustrated* magazine asked me to write about granola, I made it 23 times to get the best recipe. The winner called for toasting the oats and sweetening them lightly. Here, cardamom intensifies their warm taste even more. The only fat in this cereal comes from nuts and a bit of coconut. Besides serving granola at breakfast, snack on it in Wild Blueberry Trail Mix (page 283).

½	cup blanched almonds, halved	2	tablespoons unhulled sesame seeds
½	cup chopped walnuts	¼	cup blueberry or mesquite honey
2	cups old-fashioned rolled oats	2	teaspoons grated lemon zest
½	cup unsweetened shredded coconut	⅛	teaspoon ground cardamom
¼	cup raw sunflower seeds	⅔	cup dried blueberries

1. Preheat the oven to 325°F.

2. Stirring frequently with a wooden spoon, toast the almonds and walnuts in a large, cast-iron or other heavy skillet over medium heat until they just begin to color, 3 minutes. Mix in the oats and coconut and toast until the oats color slightly, 2 minutes, continuing to stir often. Add the sunflower and sesame seeds and continue cooking, stirring constantly until the mixture turns an even beige, 45 seconds. Off the heat, mix in the honey, lemon zest, and cardamom until all the ingredients are thoroughly coated.

3. Spread the mixture on a 10" × 15" jelly-roll pan, making an even layer. Bake for 5 minutes. Stir and respread the granola. Bake 5 minutes longer. Repeat once more, baking the granola until it is light brown, another 5 minutes. Mix in the blueberries and spread the hot granola on a baking sheet to stop the cooking. Cool it to room temperature. This granola keeps 2 weeks stored in an airtight container.

Makes 5½ cups

Per serving (½ cup): 124 calories, 7 g fat, 2 g saturated fat, 3 g protein, 14 g carbohydrates, 2 g fiber

The thick rolled oats sometimes called old-fashioned are essential for crunchy granola.

Natural food stores sell coconut without sulfites.

FOOD FACT
Sunflower seeds are rich in vitamin B-1 (thiamin).

CREAM OF OAT BRAN

Thick and rich, this hot cereal is like old-fashioned cream of wheat, but with nutty flavor and 5 grams of fiber to a bowl. The recipe can be doubled.

½   cup reduced-fat (2%) milk or plain
       soymilk
      Pinch of salt
⅓   cup oat bran

Combine the milk and ½ cup cold water in a saucepan and bring to a boil. Add the salt. Gradually mix in the bran while stirring vigorously. Cook uncovered at a medium boil for 3 minutes, stirring constantly. Off the heat, cover and set aside for 1 minute. Serve with a sprinkling of brown sugar or cinnamon.

Makes 1 serving

Per serving: 137 calories, 5 g fat, 2 g saturated fat, 9 g protein, 26 g carbohydrates, 5 g fiber

OAT BRAN MUESLI

Including oat bran and other healthy ingredients, this 1-bowl breakfast is like a bright morning pudding, especially with the whole wheat cereal, apple, and dried fruit. This muesli is easily portable and also makes a good quick lunch or afternoon snack.

½ cup old-fashioned rolled oats

⅓ cup sliced almonds

2 tablespoons oat bran

1 tablespoon sunflower seeds

¼ teaspoon salt

¼ cup chopped dates

¼ cup chopped Calimyrna figs

½ cup Grape-Nuts, or whole wheat flake cereal

1 Gala apple, peeled and coarsely shredded

1½ cups low-fat plain yogurt

In a mixing bowl, combine the oats, nuts, bran, sunflower seeds, salt, dates, figs, and cereal. Mix in the apple. Stir in the yogurt. Cover and refrigerate overnight. This muesli keeps for 2 days, tightly covered in the refrigerator.

Makes 4 servings

Per serving: 280 calories, 8 g fat, 2 g saturated fat, 11 g protein, 44 g carbohydrates, 6 g fiber

Using a quality brand of oats and oat bran like McCanns or Bob's Red Mill, which have the best flavor, will reflect in the taste of this dish.

FOOD FACT

Two dried figs contain more than 3 grams of fiber.

MUESLI IN A GLASS

This drinkable breakfast tastes like a bowl of cinnamon oatmeal. Kids who hate oatmeal go for it served this way. Pour it into a mug and take it on the road.

¼	cup raisins	½	cup unsweetened plain or vanilla soymilk
¼	cup quick-cooking rolled oats (not instant)	½	cup unsweetened applesauce
2	tablespoons walnuts	½	teaspoon ground cinnamon
2	tablespoons flax seeds	6	ice cubes

1. In a small bowl, combine the raisins, oats, nuts, flax seeds, and soymilk. Cover and refrigerate overnight.

2. Place the soaked oat mixture in a blender, add the applesauce, cinnamon, and ice cubes and blend until almost smooth. Pour into a large glass and serve immediately.

Makes 1 serving

Per serving: 479 calories, 18 g fat, 2 g saturated fat, 14 g protein, 79 g carbohydrates, 12 g fiber

FOOD FACT

Flax seed is loaded with fiber, omega-3 fatty acids, and phytoestrogens.

FRENCH TOAST WITH HIDDEN BLUEBERRIES

Usually, stuffed French toast has a filling sandwiched between slices of bread. Instead, I remove the center of the bread, combine it with berries, and put it back, creating the surprise of blueberries *in* your French toast.

FOOD FACT

Semolina flour, ground from high-protein durum wheat, has more fiber than white flour.

1	*(1-pound) loaf Italian semolina bread, with or without sesame seeds*	1	*tablespoon citrus liqueur such as Grand Marnier, Triple Sec, or*
½	*cup fresh or frozen blueberries*		*1 teaspoon grated lemon zest*
3	*large eggs*	1	*teaspoon vanilla extract*
1	*cup vanilla soymilk*	3	*tablespoons melted unsalted butter or canola oil*
			Warm maple syrup

1. Cut the bread diagonally into 1" slices, discarding the ends. Carefully pull the center from each slice, leaving about ½" of bread inside the crust. Set aside the rings of crusts. Tear the centers into ½" pieces and place them in a mixing bowl. Add the blueberries.

2. In another bowl, whisk the eggs with the soymilk, liqueur or zest, and vanilla. Pour half this mixture over the torn bread and blueberries. Add the crust rings to the remaining egg mixture. Toss gently.

3. Heat half the butter or oil in a large, heavy skillet over medium-high heat. Arrange the soaked bread rings in the pan. Spoon the moistened bread and berry mixture into the center of each ring, pressing with the back of the spoon to pack it firmly. Cook until the toast is browned on the bottom, 3 to 4 minutes. With a spatula, turn and brown the second side. Remove to a platter, and repeat until all the bread has been cooked. Serve with warm maple syrup.

Makes 4 servings

Per serving: 490 calories, 17 g fat, 8 g saturated fat, 16 g protein, 64 g carbohydrates, 4 g fiber

BUCKWHEAT OAT BRAN
PANCAKES WITH APPLE SALSA

FOOD FACT

Buckwheat flour is nearly as high in fiber as oat bran.

I first ate these substantial yet light wheat-free pancakes at a bed-and-breakfast in Great Barrington, Massachusetts. I added the fruit salsa and the extra flourish of plain yogurt mixed with vanilla extract. The mellow sweetness of the vanilla is just right with the unsweetened yogurt.

½	cup buckwheat flour	2	tablespoons walnut or canola oil
½	cup oat bran	1	large egg
1	teaspoon baking powder	½	teaspoon unsalted butter
¼	teaspoon salt		Apple Salsa (opposite page)
¼	cup defrosted orange juice concentrate	½	cup low-fat plain yogurt, optional
		½	teaspoon vanilla extract, optional

1. In a mixing bowl, combine the buckwheat flour, oat bran, baking powder, and salt. In a measuring cup or a second bowl, whisk together the orange juice concentrate, oil, and egg until well blended. Pour the liquid ingredients into the dry ingredients and mix with a whisk to combine them. The batter will be quite thick.

2. Heat a griddle or large, heavy skillet over medium-high heat. Add the butter, spreading it with a paper towel to lightly coat the pan. Pour a scant ¼ cup of batter onto the griddle for each pancake, spreading it into 5" rounds. When the top is covered with small bubbles and dry looking, 3 minutes, flip the pancakes and cook on the other side until dark brown. Serve immediately or keep the finished pancakes in a 200°F oven while making the rest of the batch. Serve topped with Apple Salsa. Add a dollop of the yogurt mixed with the vanilla, if desired.

Makes 4 servings (eight 5" pancakes)

Per pancake: 95 calories, 5 g fat, 1 g saturated fat, 3 g protein, 13 g carbohydrates, 2 g fiber

APPLE SALSA

Chunky and perfumed with honey, this fruit salsa makes a nice change from syrup on pancakes. Feel free to use blueberries or other fruit in place of the orange, and vary the kind of honey, depending on the pancakes.

1	Fuji apple, peeled, cored, and chopped	3	tablespoons dried currants
1	small navel orange, peeled and chopped	20	whole almonds, coarsely chopped
		2	tablespoons orange blossom honey

Combine the apple, orange, currants, and nuts in a mixing bowl. Mix in the honey until the fruit and nuts are coated. Use immediately or cover tightly and refrigerate up to 12 hours.

Makes 2 cups

Per serving (¼ cup): 71 calories, 2 g fat, 0 g saturated fat, 1 g protein, 13 g carbohydrates, 2 g fiber

CHOCOLATE PANCAKES

Chocolate for breakfast feels decadent in these cocoa-and-soymilk pancakes. Fresh strawberries are the perfect accompaniment. Add maple syrup, if you wish. This batter also makes crisp waffles.

1	cup unbleached all-purpose flour	1½	cups plain soymilk
2	tablespoons soy flour		Pinch of salt
¾	cup Dutch-process cocoa powder		Confectioners' sugar
2	teaspoons baking powder	1	pint fresh strawberries, hulled and
2	tablespoons granulated sugar		sliced, optional
3	large eggs		
3	tablespoons melted unsalted butter or canola oil		

1. Sift the all-purpose and soy flours, cocoa, and baking powder into a medium bowl. Mix in the granulated sugar. In another bowl, whisk the eggs with the butter or oil, soymilk, and salt until well combined. Add the wet ingredients to the dry mixture, mixing just until they are blended. The mixture should be slightly lumpy and have the consistency of cake batter.

2. Coat a medium, cast-iron skillet with cooking spray or use a nonstick pan. Place the pan over medium-high heat. Ladle a scant ¼ cup batter for each pancake into the pan. Cook until bubbles form on the surface and the edges darken, about 2 minutes. Turn and cook until the pancake resists slightly when gently pressed in the center with your finger, about 2 minutes. Repeat until all the batter is used up, keeping the cooked pancakes covered and warm in a 200°F oven until they are all ready to serve. Dust lightly with confectioners' sugar, and serve accompanied by sliced strawberries, if you wish.

Makes 5 servings (15 5" pancakes)

Per pancake: 84 calories, 2 g fat, 1 g saturated fat, 4 g protein, 12 g carbohydrates, 2 g fiber

BLUEBERRY BUTTER

Apple butter is common, but you have probably never seen blueberry butter. Making it takes about as much effort as cooking a bowl of old-fashioned oatmeal. You can even whip up a batch while doing the dinner dishes so it is ready to serve the next morning. Use cultivated berries; wild ones produce a gritty texture. Spread Blueberry Butter on toast or Scottish Oatmeal Scones (page 218), add it to yogurt, or eat it right off the spoon.

1	(10-ounce) bag unsweetened frozen blueberries	½	cup brown sugar, packed
½	Crispin apple, peeled, cored, and chopped	1	(4") cinnamon stick
		1	whole clove

1. Combine the blueberries, apple, sugar, cinnamon, and clove in a medium saucepan. Cover and bring to a boil over medium-high heat. Reduce the heat as needed to prevent boiling over, and cook until the fruit is very soft, 20 minutes. Remove the cinnamon stick, but do not worry about fishing out the clove. It gets ground up in the blender.

2. Pour the contents of the pan into a blender and puree until almost smooth. Rinse out the pan.

3. Return the pureed fruit to the pan. Cook, stirring with a wooden spoon frequently to reduce spattering and avoid sticking, until it is thick enough to show the bottom of the pan when stirred, 10 minutes.

Makes 1¼ cups

Per serving (2 tablespoons): 46 calories, 0 g fat, 0 g saturated fat, 0 g protein, 12 g carbohydrates, 1 g fiber

GINGER-TOMATO MARMALADE

Botanically a fruit, tomatoes are used so much in savory dishes that one easily forgets about their natural sweetness. The tomato skins, left on here since they contain so many vital phytonutrients, produce a texture that reminds me of marmalade. Be forewarned that this jam packs a gingery punch. Serve it with cottage cheese, and use it on sandwiches as well as on toast.

2	pounds plum tomatoes, seeded and chopped	1	navel orange
			Juice of ½ lemon
1	medium Crispin or Golden Delicious apple, peeled, cored, and finely chopped	⅔	cup brown sugar, firmly packed
		½	teaspoon ground ginger

Place the tomatoes and apple in a medium saucepan. Grate 2 teaspoons of zest from the orange, and squeeze out the juice. Add them to the tomatoes and apple. Add the lemon juice, sugar, and ginger. Cook, stirring occasionally, until the jam is thick enough to plop, 40 to 45 minutes. Off the heat, stir vigorously to give the jam a pulpy texture. Spoon it into glass jars or a plastic container, seal, and cool to room temperature. The marmalade keeps, tightly covered in the refrigerator, for 1 month.

Makes 2 cups

Per serving (2 tablespoons): 50 calories, 0 g fat, 0 g saturated fat, 1 g protein, 13 g carbohydrates, 1 g fiber

OH MY GOD! HOT CHOCOLATE

The name may seem extreme, but when people taste it, that's what they say. Hot chocolate does not get any richer or more decadent than this one cup. Using soymilk actually makes it creamier than dairy milk, and you get zero cholesterol, too. You can make up to 6 cups at a time simply by multiplying the recipe.

⅓   cup Chocolate, Chocolate, Chocolate (page 270)

¾   cup vanilla soymilk

1   (6"–8") cinnamon stick, optional, for garnish

Combine the chocolate and soymilk in a saucepan. Set the pot over medium heat and cook, whisking slowly, until the chocolate and milk are blended and hot. Pour the hot chocolate into a mug. Serve garnished with a long cinnamon-stick stirrer, if desired.

Makes 1 serving

Per serving: 201 calories, 11 g fat, 4 g saturated fat, 7 g protein, 25 g carbohydrates, 2 g fiber

FROZEN HOT CHOCOLATE

This frozen chocolate slush is my version of the world-famous Frrrozen Hot Chocolate served in an immense ice-cream parlor goblet at Serendipity in New York City. It is a grown-up drink, even though drinking it will make you feel like a well-indulged child. Advance planning is necessary, but the steps are easy.

> *Ice cubes*
> *Oh My God! Hot Chocolate*
>   *(opposite page)*
> 1   *tablespoon grated chocolate*

1. Fill a 10-ounce glass with ice. Pour 1 serving of the hot chocolate over it.

2. When the ice melts, pour the chilled chocolate into an ice cube tray, using all the compartments. Freeze until hard. If desired, store the frozen cubes in a plastic bag for up to 1 week. For multiple servings, you can make all the hot chocolate at once, but use a separate ice cube tray for each serving.

3. Place the frozen chocolate cubes in a blender and whirl until they are an icy slush.

4. To serve, fill a large wine glass three-quarters full with the slush. Immediately top with grated chocolate and serve.

Makes 1 serving

Per serving: 201 calories, 12 g fat, 7 g saturated fat, 3 g protein, 19 g carbohydrates, 3 g fiber

WILD BLUEBERRY LEMONADE

A combination of fresh lemon juice and lemon peel with the pith gives this iced drink the quintessence of lemon. Blueberry juice adds a deep rosy blush. For the blueberry juice, I prefer using a fruit-sweetened blend because it is sweeter than pure blueberry juice.

Strain the lemon juice, pressing to eliminate the seeds but keep most of the pulp.

1	cup lemon juice, about 6 large lemons	1	cup wild blueberry juice
½	lemon, preferably organic, cut in 16 pieces	12	ice cubes, about 2 cups + additional for serving
¾	cup superfine sugar	4	mint sprigs, optional, for garnish

1. Place the lemon juice, lemon pieces, and sugar in a blender. Add the blueberry juice and 12 ice cubes. Whirl on high speed until the lemonade is frothy and looks creamy.

2. Fill four 12-ounce glasses halfway with the additional ice cubes. Fill with the lemonade. Garnish with the mint, if using. Serve immediately.

Makes 4 servings

Per serving: 174 calories, 0 g fat, 0 g saturated fat, 0 g protein, 46 g carbohydrates, 0 g fiber

BLUE MOON SMOOTHIE

The tropical flavor of this smoothie can take you to that island you dream about once in a blue moon.

½   frozen banana, sliced
½   cup frozen diced papaya

⅓   cup frozen blueberries
¾   cup blood orange juice

In a blender, combine the banana, papaya, blueberries, and blood orange juice. Blend until smooth. Serve immediately.

Makes 1 serving

Per serving: 227 calories, 1 g fat, 0 g saturated fat, 3 g protein, 57 g carbohydrates, 5 g fiber

WILD BLUEBERRY–BUTTERMILK REFRESHER

If you use cultivated blueberries, add a tablespoon of blueberry jam to intensify the flavor. This recipe can be doubled.

¾   cup fresh or frozen wild blueberries
½   frozen banana, sliced
¾   cup buttermilk

1   tablespoon honey
3 or 4 grinds of black pepper optional
Mint sprig, optional, for garnish

In a blender, combine the blueberries, banana, buttermilk, honey, and pepper, if using. Blend until smooth. Garnish with a mint sprig, if desired, and serve immediately.

Makes 1 serving

Per serving: 253 calories, 2 g fat, 1 g saturated fat, 7 g protein, 56 g carbohydrates, 5 g fiber

BLUEBERRY BUZZ

The buzz in this brisk cooler comes from ginger.

¾ cup frozen blueberries
1 cup frozen cubed watermelon
½ cup unfiltered apple juice

2 teaspoons minced ginger
Juice of ½ lemon

In a blender, combine the blueberries, watermelon, apple juice, ginger, and
lemon juice. Blend until smooth. Serve immediately.

Makes 1 serving

Per serving: 252 calories, 2 g fat, 1 g saturated fat, 7 g protein, 55 g carbohydrates, 5 g fiber

WATERMELON-BLUEBERRY SLURPY

This frosty slush is most refreshing on a hot day.

1 cup frozen cubed seedless red
   watermelon
¾ cup frozen blueberries

2 teaspoons finely chopped fresh ginger
½ cup unfiltered apple juice
Juice of ½ lime

In a blender, combine the watermelon, berries, ginger, apple juice, and
lime juice. Blend until pureed and still slightly pulpy. Pour into a wide
glass and serve with a spoon.

Makes 1 serving

Per serving: 192 calories, 2 g fat, 0 g saturated fat, 2 g protein, 47 g carbohydrates, 6 g fiber

SIPPIN' SALSA

This sizzling drink gets its swagger from chile pepper and raw onion. Control its heat by the size of the chile pepper you use. If you do not have a juicer, using a blender turns this piquant drink into a savory smoothie. Either way, spike it with tequila, if you like.

6	*large plum tomatoes, quartered lengthwise*	1	*jalapeño chile pepper, halved and seeded*
½	*small yellow onion, halved lengthwise*		*Juice of 1 lime*
10–12	*cilantro sprigs*		*Salt*
		2	*large scallions, for garnish*

1. Place 2 tall glasses in the freezer to chill.

2. Juice the tomatoes, onion, cilantro, and jalapeño pepper, feeding a few pieces of each alternately into the machine. Add the lime juice. Season the juice to taste with salt. Refrigerate until well chilled, at least 2 hours.

3. To serve, mix until the pink pulpy top and clear bottom liquid are recombined. Check and adjust the seasoning. Divide the drink between the 2 chilled glasses. For garnish, trim the bottoms of the scallions, and cut the green tops off so the scallions stick up 3" or 4" above the rim of the glass. Add a scallion to each glass. Serve immediately.

Makes 2 servings

Per serving: 67 calories, 1 g fat, 0 g saturated fat, 2 g protein, 15 g carbohydrates, 4 g fiber

GREEN GODDESS

This light, bright-emerald juice is pleasantly mild and slightly sweet, especially if you use flat-leaf spinach.

3½	*ounces spinach (⅓ bunch)*	3	*large kale leaves*
2	*ribs celery, with leaves*	1	*teaspoon fresh lime juice*
10	*flat-leaf parsley sprigs*		

In an electric juicer, juice the spinach, celery, parsley, and kale, in that order. Mix in the lime juice and serve immediately.

Makes 1 serving

Per serving: 15 calories, 0 g fat, 0 g saturated fat, 3 g protein, 2 g carbohydrates, 0 g fiber

GOLDEN GLOW

The color of a Hawaiian sunset, this juice is sweet with a tropical taste.

1	*medium Garnet, Jewel, or Beauregard yam*	¾	*cup diced cantaloupe*
1	*large carrot*	1	*tablespoon frozen orange juice concentrate*
½	*Fuji apple*		

In an electric juicer, juice the yam, carrot, apple, and melon, in that order. Mix in the orange juice concentrate and serve immediately.

Makes 1 serving

Per serving: 135 calories, 1 g fat, 0 g saturated fat, 2 g protein, 30 g carbohydrates, 0 g fiber

Clockwise from right: Ruby Zinger (opposite page), Golden Glow (page 313), Green Goddess (page 313)

RUBY ZINGER

Sparkling in color and taste, this juice is tangy, with a hint of earthiness and a ginger buzz. Stay with these proportions so the beet does not overpower the other ingredients.

1	*medium beet (5 ounces)*		1	*(2½") piece of ginger (1½ ounces)*
3	*ripe plum tomatoes*		⅛	*teaspoon salt*
1½	*cups diced pineapple*			

In an electric juicer, juice the beet, tomatoes, pineapple, and ginger, in that order. Mix in the salt and serve immediately.

Makes 2 servings

Per serving: 103 calories, 0 g fat, 0 g saturated fat, 2 g protein, 24 g carbohydrates, 0 g fiber

GLOSSARY

The following terms relate to phytochemicals, vitamins, minerals, and other substances that the 12 Best Foods, as well as the other ingredients used in these recipes, provide.

Allicin—The active sulfur compound found in garlic that plays a role in cancer prevention and heart disease.

Alpha lipoic acid—One of the three antioxidants the body produces (the other two are coenzyme Q_{10} and glutathione), alpha lipoic acid is important to help boost glutathione levels. Good food sources include spinach, broccoli, and tomatoes.

Anthocyanins—The red, purple, and blue pigments found in fruits and vegetables. These antioxidant flavonoids help prevent cancer and heart disease and may improve memory. Sources include berries, cherries, red cabbage, red grapes and wine, and red onions.

Antioxidants—Substances that protect the body from oxidation, a natural process that creates harmful molecules called free radicals that accelerate aging and lead to disease. Antioxidants neutralize free radicals and minimize the cellular damage they cause.

Arginine—An amino acid that plays a role in maintaining the vascular system by helping to keep blood vessel walls relaxed and smooth, promoting increased blood flow.

Beta-carotene—A pigment found in dark leafy greens and deep-orange fruits and vegetables. Beta-carotene is a precursor to vitamin A. This antioxidant and carotenoid helps to reduce the risk of cancer and heart disease. Good sources include carrots, sweet potatoes, pumpkin, apricots, cantaloupe, spinach, kale, red bell peppers, and chile peppers.

Betaine—This derivative of choline plays a role in reducing elevated blood levels of homocysteine that can lead to atherosclerosis and stroke. Good sources of betaine include wheat bran, wheat germ, whole wheat bread, spinach, and cooked beets.

Caffeic acid—A cancer-blocking phenolic acid. Sources include apples, artichokes, blueberries, citrus fruits, sour cherries, and spinach.

Calcium—A mineral essential for formation of bones and teeth, nerve and muscular function (including the heart), blood pressure, and blood clotting. Vitamin D helps the body absorb calcium, and together they aid in preventing osteoporosis, heart disease, and stroke. Good sources of calcium include dairy products, canned sardines and salmon with bones, collards, mustard greens, broccoli, and soybeans.

Carotenoids—Red, orange, and yellow pigments found in fruits and vegetables. They include alpha- and beta-carotene, beta-cryptoxanthin, lutein, lycopene, and zeaxanthin. These plant pigments, also called phytochemicals, help to reduce the risk of cancer and protect against heart disease and age-related macular degeneration. Good sources include carrots, sweet potatoes, winter squash, yellow corn, tomatoes, apricots, peaches, pink grapefruit, watermelon, and dark-green vegetables such as kale, collards, and spinach, in which chlorophyll masks their color.

Catechins—A type of flavonoid found in green tea, black tea, red wine, grapes, and chocolate. This group of compounds may help to protect against cancer and heart disease.

Chlorogenic acid—An antioxidant in tomatoes that seems to inhibit the formation of carcinogenic nitrosamines in the body.

Choline—A water-soluble vitamin present in a wide variety of foods that plays a role in memory and learning. Food sources include soy, eggs, cauliflower, peanut butter, and tomatoes.

Coenzyme Q_{10} (CoQ_{10})—One of three antioxidants the body produces (the other two are glutathione and alpha lipoic acid), CoQ_{10} is important to protect cells from free radicals. Good food sources include spinach and broccoli.

Copper—A mineral vital to the formation of red blood cells, copper helps keep bones, blood vessels, and the nervous system healthy. It is found in shellfish, nuts, legumes, and mushrooms.

Curcumin—The yellow pigment in turmeric, this antioxidant and anti-inflammatory apparently helps prevent polyps and colon cancer, based on animal tests.

DHA—An omega-3 fatty acid that helps reduce blood cholesterol and the risk of arterial plaque formation. Main sources are oily fish and some plants, including salmon, sardines, mackerel, shrimp, walnuts, flaxseed, canola oil, spinach, kale, purslane, and other dark leafy greens.

Diallyl disulfide—A pungent sulfur compound in onions and garlic that may be anticarcinogenic.

D-limonene (limonene)—One of the many antioxidant terpenes found in citrus fruits, especially in their peel, with anti-cancer powers. May also help lower LDL cholesterol.

Ellagic acid—A phenolic acid, this antioxidant seems to help prevent cancer. Sources include walnuts, raspberries, strawberries, and cranberries.

EPA—An omega-3 fatty acid found mainly in oily fish that helps reduce blood cholesterol and the risk of arterial plaque formation. Sources include salmon, mackerel, sardines, shellfish, and tuna.

Essential fatty acids (EFAs)—Required for many body functions, hence essential, these omega-3, omega-6, and omega-9 fatty acids can only reach the body through dietary sources. They include vegetable oils, oily fish, nuts, flaxseed, and some dark greens.

Ferulic acid—Another of the cancer-blocking phenolic acids. Sources include oats and other whole grains, tomatoes, apples, green bell peppers, and grapefruit.

Fiber—A general term given to the parts of plants that cannot be digested. Dietary fiber is broken down into two categories—soluble and insoluble fiber. Soluble fiber, including pectins and gums, reduces blood cholesterol (particularly LDL), reducing the risk of heart disease, and helps to stabilize blood sugar levels. Oats, apples, beans, and citrus are good sources. Insoluble fiber, including cellulose and lignins, absorbs water to speed the passage of waste through the intestines, reducing the risk of colon cancer. Wheat bran, whole grain breads and cereals, and vegetables are good sources.

Flavanol—An antioxidant flavonoid found in cocoa beans, cocoa, and chocolate.

Flavonoids—A large group of potent antioxidant phytochemicals including anthocyanins, catechins, isoflavones, lignans, quercitin, and theaflavins, which are antioxidants that help protect against cancer.

Folacin (folic acid, folate)—This B vitamin prevents birth defects and helps break down homocysteine, an amino acid whose presence is related to a high risk of heart disease. This water-soluble vitamin, which also protects against cancer, is found abundantly in spinach and other dark leafy vegetables, oranges, whole grains, nuts, and dried beans.

Free radicals—Unstable molecules that cause oxidation by attacking other molecules. Oxidation produces cell damage that leads to aging, etc.

Fructooligosaccharides (FOS)—These prebiotics, a form of fiber that nourishes beneficial bacteria in the gut, may help protect against colon cancer and benefit bones by improving the body's absorption of calcium and other minerals. Onions, bananas, legumes, and yogurt provide them.

Glutathione—One of the three important antioxidants the body produces (the other two are alpha lipoic acid and coenzyme Q_{10}) to boost the immune system, repair DNA, reduce inflammation, and help the body detoxify. Food sources include spinach, asparagus, avocados, okra, potatoes, and strawberries.

Homocysteine—An amino acid whose presence in high levels appears to be a signal for heart disease.

Indoles—Cancer-fighting phytochemicals found in cruciferous vegetables, indoles work by blocking estrogen receptors and helping to balance estrogens in the body. Abundant in broccoli, cabbage, Brussels sprouts, kale, collard greens, bok choy, and turnips.

Iron—A mineral essential for the production of hemoglobin and the oxygenation of red blood cells. Red meat contains heme iron. Vegetables contain nonheme iron, a form that benefits from the presence of vitamin C for absorption. Iron-rich foods include broccoli, spinach, kale, liver and other red meat, whole wheat, and enriched or fortified grains and cereals.

Isoflavones—Plant estrogens that particularly help to alleviate symptoms of menopause, lower the risk of some forms of breast and prostate cancer, and also act as antioxidants. Found mainly in soy foods.

Lignans—Plant estrogens found in broccoli, flaxseed, whole grains, and soy that help to block some forms of cancer.

Lutein—A yellow pigment usually found together with zeaxanthin. These antioxidant carotenoids help prevent age-related macular degeneration and cataracts and may also help reduce the risk of heart disease and cancer. Sources include yellow corn, spinach, kale, collards, and turnip greens.

Lycopene—The red pigment abundant in tomatoes that tends to protect the prostate and lungs particularly against free radicals to reduce cancer risk. Other sources for this antioxidant carotenoid include watermelon, pink grapefruit, paprika, and guavas.

Magnesium—A mineral important for healthy bones, teeth, muscles, and metabolism. Sources include chocolate, leafy green vegetables, whole grains, legumes, nuts, and seeds.

Manganese—A mineral important for metabolism and building strong bones. Good sources are whole grains, legumes, nuts, and leafy green vegetables.

Niacin (nicotinic acid)—A water-soluble B vitamin necessary for healthy nerves and skin, niacin helps regulate blood cholesterol levels. Sources include oats and other whole grains, black beans and other legumes, poultry, fish, and peanut butter.

Omega-3 fatty acids (see *Essential fatty acids*)—The essential fatty acids found in oily fish (see EPA and DHA) and some plants (see DHA), these help reduce inflammation and promote heart health. They are found in salmon, mackerel, sardines, shellfish, tuna, walnuts, flaxseed, canola oil, spinach, kale, purslane, and other dark leafy greens.

P-coumaric acid—An antioxidant phenolic acid in tomatoes that seems to inhibit the formation of carcinogenic nitrosamines in the body.

Phenols (polyphenols)—A large group of antioxidant compounds found in plants, including phenolic acids and flavonoids. These antioxidants include anthocyanins, catechins, ellagic acid, quercitin, and other substances.

Phosphorus—A mineral essential for healthy bones and metabolic function. Sources include fish, meat, poultry, dairy products, eggs, nuts, and beans.

Phytates (phytic acid)—Compounds found in soybeans, bran, nuts, and seeds, phytates appear to help protect against cancer. They also bind calcium, iron, zinc, and other minerals, making them unavailable to the body.

Phytochemicals (phytonutrients, functional foods)—Natural compounds found in plants that appear to be potent disease fighters due to their antioxidant properties and health-promoting actions in the body.

Phytoene—A colorless carotenoid in tomatoes that is an antioxidant.

Phytoestrogens—Plant hormones including isoflavones and lignans, akin to but weaker than human hormones, that may reduce the risk of breast and prostate cancer. Soy and other legumes and flaxseed are the main sources.

Phytofluene—A colorless carotenoid in tomatoes that is an antioxidant.

Phytosterols (sterols)—A type of plant fat that actually helps to reduce cholesterol by slowing its absorption in the body and lowering LDL. May also be anticarcinogenic. Found in walnuts, peanuts, sesame and sunflower seeds, avocados, and edamame.

Potassium—A mineral essential for the nervous system, the heart muscle, and the body's fluid balance.

Proanthocyanins—Forms of bitter-tasting antioxidant catechins that give an astringent flavor to chocolate, wine, and fruits such as grapes, persimmons, and peaches when they are unripe.

Protease inhibitors—Found in soy and other beans, these phytochemicals appear to help prevent cells from turning cancerous and multiplying.

Quercitin (Rutin)—An anti-inflammatory flavonoid that may boost HDL, help thin the blood, and aid in reducing asthma symptoms. Sources include onions, red grapes, and apples.

Resveratrol—A powerful antioxidant that helps lower LDL levels in the blood. Found in blueberries, red grapes, and red wine.

Riboflavin (vitamin B$_2$)—A water-soluble, light-sensitive vitamin that helps metabolism and is essential for healthy body tissue and making red blood cells. Sources include meat, dairy products, whole grains, spinach, and broccoli.

Selenium—A mineral that, as an antioxidant, boosts HDL and lowers LDL to help protect against heart disease, selenium may also protect against prostate and other forms of cancer. Sources include Brazil nuts, salmon and other seafood, eggs, lean meats, broccoli, legumes, and mushrooms.

Sterol (plant sterol)—Plant compounds that help to lower cholesterol levels and that may reduce the risk of cancer. Top sources include almonds, avocados, hazelnuts, peanuts, walnuts, and certain margarines, such as Benecol.

Sulforaphane—An antioxidant found in cruciferous vegetables that decreases cancer risk by stimulating the body's production of cancer-fighting enzymes and blocking free radicals. Top sources include broccoli, cauliflower, cabbage, kale, Brussels sprouts, and radishes.

Theaflavin—A flavonoid found in chocolate that has antioxidant and anti-inflammatory benefits and may protect against heart disease and help lower blood cholesterol.

Theobromine—The stimulating substance related to caffeine found in cocoa beans, cocoa, and chocolate.

Thiamine (vitamin B$_1$)—A water-soluble vitamin important for a healthy nervous system. Found in meats, beans, nuts, whole grains, and enriched breads and cereals.

Vitamin A—Helps the body grow and repair itself, supports the immune system, and helps night vision.

Vitamin B$_6$—A water-soluble vitamin found in green and leafy vegetables, meats, fish, poultry, beans, fruits, and whole grains.

Vitamin B$_{12}$—A water-soluble vitamin that helps produce red blood cells and build and maintain healthy nerve tissue. Not found in plant foods, but good sources include meat, fish, dairy products, poultry, and eggs.

Vitamin C—This water-soluble vitamin acts as one of the first-line antioxidants in the body, along with vitamin E.

Vitamin E—One of the body's major antioxidants, it neutralizes and destroys free radicals and helps protect against oxidation of cholesterol.

Vitamin K—Helps clot blood and aids in maintaining strong bones.

Zeaxanthin—A yellow pigment often found along with lutein, zeaxanthin functions similarly as an antioxidant carotenoid to help prevent age-related macular degeneration and cataracts and may also help reduce the risk of heart disease and cancer. Sources include yellow corn, spinach, kale, collards, and turnip greens.

Zinc—A mineral essential for producing DNA, RNA, protein synthesis, immune reactions, and sperm. Sources include seafood, meat, milk, poultry, nuts, and whole grains.

RESOURCES

Food products nationally available in supermarkets and natural food markets unless specified, and useful information resources

All-Clad Metalcrafters
424 Morganza Road
Canonsburg, PA 15317
Phone: (800) 255-2523
Fax: (724) 746-5035
Web site: www.allclad.com
Produces stainless steel cookware

Applegate Farms
750 Route 202 South, Third Floor
Bridgewater, NJ 08807
Phone: (866) 587-5858
Fax: (800) 358-8289
Web site: www.applegatefarms.com
Produces natural and organic pork, poultry, and meat products

Bob's Red Mill Natural Foods
5209 SE International Way
Milwaukie, OR 97222
Phone: (800) 349-2173
Fax: (503) 653-1339
Web site: www.bobsredmill.com
Produces oats and other specialty organic grains and flours

The Chocolate Information Center
Web site: www.chocolateinfo.com
Funded by Mars, Inc., to provide information on chocolate and health

Coleman Natural Products
5140 Race Court, Unit 4
Denver, CO 80216
Phone: (800) 442-8666
Fax: (303) 297-0426
Web site: www.colemannatural.com
Produces natural beef

Diamond of California
P.O. Box 1727
Stockton, CA 95201
Phone: (209) 467-6000
Web site: www.diamondnuts.com
Cooperative of family farms for California walnuts, almonds, and other nuts

Diamond Organics
Highway 1
Moss Landing, CA 95039
Phone: (888) 674-2642
Fax: (888) 888-6777
Web site: www.diamondorganics.com
Purveyor of organic food and produce

Earthbound Farms/Natural Selection Foods
1721 San Juan Highway
San Juan Bautista, CA 95045
Phone: (800) 690-3200
Web site: www.ebfoods.com
Grows organic baby spinach and produce

Eden Foods
701 Tecumseh Road
Clinton, MI 49236
Phone: (888) 441-3336
Fax: (517) 456-6075
Web site: www.edenfoods.com
Produces organic black soybeans, Eden Shake, and other whole foods

Eggology
6728 Eton Avenue
Canoga Park, CA 91303
Phone: (888) 441-3336
Fax: (818) 610-2223
Web site: www.eggology.com
Produces 100% pure liquid egg whites

Flavorganics
268 Doremus Avenue
Newark, NJ 07105
Phone: (973) 344-8014, ext. 109
Fax: (973) 344-1948
Web site: www.flavorganics.com
Produces organic vanilla and other flavorings

Florida Tomato Committee
800 Trafalgar Court
Suite 300
Maitland, FL 32751
Phone: (407) 660-1949
Fax: (407) 660-1656
Web site: www.floridatomatoes.org
Regulates handling of tomatoes

The Hain Celestial Group
4600 Sleepytime Drive
Boulder, CO 80301
Phone: (800) 434-4246
Web site: www.hain-celestial.com
Produces Arrowhead Mills organic flours, Westbrae beans, and Hain broths

House Foods America
7351 Orangewood Avenue
Garden Grove, CA 92841
Phone: (877) 333-7077
Fax: (714) 901-4235
Web site: www.house-foods.com
Produces House Brand tofu steaks
and Hinoichi tofu

Lightlife Foods
153 Industrial Boulevard
Turners Falls, MA 01376
Phone: (800) 769-3279
Fax: (413) 863-8502
E-mail: info@lightlife.com
Web site: www.lightlife.com
Makes tempeh and soy meat
alternatives

Louisiana Sweet Potato Commission
P.O. Box 2550
Baton Rouge, LA 70821
Phone: (225) 922-1280
Fax: (225) 922-1289
Web site: www.sweetpotato.org
Provides information about health
and using sweet potatoes

Manicaretti
5332 College Avenue
Oakland, CA 94618
Phone: (800) 799-9830
Fax: (510) 655-2034
Web site: www.manicaretti.com
Imports and distributes artisanal olive
oils, balsamic vinegars, and
Rustichella d'Abruzzo farro (spelt)
pasta

Melissa's/World Variety Produce
P.O. Box 21127
Los Angeles, CA 90021
Phone: (800) 588-0151
Fax: (323) 588-9774
Web site: www.melissas.com
Distributes specialty and exotic pro-
duce, Asian and Latin foods, and soy
products

Myers of Keswick
634 Hudson Street
New York, NY 10014
Phone: (212) 691-4194
Fax: (212) 691-7423
Web site: www.myersofkeswick.com
Purveyors of Scott's Porridge Oats

National Onion Association
822 Seventh Street, Suite 510
Greeley, CO 80631
Phone: (970) 353-5895
Fax: (970) 353-5697
Web site: www.onions-usa.org
Provides information about health
and using onions

North American Blueberry Council
P.O. Box 1036
Folsom, CA 95763
Phone: (916) 983-0111
Fax: (916) 983-9022
Web site: www.nabcblues.org
Encourages use of cultivated
blueberries

Scharffen Berger Chocolate Maker
914 Heinz Avenue
Berkeley, CA 94710
Phone: (800) 930-4528
Fax: (510) 981-4051
Web site: www.scharffenberger.com
Makers of premium baking chocolate

Seafood Choices Alliance
1731 Connecticut Avenue NW,
Fourth Floor
Washington, DC 20009
Phone: (866) 732-6673
Web site: www.seafoodchoices.com
Sustainable seafood shopping
information

South River Miso
888 Shelburne Falls Road
Conway, MA 01341
Phone: (413) 369-4057
Fax: (413) 369-4299
Web site: www.southrivermiso.com

Makers of organic small-batch miso,
in special varieties

The Soy Daily
122 Avenida Adobe
San Clemente, CA 92672
Phone: (949) 481-4044
Web site: www.thesoydailyclub.com
Provides information on soy history
and soy products

Soyfoods Association of North
    America
101 Connecticut Avenue NW,
    Suite 1120
Washington, DC 20036
Phone: (202) 659-3520
Web site: www.soyfoods.org
Provides comprehensive information
about soyfoods and health issues

Spectrum Organic Products
5341 Old Redwood Highway,
    Suite 400
Petaluma, CA 94954
Phone: (707) 778-8900
Fax: (707) 765-1026
Web site: www.spectrumorganics.com
Makers of specialty and organic oils

Thai Kitchen/Epicurean
    International
30315 Union City Boulevard
Union City, CA 94587
Phone: (800) 967-8424
Web site: www.thaikitchen.com
Makers of organic and regular
coconut milk without sulfites

Jasper Wyman and Son
P.O. Box 100
Milbridge, ME 04658
Phone: (800) 341-1758
Fax: (207) 546-2074
Web site: www.wymans.com
Producers of wild blueberry products

BIBLIOGRAPHY

The American Institute for Cancer Research. *Stopping Cancer Before It Starts.* New York: Golden Books, 1999.

Anderson, Jean, M.S., and Barbara Deskins, Ph.D., M.D. *The Nutrition Bible.* New York: William Morrow, 1995.

Beling, Stephanie, M.D. *Power Foods.* New York: HarperCollins, 1997.

Bishop, Jack. *Vegetables Every Day.* New York: HarperCollins, 2001.

Brown, Catherine. *Scottish Regional Recipes.* London: Penguin Books, 1981.

Corriher, Shirley O. *CookWise.* New York: William Morrow, 1997.

Davidson, Alan. *The Oxford Companion to Food.* New York: Oxford University Press, 1999.

Draine, Betsy, and Michael Hinden. *The Walnut Cookbook.* Berkeley, CA: Ten Speed Press, 1998.

Gebhardt, Susan E., and Robin G. Thomas. *United States Department of Agriculture Home and Garden Bulletin Number 72: Nutritive Values of Foods.* Beltsville, MD: U.S. Department of Agriculture, Agricultural Research Service, Nutrient Data Laboratory, 2002.

Gow, Rosalie. *Modern Ways with Traditional Scottish Recipes.* Gretna, LA: Pelican Publishing Company, 1981.

Greene, Bert. *The Grains Cookbook.* New York: Workman Publishing, 1988.

———. *Greene on Greens.* New York: Workman Publishing, 1984.

Herbst, Sharon Tyler. *The New Food Lover's Companion.* New York: Barron's Educational Series, 1995.

Hibler, Janie. *The Berry Bible.* New York: William Morrow, 2004.

Ibsen, Gary, with Joan Nielsen. *The Great Tomato Book.* Berkeley, CA: Ten Speed Press, 1999.

Johari, Harish. *The Healing Cuisine.* Rochester, VT: Healing Arts Press, 1994.

Joseph, James A., Ph.D., Daniel A. Nadeau, M.D., and Anne Underwood. *The Color Code.* New York: Hyperion, 2002.

La Spada, Angelita, and Lucio Falcone. *Cucina Eoliana.* Siracusa, Italy: Pungitopo, 1997.

London, Sheryl, and Mel London. *The Versatile Grain and the Elegant Bean.* New York: Simon and Schuster, 1992.

Margen, Sheldon, M.D., and the editors of the University of California at Berkeley Wellness Letter. *The Wellness Encyclopedia of Food and Nutrition.* New York: Rebus, 1992.

Medrich, Alice. *Bittersweet: Recipes and Tales from a Life in Chocolate.* New York: Artisan, 2003.

Oster, Maggie. *The Potato Garden.* New York: Harmony Books, 1993.

Pensiero, Laura, R.D., and Susan Oliveria, Sc.D., M.P.H., with Michael Osborne, M.D. *The Strang Cookbook for Cancer Prevention.* New York: Dutton, 1998.

Peterson, James. *Essentials of Cooking.* New York: Artisan, 1999.

Pratt, Steven, M.D., and Kathy Matthew. *SuperFoods Rx.* New York: William Morrow, 2004.

Precilla, Maricel E. *The New Taste of Chocolate.* Berkeley, CA: Ten Speed Press, 2001.

Reader's Digest. *Foods That Harm, Foods That Heal.* Pleasantville, NY: The Reader's Digest Association, 1997.

Rombauer, Irma S., Marion Rombauer Becker, and Ethan Becker. *Joy of Cooking.* New York: Scribner, 1997.

Schneider, Elizabeth. *Uncommon Fruits and Vegetables.* New York: Harper and Row, 1986.

Schwartz, Arthur. *Naples at Table.* New York: HarperCollins, 1998.

Shurtleff, William, and Aoyagi Akiko. *The Book of Miso.* Berkeley, CA: Ten Speed Press, 1976.

———. *The Book of Tofu.* Berkeley, CA: Ten Speed Press, 1975, 1998.

Siguel, Edward N., M.D., Ph.D. *Essential Fatty Acids in Health and Disease.* Brookline, MA: Nurek Press, 1994.

Tantillo, Tony, and Sam Gugino. *Eat Fresh, Stay Healthy.* New York: Macmillan, 1997.

United States Department of Agriculture National Nutritional Database for Standard Reference, Release 17. Washington, D.C.

Visson, Lynn. *The Russian Heritage Cookbook.* Woodstock and New York: The Overlook Press, 1998.

Waters, Alice, and the cooks of Chez Panisse. *Chez Panisse Vegetables.* New York: HarperCollins, 1996.

Willett, Walter C., M.D., with The Harvard School of Public Health. *Eat, Drink, and Be Healthy: The Harvard Medical School Guide to Healthy Eating.* New York: Simon & Schuster Source, 2001.

Zeitoun, Edmond. *250 Recettes de Cuisine Tunisienne.* Paris: Jacques Grancher, 1977.

INDEX

Note: <u>Underscored</u> page references indicate boxed text.
Boldfaced page references indicate photographs.

Conversion Chart

These equivalents have been slightly rounded to make measuring easier.

Volume Measurements

U.S.	Imperial	Metric
¼ tsp	–	1 ml
½ tsp	–	2 ml
1 tsp	–	5 ml
1 Tbsp	–	15 ml
2 Tbsp (1 oz)	1 fl oz	30 ml
¼ cup (2 oz)	2 fl oz	60 ml
⅓ cup (3 oz)	3 fl oz	80 ml
½ cup (4 oz)	4 fl oz	120 ml
⅔ cup (5 oz)	5 fl oz	160 ml
¾ cup (6 oz)	6 fl oz	180 ml
1 cup (8 oz)	8 fl oz	240 ml

Weight Measurements

U.S.	Metric
1 oz	30 g
2 oz	60 g
4 oz (¼ lb)	115 g
5 oz (⅓ lb)	145 g
6 oz	170 g
7 oz	200 g
8 oz (½ lb)	230 g
10 oz	285 g
12 oz (¾ lb)	340 g
14 oz	400 g
16 oz (1 lb)	455 g
2.2 lb	1 kg

Length Measurements

U.S.	Metric
¼"	0.6 cm
½"	1.25 cm
1"	2.5 cm
2"	5 cm
4"	11 cm
6"	15 cm
8"	20 cm
10"	25 cm
12" (1')	30 cm

Pan Sizes

U.S.	Metric
8" cake pan	20 × 4 cm sandwich or cake tin
9" cake pan	23 × 3.5 cm sandwich or cake tin
11" × 7" baking pan	28 × 18 cm baking tin
13" × 9" baking pan	32.5 × 23 cm baking tin
15" × 10" baking pan	38 × 25.5 cm baking tin (Swiss roll tin)
1½ qt baking dish	1.5 liter baking dish
2 qt baking dish	2 liter baking dish
2 qt rectangular baking dish	30 × 19 cm baking dish
9" pie plate	22 × 4 or 23 × 4 cm pie plate
7" or 8" springform pan	18 or 20 cm springform or loose-bottom cake tin
9" × 5" loaf pan	23 × 13 cm or 2 lb narrow loaf tin or pâté tin

Temperatures

Fahrenheit	Centigrade	Gas
140°	60°	–
160°	70°	–
180°	80°	–
225°	105°	¼
250°	120°	½
275°	135°	1
300°	150°	2
325°	160°	3
350°	180°	4
375°	190°	5
400°	200°	6
425°	220°	7
450°	230°	8
475°	245°	9
500°	260°	–